PENGUIN BOOKS
INDIA IN SLOW MOTION

Mark Tully was born in Calcutta and educated in England. He was Correspondent for the BBC in South Asia for twenty-five years. He now works as a journalist in New Delhi with his colleague and partner, Gillian Wright, who also translates Indian-language fiction into English. Together they have worked on a number of books including Mark Tully's highly acclaimed *No Full Stops in India* and *The Heart of India*.

India in Slow Motion

MARK TULLY

and

GILLIAN WRIGHT

PENGUIN BOOKS

PENGUIN BOOKS
Published by the Penguin Group
Penguin Books India Pvt. Ltd, 11 Community Centre, Panchsheel Park,
New Delhi 110 017, India
Penguin Group (USA) Inc., 375 Hudson Street, New York, New York 10014, USA
Penguin Group (Canada), 90 Eglinton Avenue East, Suite 700, Toronto, Ontario, M4P
2Y3, Canada (a division of Pearson Penguin Canada Inc.)
Penguin Books Ltd, 80 Strand, London WC2R 0RL, England
Penguin Ireland, 25 St Stephen's Green, Dublin 2, Ireland (a division of Penguin Books
Ltd)
Penguin Group (Australia), 707 Collins Street, Melbourne, Victoria 3008, Australia (a
division of Pearson Australia Group Pty Ltd)
Penguin Group (NZ), 67 Apollo Drive, Rosedale, Auckland 0632, New Zealand
(a division of Pearson New Zealand Ltd)
Penguin Group (South Africa) (Pty) Ltd, Block D, Rosebank Office Park, 181 Jan
Smuts Avenue, Parktown North, Johannesburg 2193, South Africa

Penguin Books Ltd, Registered Offices: 80 Strand, London WC2R 0RL, England

First published in India in Viking by Penguin Books India 2002
First published in Penguin Books 2003

Copyright © Mark Tully and Gillian Wright 2002

25 24 23 22 21 20 19

ISBN 9780143030478

For sale in the Indian Subcontinent only

Printed at Repro India Ltd., Navi Mumbai

To all those who are striving
for the good of India

Contents

Acknowledgements

We would like to thank all those who have helped us during our travels for this book, especially I. B. Singh, Madhukar Shah of Orcha, Mario Miranda and his family, Percival Naronha, Frederick Naronha, Claud Alvares, G. S. Radhakrishna, Uday Mahurkar, Yusuf Jameel, Pushkar Johari, all those who gave us their time on our travels, and the team in our home in Delhi – Ravi Prasad Narayanan in the office, and Ram Chander and Bubbly in the kitchen.

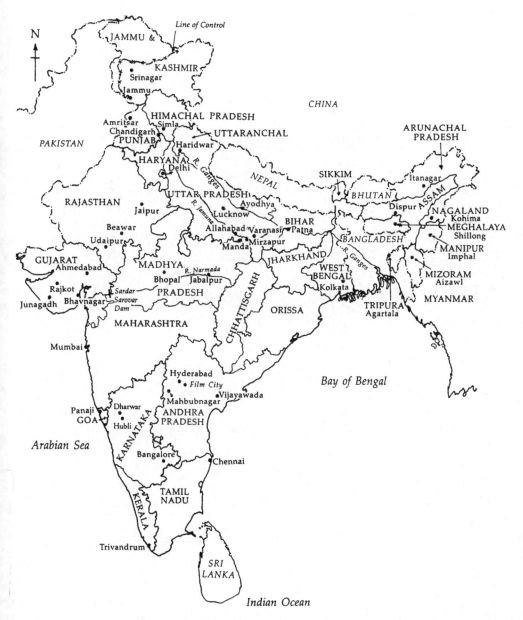

The international boundaries of the map on this page are neither purported to be correct nor authenticated by the Survey of India.

Introduction

Not a word passed between them as they strode towards the town of Orcha with its temples to visit and its sacred river to bathe in. These were peaceful pilgrims, they carried peacock feathers as standards and sticks for dancing, not for doing battle. They were robed for rejoicing, with cowbells tinkling on their cross-belts, while round their waists gaudy green and red pom-poms bounced. Some wore vests embroidered with rosettes, and some pointed multicoloured clowns' hats. There would have been loud praising of their gods too had this not been the end of a week of abstinence when not a word was to be spoken. The men of the villages of Bundelkhand, a region of central India, were on their way to celebrate one of their immemorial festivals when their silence was broken by the wail of a siren. An inspector of police in khaki uniform clutching the handle of his motorbike in one hand and imperiously waving everyone off the road with the other appeared round the corner. He was followed by a white car with a blue light revolving on the roof and one star above black number plates, the badge of office of a deputy inspector general of police. The convoy, completed by a pick-up full of armed policemen, hurtled past, scattering the pilgrims in a cloud of dust. They couldn't see whether the superintendent of police, the representative of the Raj which succeeded the British, even bothered to glance at their discomfiture shielded as he was from those he ruled by firmly closed, heavily tinted windows. Waiting in our car to pass the pilgrims I was reminded of the senior Indian civil servant who had said to me, 'Our police are only for the poor. They don't touch the rich and the influential.'

We were on our way to see a cyber-café that a non-governmental organization had set up in a remote village. There we were told that the computers had been much more useful when they could pull down material from a satellite. But then some bureaucrat had discovered that the NGO needed an Internet Service Provider Licence II and had ordered them to dismantle the aerials. The government itself had proved quite unable to provide any connection with the outside world. There was a wireless mast for one public telephone but the villagers said no one had come to maintain the battery for years. The villagers themselves were of course not allowed to touch government property. As I have found so often in India the government was the problem not the solution.

The police officer with his convoy, and the bureaucrats who ordered the aerials to be dismantled, were the unchanging India, the India which is still shackled by a colonial bureaucracy, the India which has become a byword for red-tape and corruption, the India described by one of its most distinguished civil servants as a kleptocracy. This was the India that, according to a recent World Bank report, still has social indicators that are 'poor by most measures of human development'. But there is a changing India too. In the same report the World Bank also said that India's economy had, since the 1980s, been among the fastest growing in the world. Indian democracy has brought about a social revolution. The lower castes, because they are largest in number, have come to dominate the political scene. There is a sophisticated Indian elite and a sizeable well-educated middle class: thoroughly professional lawyers, bankers and accountants, academics, engineers, doctors, all admired by their peers in other parts of the world. India is renowned for its information technology skills. Civil society is vibrant, India has become the NGO capital of the world. Television has grown from a drab purveyor of government propaganda to a multi-channel independent media. The press, once obsessed with politics, now provides news and a bewildering variety of views on every aspect of Indian life, including the misdeeds of those who wield power.

Why then is India still in slow motion? Part of the answer lies in this story from the Indian Institute of Technology in Delhi, or IIT, a symbol of modern India's potential – a first-class university, teaching the cream of India's science students. Rukmini Bhaya Nair is an effervescent enthusiast for the humanities, charged with persuading IIT students that there is more to knowledge than just science and technology. Apparently, if she travels on official business she is asked to fill in a form on which she can still claim for travelling by camel, or canal, depending on the version. The small print also sets out the rules for claiming second-class fare (without meals) on steamers, and mentions the furlongs travelled by trolley. What about more modern forms of travel? According to Rukmini Bhaya Nair: 'Our clerks of the government of India have simply added air-travel to the list of possible conveyances – a final palimpsest layer.' And what conclusion does she draw from this? 'Despite our flirtation with the latest computer technology, our gleaming machines, and the constant talk of efficiency, we at the hi-tech IIT remain the hostages of history. The obfuscatory rites of colonial administration are with us still and everyone is caught equally helplessly in the toils of the paper chase.' Those obfuscatory rites would have been done away with if politicians had concentrated on the most obvious issue facing India – bad governance. That would go against their own vested interests so they have distracted the voters' attention by raising issues of caste and creed.

There have been many explanations for the failures of India. Some centre on India's past, its history of invasions and foreign domination – Naipaul has described it as a wounded civilization. Some blame India's culture, and its religions, seeing it as a land of fatalism, a society set in stone by the caste system. Some even blame the climate, saying it has sapped the will of the people. These explanations denigrate India, Indians, and an ancient culture that has been described by the poet Kathleen Raine as 'having more fully than any other civilization on earth, past or present, explored and embodied the highest and the most embracing realization of our human scope'. It is these critiques that are fatalistic for they suggest that there is nothing that can be done, the flaws are fatal and India is fated to be a poor and backward country.

In this book we argue that one of the fundamental problems of India is a peculiarly Indian form of bad governance. The need to do something about governance was acknowledged by the Prime Minister of India, Atal Behari Vajpayee when he addressed the

National Development Council in 1999. There he admitted, 'People often perceive the bureaucracy as an agent of exploitation rather than a provider of service. Corruption has become a low risk and high reward activity. Frequent and arbitrary transfers of government officials combined with limited tenures are harming the work ethic and lowering the morale of honest officers. While expecting discipline and diligence from the administration the political executive should self-critically review its own performance.' Three years later his party became the junior party in a coalition in Uttar Pradesh, India's most populous state, headed by Mayawati, a formidable Dalit politician who when heading an earlier administration earned the nickname of 'Transfer Chief Minister'. On assuming power this time she transferred two hundred and fifty officials within ten days.

The stories in this book tell not just of bad governance, but of the reason for it and also of those who are battling against it. We do not suggest that bad governance is the root of all India's problems, but, unlike so many of the more exotic diagnoses, there can be no doubt that it's a brake slowing down a country with enormous but unrealized potential.

The Reinvention of Rama

On 6 December 1992 Gilly and I were standing on the roof of a building with a clear view of a somewhat dilapidated Mughal mosque in the north Indian town of Ayodhya, a place of pilgrimage, hallowed by tradition as the home town of the god Rama. The right-wing Hindu nationalist Bharatiya Janata Party and its sister organization the VHP, the Vishwa Hindu Parishad, or World Council of Hindus, had been campaigning for six years to pull down this mosque, which they claimed had been built on the site of a Hindu temple marking Rama's birthplace. This was the day the BJP and the other organizations supporting it were to begin work on building the temple, but they had given a commitment to the government and to the courts that it would only be a symbolic start, a religious ceremony, and the mosque would not be touched. Below us saffron-robed Hindu holy men jostled with each other for a place on the platform where the religious ceremony was to be conducted. Arrogant, officious young men strode around ejecting anyone they thought had no right to be there. Khaki-clad police held back the throng threatening to break through the bamboo barriers. A former head of the Uttar Pradesh police, now himself a political Hindu holy man, gave orders to officers he had once officially commanded. At what the police hoped would be a safe distance from the mosque, a vast crowd, perhaps 150,000 strong, some of whom had been camping near the mosque for ten days, roared encouragement to speakers who threatened they would pull down the building erected by the Mughal conquerors. Sitting on the VIPs' platform, the former Maharani of Gwalior, wearing the white sari of a widow, clapped when the mosque was described as 'a symbol of slavery, an insult to Hinduism'. Beside her, Lal Krishan Advani, the politician who had masterminded the Ayodhya campaign, was strangely silent and disapproving.

Trouble first broke out in the space below us when young men wearing canary-yellow headbands managed to break through the barriers. The police stood by and watched, but the unofficial guardians of the law appointed by the organizers, and wearing saffron headbands, did put up some resistance. They soon gave up, however, and joined the intruders in beating up television journalists, smashing their cameras, and trampling on their tape-recorders. Encouraged by this first victory, thousands charged towards the outer cordon of police protecting the mosque itself shouting, 'Jai Shri Rama!', 'Victory to Lord Rama!', 'We will build the temple here!', 'We won't tolerate this symbol of slavery!' Slogans inciting hatred of Muslims were also shouted. Thick clouds of dust rose, making it impossible to see what was happening, but in what seemed like no time at all the outer cordons collapsed, and then we saw young men clambering along the branches of trees, dropping over the final barricade and rushing towards the mosque. Above the raucous slogans and the bellowing of conch shells, we heard a leader of the BJP shout through a microphone, 'Police, don't interfere!' He needn't have worried, the police had no intention of interfering. The last line of defence retreated from the mosque holding their wicker shields above their heads as protection from the stones raining down on them. We saw one police officer pushing through his men to ensure that he got out of danger first. As the police walked away, two young men scrambled on to the top of the mosque's central dome, hoisted a saffron flag, and started hacking away the mortar.

That was the last we saw of what was known as the Babri Masjid, the mosque of the emperor Babur. All communications with Ayodhya had been broken and so I drove to Faizabad, some ten miles away, to phone my story to London. On returning to Ayodhya, I was surrounded by an angry crowd shouting, 'Foreign journalists! CIA agents!' They prodded me with tridents, Hindu emblems, as they debated my fate. Some were for beating me up, but they were restrained by a young sadhu. He persuaded them to lock me up in a temple dormitory, where I was soon joined by the Indian journalists who had driven to Ayodhya with me. They refused to leave until I was released, although my captors insisted they had nothing against them. We were eventually rescued by a local official assisted by the head priest of one of Ayodhya's best-known temples, and driven to Faizabad in a police lorry with other journalists who had been forced to hide from the mobs. By then the mosque was a pile of rubble.

The BJP is a member of 'the family' of a Hindu sect, the Rashtriya Swayamsevak Sangh or National Volunteer Corps. For the RSS, India's past is a story of humiliation by foreign rulers and the future lies with a united, militant Hinduism restoring the nation's pride and standing up to fundamentalist Islam and missionary Christianity. The ideology of the Nehru-Gandhis' Congress Party, which has ruled India for most of the years since Independence, is dismissed by the RSS as pseudo-secularism. They are particularly critical of Nehru's decision to allow Muslims to keep their family law, and to give a special status to Kashmir, India's only Muslim majority state. With its nationalist agenda and its quasi-military parades, the sect has been accused of fascism. The BJP has veered between the hard-line Hindu agenda of the RSS and policies which would have a broader appeal. The campaign to destroy the mosque was on the RSS agenda and marked the temporary dominance of the hardliners in the BJP.

For six years the BJP had kept Ayodhya centre stage. They had persuaded Indians all over the country to send sacred bricks for the Rama temple, which were transported to Ayodhya by the truckload. In the 1989 election the secular Rajiv Gandhi was so alarmed by the success of the Ayodhya campaign that he allowed the foundation stone of the temple to be laid in an unsuccessful attempt to prevent the BJP running away with the Hindu vote. The next year, Advani set out on a 10,000 kilometre journey from the west coast of India to Ayodhya in a vehicle decorated like Rama's chariot, making inflammatory speeches about the mosque wherever he stopped. He was arrested before reaching his destination, but thousands of BJP supporters did manage to reach Ayodhya's bridge over the sacred River Saryu. A naked holy man drove a bus through the police cordon blocking entry to the town. The crowd surged through the narrow lanes to the mosque, broke through the gates, and hoisted a saffron flag on one of the domes before the police opened fire, killing, they say, six people. The BJP claims fifty. The next day there was a renewed attack on the mosque. This time the casualty figures were put at fifteen by the police and fifty-nine by the BJP.

Now in 1992, a year or so later, all too aware of the political potency of the issue, the Congress Prime Minister, P. V. Narasimha Rao, was heading a minority government and hadn't felt secure enough to ban this assembly at Ayodhya. He moved 195 companies of paramilitary police to the neighbouring town of Faizabad, but he didn't order them to save the mosque for fear that they would open fire and create martyrs for the BJP.

Although the destruction of the mosque was the culmination of a campaign launched by the BJP, Lal Krishan Advani was a disappointed man. Indian journalists hung their heads in shame. One commentator said the Mahatma had been assassinated again, another spoke of 'the nation's shame', and the *Times of India* editorial was headlined 'The Republic Besmirched'. In the international press the bell tolled for Indian secularism. In the London *Times*, Conor Cruise O'Brien asked, 'Will India fall to the zealots?' *Newsweek* wrote of 'the ancient conflict between Hindus and Muslims'. The *Washington Post* identified 'centuries old religious hatred' combined with 'modern day economic depression' as the cause of the desecration of the mosque.

Serious riots did indeed break out in different parts of India. In Mumbai, then still called Bombay, they turned into ugly attacks by the police on Muslims. But as has so often happened since independence India pitched and rolled alarmingly in seas which would have caused a smaller, less stable craft to capsize, but weathered the storm. The riots died down. The country didn't fall to the zealots. Perhaps one reason for this is that there is in truth no ancient history of religious hatred. There are many who view the theory that there was such hatred as a colonial version of history, a version on which the case for Pakistan as a separate homeland for Muslims was constructed, a version which requires two cohesive communities united in opposing one another. But a religion as diverse as Hinduism has never produced a united pan-Indian community. In fact some scholars question the very existence of anything that could be called Hinduism. Muslims in India, too, were not one community, nor were they necessarily hostile to Hindus. In an essay entitled 'The Myth of Unity', the Indian Muslim historian Mushirul Hasan has written of an Islamic tradition with its roots firmly anchored in Indian soil, and quotes one British civil servant reporting from Uttar Pradesh 'that there was a strong tendency among Muslims to assimilate in all externals with their Hindu neighbours'. Apparently he found Muslims wearing the Hindu dhoti and greeting each other in the name of Rama. To the east in Bengal, another civil servant described Hindu-Muslim mutual dependence and friendship as 'an old and cherished tradition'. This was confirmed by Lord Lytton, the Governor of Bengal who commented on how the rank and file of the communities in his province got on well with each other in all the daily business of life. Although that tradition does not suit the RSS, and does not make good copy for journalists, events after the destruction of the mosque in Ayodhya would suggest it is still alive.

Once the storm subsided it became clear that the destruction of the mosque and widespread riots had even alarmed many supporters of the BJP, and pushed the party into a corner where it was impossible for most other political parties to have any relationship with it. The plight of the BJP became clear the next year when it lost elections in three states it had ruled.

Before Ayodhya became the fulcrum on which Indian politics hinged, it had never been one of the premier destinations on India's pilgrimage circuit. Although Rama was one of the most popular members of the Hindu pantheon, Ayodhya was a town of crumbling mansion-like temples and rest houses, symbols of a past history when it had been capital of a Muslim kingdom. Cycle rickshaws, not cars, jammed the narrow lanes. It was bereft of hotels and the tourists to fill them. Its pilgrims could only afford to sleep in temple rest houses. They came from the surrounding villages and small towns. Ayodhya didn't attract the faithful from far and wide like Shiva's city of Varanasi, Haridwar, where the Ganges flows out of the Himalayas into the plains, Allahabad, the site of the Kumbh

Mela, the world's largest religious festival, or Tirupati in the south, said to have the most ample cash-flow of all Indian temples. The cremation ghats on the banks of Ayodhya's sacred river, the Saryu, couldn't compete with the all-India death-industry on the steps leading down to the Ganges in Varanasi. But when the mosque was destroyed, the World Council of Hindus, the VHP, had called for Ayodhya to become the Vatican of Hindus.

It was hardly surprising that the VHP dreamed of a Hindu Vatican. The council had been set up to overcome what the RSS saw as Hinduism's disadvantages, its lack of an organization like the church and its traditional reluctance to proselytize. Swami Chinmayananda, who had first proposed the establishment of a Hindu council, said, 'I know that religious organization is against the very principle of Hinduism, but we have to move with the times. We seem to have entered today all over the world, in every walk of life, in every field of endeavour, an age of organization ... Therefore, in the spiritual field, even though the individuals proceed forward and develop, if religion wants to serve the society, it also has to get organized.'

The missionaries the VHP sent out to proselytize tended to simplify Hinduism. In the same way that the Christian church taught a simple faith based on one God and one Bible, they emphasized Rama and the Ramayana.

Seven years after we had watched the destruction of the Babri Masjid, we decided to return to Ayodhya to see how far the VHP had succeeded in creating a Hindu headquarters, converting Hindus to their Rama, and putting the town on the national pilgrimage map. We went to one of the major festivals of the year, the Panch Kosi Parikrama, when pilgrims walk around the boundaries of what they believe was Rama's city.

On reaching Lucknow, the capital of Uttar Pradesh, we found that whatever else the BJP might have done for Ayodhya's status it had not been able to improve access to the town. There was still no airport. There were, we knew, a few trains but when we asked about the afternoon service there wasn't one. 'Take a bus,' the railway enquiries in Lucknow advised us. Although they were more plentiful than the trains, buses were even slower, and we wanted to get to Ayodhya before nightfall when, according to newspapers, the town would be 'sealed off' by the police to prevent traffic interfering with the pilgrims. So we fell back on a taxi.

Even in the taxi, we were still on the road after dark, and so were delayed by police enforcing the ban on traffic reaching Ayodhya. Officially only heavy vehicles were to be stopped, but they had blocked the road to all vehicles. When I asked a police officer why the lorries were parked in the middle of the road he replied, 'They are not parked. They are stopped.'

'Yes,' I agreed, 'but even then wouldn't it be better if they were stopped on the side of the road?'

'I suppose it would,' the police officer grunted, and walked off leaving the lorries exactly where they were.

We did eventually thread our way through the roadblocks, but fearing further unpleasantness with the police we decided to stop at Faizabad, a sizeable town and district headquarters, just a few kilometres short of Ayodhya. We booked into the Shan-e-Avadh Hotel – certainly not five-star, but very friendly. It had been the headquarters of the world press when the mosque was pulled down.

The next morning, after more trouble with the police, who insisted that we walked the last kilometre or so, we reached Ayodhya's only bridge over the River Saryu. The town lay before us. The spindly minarets of a mosque could still be seen standing above the forest of temple towers, some slanting like steeples, some curving to a point, some tapered wedges. As part, perhaps the only part, of the government's 'Beautify Ayodhya' campaign, the temples along the banks of the river had been painted to look like pink sandstone. The parikrama was already under way. A stream of pilgrims flowed down the road leading into the town, watched by police perched on tall watchtowers. The names of lost children blared from the public address system. Parents were advised: 'Please put a note with your child's name on it in one pocket. We have a girl here who can't give us her name.'

We joined the pilgrims, not, I am ashamed to say, barefoot as they were. It wasn't long before we were asked the inevitable question, 'What country are you from?' Our first interrogator gave us the impression that perhaps Ayodhya's festivals had progressed from local to international affairs. He was a young man who explained that he had travelled for thirteen and a half hours by bus and train from Kathmandu, the capital of Nepal, the world's only Hindu kingdom, 'to see Rama's kingdom'. He went on to say, 'When I was a boy many old people told me to worship Rama every morning and evening and so I do.' How many Western Christian parents and priests must wish that inspiring a lasting faith in the young was always so simple.

We mistook one young man, with his head shaved except for a tuft at the back and wearing yellow robes, for a sadhu, a potential recruit for the VHP, if not already a member. But he told us very firmly he was not. He was a Brahmin training to follow in his father's footsteps as a priest who would perform all the rituals that mark an orthodox Hindu's passage through life. He'd come to Ayodhya to study Sanskrit.

Two men, failing to mingle inconspicuously with the pilgrims, listened to our conversation. When Gilly told them she'd recognized them as intelligence officers from their uniform – tight-fitting safari suits – they moved off.

The young Brahmin was not interested in the Rama temple controversy. 'That's politics,' he said. 'I don't understand political matters in depth and so I don't think it's right for me to comment. I just want to become a perfect Brahmin.' He spoke excellent English and was well aware that his ambition might seem to be rather outdated. 'These are new times,' he said, 'I know that. A scientific education is important, but we shouldn't forget our traditions, and we should be proud of them.'

The stream flowed along what passes for Ayodhya's high street and turned off down a lane flanked by temples. We sat outside a small shop to watch the never-ending procession pass by. Religion in India doesn't just attract the elderly. Young mothers with babies in their arms, and fathers carrying children on their shoulders, villagers of all ages, their clothes dusty, their supplies and cooking utensils on their heads, smartly dressed middle-class families, all strode purposefully towards their destination. Two boys wearing jeans and listening intensely to Walkmans overtook a pot-bellied, self-important man, possibly a politician. A woman stopped, cupped her hand under a tap beside us and scooped water into her child's mouth. Two old ladies hobbled along bent over their sticks. A young man lifted his paralysed leg with his hands for each step he took as he struggled to keep up with his colleagues. There were countless sadhus clad in loose-fitting robes, with ill-kempt hair and beards, carrying staffs and small pots full of water from the Saryu. A train of sadhus, two blind led by one with sight, coupled by walking sticks, passed at a remarkable speed. There were saffron-robed women too who had taken vows of chastity and poverty. Two local journalists stopped to talk to us. When I asked what role the members of the RSS family were playing in the pilgrimage, they pointed out that no one was wearing their uniform saffron headbands, or shouting their slogans.

We moved on, leaving the shopkeeper massaging his feet swollen by completing an even longer parikrama a few days earlier. He said, 'We were so tired that we didn't think we could take another step, then we saw the enthusiasm of others, we said *chalo*, let's go. There's something about Ayodhya that no matter how bad they are, people become good here.'

As we approached the shrine of the Five-Faced Hanuman, the monkey god who was Rama's loyal, efficient, and effective lieutenant, we saw a banner across the road reading 'Minister of State for Energy, Lallu Singhji heartily welcomes all Rama Bhakts', our first sign of BJP activity. Outside the temple was a stall run by the youth wing of the BJP offering free tea to the pilgrims. A young man insisted, 'You must avail of this facility', and so we sat under a canvas awning draped in the party colours to drink tea and be introduced to the president of the party's youth wing, Rishikesh Upadhyaya. He was proud to have been present when the mosque was pulled down but reluctant to explain the role he had played. Clean-shaven, neatly dressed in shirt and trousers, it was hard to imagine him as one of the hooligans swarming over the mosque and through the lanes of Ayodhya, shouting obscene slogans against

Muslims on that day. When I asked whether he was also proud that the BJP had failed to live up to its commitment to ensure the mosque would not be harmed, that there would only be a ceremonial start to the work on the temple, he replied, 'The BJP didn't do it. It was the spirit of the devotees which carried them away.' A surly man pouring cartons of milk into a vast pan of tea added, 'The BJP would have been thrashed if they'd tried to stop it.' It was now six years after that incident but not a brick of the temple had yet been laid. Nevertheless Rishikesh Upadhyaya assured me it would be built by the Panch Kosi Parikrama in 2001. His forecast was not fulfilled. Nothing happened in 2001, and in 2002 the VHP tried to make just a ceremonial start to the construction of the temple but the government forestalled it.

We decided to get on with this parikrama, and rejoined the pilgrims who were marching on doggedly, entirely intent on completing the course, rarely even turning their heads to look at the temples they passed. We came to the headquarters of the VHP. The gates of the spacious garden were closed. Inside a few members of the VHP hierarchy sat talking under a tree. They evoked no interest in the pilgrims, and were not much interested themselves in this traditional pilgrimage, with the many different temples it encompassed and the diverse beliefs of the devotees. They were propagating one temple and one Rama. The pilgrims also walked straight past the compound where stonemasons were chiselling sandstone, carving pillars to be ready for when construction of the temple started. There had been an uproar about this in parliament, with opponents of the BJP government demanding that a stop be put to these preparations, but nobody in Ayodhya seemed particularly bothered either way. We came on two young boys dressed as Rama and his wife, Sita, wearing crowns taller than they were, sitting under a canopy by the roadside with their arms raised in blessing. They were of some interest to the pilgrims who dropped coins in their metal begging bowl. The humble paisa was still the currency of most Ayodhya pilgrims. They couldn't afford to offer rupees.

Breaking away from the pilgrimage, we walked to the site where

the mosque had stood and found ourselves the only visitors. The
police didn't allow us past the massive fortifications protecting the
images of Rama and Sita now installed there because we didn't have
our passports. They were unamused when Gilly asked, 'Do we need
a passport to see God?'

Returning disappointed, we passed some villagers outside a
temple, resting after completing the parikrama. An elderly woman
was rubbing her leg, the men were lying down. They came to the
festival in a party from a village in the neighbouring Gorakhpur
district every year. The leader of the group was a staunch supporter
of the BJP's opponents, the Gandhi family's Congress Party, but he
was in favour of building the temple. 'Yes,' he said, 'it is important
to build a temple. In their raj the Muslims destroyed our temple, so
in our raj why can't we have a place for our god?'

So, at the end of the day, we couldn't say there was no interest
in building the temple, but it wasn't top priority in the pilgrims'
minds. What mattered was still the old tradition of beating the
bounds of Rama's city. At the same time there was little evidence of
the pilgrimage drawing the faithful from afar.

We walked back into the heart of Ayodhya, to Kanak Bhavan, the
temple where we were to sleep that night. The Maharaja of Orchha,
Madhukar Shah, the chairman of the temple trust, had kindly
arranged for us to stay there. As guests of the maharaja we had been
give the VVIP accommodation. We had all to ourselves the two
large bedrooms with thick cotton mattresses arranged on the floor
and a pleasant verandah protected by wire mesh from mosquitoes
and monkeys. A cook borrowed from the local bazaar had occupied
the simple kitchen, where he sat on the floor cutting up vegetables,
which he smuggled into the resthouse under his clothes for fear of
monkeys.

The maharaja had told us that the temple was built by his great-
great-grandmother who had collected silver rupees to 'do religion'.
The maharani didn't trust the banking system of those days and so
the silver rupees were transported to Ayodhya for the construction
of the temple which took twelve years and was completed in 1901.
The maharaja still has the deeds on Victorian stamp paper signed

by the British sub-registrar of Ayodhya. The family bought some villages to provide for the maintenance of the temple. Land reforms after Independence took away most of the income from those villages but the trust still receives 2,300 rupees a year. To bridge the gap, and it's a wide gap, between its much depleted endowment and the costs incurred in running the temple the trust now has to depend on donations.

As we were unpacking, there was a knock on the door and a man diffidently announced himself as Ajai Kumar Chhawchharia, a member of the temple's management team, who had been deputed by the maharaja to look after us. He was thin almost to the point of emaciation, short, with a delicate, scholarly face, thick spectacles, closely cropped greying hair and wearing a brown shirt outside his baggy white cotton pajama trousers. As so often occurs in India he made me feel very large and clumsy.

Sitting on the verandah over the cup of sweet tea, which forms the start of most relationships, he told me that he kept the temple accounts. The next stage in getting to know each other was to discover that Ajai came from Bengal. His name wasn't Bengali, and so I thought he might be a Marwari. They are a community, originally of moneylenders, from Rajasthan. Many of them migrated to Bengal during the Raj, where they flourished, eventually buying out the British businesses when Nehru's socialism, and the bureaucracy that went with it, became too much for their owners to cope with.

Ajai confirmed that his father had been a wealthy Marwari who had supplied timber props to coal mines. Ajai himself had done well at school and university. After that he'd collected postgraduate diplomas in tax law, transport management, and hotel management too. He had been selected as a management trainee by the prestigious Taj group of hotels, but eventually went back to work in the family business. There he found that his father had to pay ten per cent of the money he was owed to the clerks of the nationalized collieries before they would clear his bills. He would charge for twelve lorryloads of timber when he'd only sent ten to pay all the bribes required to get business, and be paid for it. Disgusted by this corruption, Ajai had given it all up and come to live a celibate life in Ayodhya.

'Why did you take such an extreme step?' I asked. 'After all, with your qualifications there were plenty of other avenues open to you.'

'Well, you can say that from my childhood I was religious, so I suppose I always had this in the back of my mind. I adore Rama, he is my family, my father, my brother, and my friend.'

'But by now you might have been a manager of a magnificent palace hotel, a latter-day maharaja. Don't you regret that?'

'No,' he replied without hesitation. 'Now I'm looking after Rama's palace.'

Ajai insisted that his Rama was not the Rama of the VHP. So where do the different Ramas come from, and how many are there? In Sanskrit, the sacred language of Brahmin priests, there are more than twenty-five different versions of the Ramayana. The epic has been told in countless other languages too. In different versions down the centuries the hero has been adapted to the times, and to the purposes of those who have retold the epic. There is a legend told about the monkey god Hanuman going down to the netherworld to find a ring Rama had lost. After narrowly avoiding being eaten by the King of Spirits he was shown a platter on which there were thousands of rings, and told to pick the one Rama had lost. But Hanuman didn't know which ring it was. The King of Spirits said, 'There have been as many Ramas as there have been rings on this platter. Whenever Rama is coming to the end of an incarnation his ring drops down to me here. When you return to earth you will not find your Rama, his incarnation is over.'

Most scholars agree that the Sanskrit Ramayana of Valmiki is the earliest written version we have. He tells of Rama, the heir to the throne of Ayodhya who is robbed of his inheritance by his father's favourite wife. When the king abdicates she persuades him to choose her son as his successor, and send Rama into exile. Rama willingly accepts his father's decision and retires to the forest to live with his wife, Sita, and his brother, Lakshman. There Sita is abducted and carried off by the demon king Ravana to Lanka. With the help of Hanuman and his army of monkeys Rama kills Ravana and

rescues Sita. He returns to Ayodhya where his brother rejoices to
see him again and hands over the throne. When Rama was exiled
his brother had refused to sit on the throne, putting Rama's sandals
there instead, and telling his people that he was only their regent.
Rama becomes the perfect king. Because the ancient Indian tradition
of royalty is remarkably democratic – a king has no right to rule
if he doesn't satisfy his subjects – Rama used to move around his
capital after dark, disguised, to find out what the people thought
of his rule. One night he overheard a washerman saying that he
shouldn't have taken Sita back because she had stayed with another
man, even though she had been through an ordeal by fire to prove
her innocence. Rama accepted the verdict of his people and sent Sita
back to the forest.

The Ramayana Ajai was brought up on doesn't include the last
section of Valmiki's version – Sita's banishment. Ajai's mother used
to read to him from a much later version of the epic written by
the poet Tulsi Das in the seventeenth century. Revered as a saint
by Hindus, Tulsi Das started writing his Ramayana in Ayodhya,
but later moved to Varanasi. He called his retelling of the epic the
Ramacharitmanas. Valmiki wrote in Sanskrit, the language of the
priests, but the Ramayana of Tulsi Das was written in Avadhi, a form
of Hindi, the language of the people, and so became the Vulgate,
the people's version of the epic. To this day it remains probably
the most influential book in north India. The Brahmins were not
amused when their monopoly of the Ramayana ended. Nor did
they like Tulsi Das's emphasis on personal devotion to Rama, which
diminished the importance of the rituals they performed. According
to tradition, they decided to test the Ramacharitmanas in Varanasi's
most sacred Shiva temple. It was placed under copies of the four
Vedas, the original Hindu scriptures, and left overnight. The next
morning it was discovered on top of the pile, and thereafter was
regarded as the essence of the Vedas.

Tulsi Das followed the *bhakti* tradition of personal devotion to
one of the manifestations of the supreme being. So the divinity of
his Rama was established from the very beginning. Valmiki's Rama
didn't realize he was a god until after he had slain the demon king.

Only then was he informed that he was an incarnation of Vishnu. To Tulsi Das, Rama was 'the benevolent Lord' who is 'compassionate beyond our deserts', 'an ocean of amiability and gentleness', 'the formless, invisible, and uncreated Immaterial'. But at the same time Rama became a man out of love for his devotees 'as water crystallizes into ice'. He was a companion 'dwelling in the hearts of those who are all men's friends and are friendly to all: to whom pleasure and pain, praise and abuse, are all alike, who are careful to say what is both true and kind'.

Rama certainly dwelt in Ajai's heart. He told us he loved 'his Rama'. There was 'no formality in his relationship with his God'. 'It is enough,' he said, 'if you thrill and the fine hairs of your body stand on end at the mention of Rama's name.' He hoped to die laying his head on Rama's arm as his pillow.

Before we set off to see the image of Rama at Kanak Bhavan, the Rama we thought would be Ajai's God, he armed himself with a stick. That seemed surprising for such a mild-mannered man, but he explained to us that it was for 'the monkey menace'. 'You have to be very careful of them,' he said. 'You shouldn't actually hit them or they will attack you, but they won't come near you if you show them the stick. The worst thing you can do is to look them in the face, and don't smile at them, or they get very angry.'

There are enough rhesus macaques with protruding red bottoms in Ayodhya to provide the recruits for several armies of Rama's lieutenant Hanuman. Mothers with infants slung under their bellies pouncing on unsuspecting pilgrims and snatching the fruit intended for the gods, youngsters shinning up electricity poles, or picking fleas out of each other's hair, indicate that the population problem is getting worse. But no one dares to do anything about that in Ayodhya where Hanuman is second only to Rama and his wife Sita.

We crossed the compound safely, walked up a flight of steps, through an ornate arch into a courtyard paved with black and white marble. It was surrounded by a two-storeyed-white building, surmounted by small domed pavilions. The temple could well have been one of those Rajput palace hotels, so popular with tourists, which Ajai might have managed. The congregation for the evening *aarti*, or worship, was assembling in the high-ceilinged hall on the far side of the courtyard. We sat cross-legged on the floor in front of the curtain hiding the sanctum sanctorum and the gods inside it. As the hands of the distinctly un-ornate electric clock on the wall moved towards the time for the aarti, the congregation fell silent. The curtains were drawn back, revealing the images and the *pujari*, or priest, standing in front of them with a bell in one hand and a lamp lit by seven wicks of cotton wool dipped in ghee in the other. Many in the congregation prostrated themselves, but Ajai didn't. 'I don't bow down,' he whispered, 'because I regard Rama more as my brother than as a god.'

Unlike the deliberately dishevelled sadhus who throng the narrow lanes of Ayodhya, the pujari was a smart young man, his sleek, oiled, black hair neatly trimmed, his *kurta* and dhoti clean and pressed. The flames flickered as he circled the lamp in front of the images chanting Sanskrit prayers. There were three images of the couple sitting under the ornate gold canopy. The largest couple were joined by a huge marigold garland, the smallest were so small I would probably have missed them if Ajai hadn't pointed them out to me. The tinkling of the bell in the pujari's hand was almost drowned by the clang of a temple bell and the cacophony produced by a Heath-Robinson contraption driven by an electric motor which managed to ring yet more bells, clash cymbals and beat a drum all at the same time. Ajai whispered in my ear, 'I dislike that thing. The way things are going they will soon be automating the aarti itself.'

The congregation sat enthralled by the *darshan*, or sight of Rama and Sita, whose blank, black almond-shaped eyes stared back. Emotion rarely plays any part in Hindu iconography. Just in front of us a young man in a khaki shirt was talking to his prayer beads fervently. After the ceremony he introduced himself as 'Rama's security guard'. He was a constable from one of the fourteen companies of police protecting the site of the mosque and the images of Rama and Sita installed there. 'I stand just by Rama,' he said proudly.

Ajai's attitude to Rama was not entirely consistent, as we discovered after the aarti when he took us into a small room where the royal couple's robes were stored. They changed clothes each day, and Ajai was responsible for looking after their wardrobe. Although he hadn't prostrated himself before the images because he regarded Rama as his brother, he handled the royal robes with the greatest reverence saying, 'I love this because I am touching the clothes my Lord has worn.' I had been surprised to notice during the aarti that Rama had been wearing a cap not a crown. Ajai explained that he wore a crown during the day, when he was about his official duties, but in the evening he was relaxing. 'You will notice too,' he added, 'that Rama and Sita are seated when they are usually seen standing. This is because Kanak Bhavan is their home. That's why Rama's brother Lakshman who you usually see with him isn't here too. You see in our custom a younger brother-in-law is not allowed to enter his sister-in-law's house.'

According to tradition, Kanak Bhavan is the palace in which Rama and Sita lived after they were first married. It's a temple of *rasik* Hindus. For them Rama is the young husband ecstatic in his love for his new bride, and they respond by adoring Rama as Sita did. Their love is feminine, the passion of a young bride for her noble, handsome husband. When the pujari performs the aarti he covers his head to symbolize that he is worshipping Rama as a woman would. Although Ajai has devoted his entire life to serving the Rama of Kanak Bhavan, without incidentally being paid a paisa, he is not a rasik. 'I have nothing to do with sects,' he insisted, 'I stick by my Rama that's all. I wouldn't even necessarily call myself a Hindu, because if Rama had been a Muslim I would have been a Muslim. I love my Rama, no one else's.' From the robing room we climbed a flight of stairs to the private chamber where the royal couple live.

On the first floor, right above the sanctum sanctorum, there was a low-ceilinged room with a silver bed, open on all sides and surrounded by smaller rooms – a music room with a sitar in the corner, a dining room, a room for recreation complete with chessboard, a bathroom, a wardrobe with a cupboard for the crowns, and even a room for those who prepare *paan*, or betel nut, for Rama and his wife to chew after their meals. Ajai told us the images were not brought up to the private chambers but Rama does receive petitions and letters every day, some delivered by hand and some by post. These are brought up to the private chambers at night and then taken to be immersed in the river. 'Rama does sometimes reply to letters,' said Ajai, drawing our attention to a letter which had been framed and hung on the wall of the bedroom. It was Rama's reply to a Srimati Hemlata Devi in a dialect of Hindi neither Gilly nor I understood. Ajai carefully pieced together its meaning.

> I come to your garden, Beloved
> Every day in the early morning.
> I am pleased and please you.
> Come to my palace
> To my chamber, Beloved,
> Come in the month of Magh
> In the evening I will call you
> Come, Sakhi,
> To my palace
> Come, do come,
> In the darkness
> Don't forget.

The next morning we woke up to a dawn chorus of devotees chanting 'Sita Rama, Sita Rama', with a monotonous harmonium accompaniment. This was soon drowned by cassette stalls broadcasting their wares. After the mosque was pulled down, Ayodhya was flooded with cassettes revelling in the insult to Islam. Now, seven years later, the tone seemed to be much more moderate. One cassette we bought even described that event as 'a black day'. After we'd breakfasted on bananas and toast – no eggs and, of course, no meat are allowed inside Kanak Bhavan – Ajai arrived to take us to someone who was a rasik.

On our way to the Lakshman temple where the rasik, Dr Sunita Shastri, lived, our car was surrounded by *pandas*, the priests who act as guides, and take a commission from the temples for the donations pilgrims in their charge give. They offered their services to us for one thousand rupees a day. 'There you are,' said a deeply offended Ajai. 'You wanted to have a panda as a guide and I told you they were all rogues. One thousand rupees for one day, that's more than most Indians can earn in one month.'

Dr Shastri's room was in an airy corner high up in the Lakshman temple complex, known as a *qila*, or fort, which is exactly what it resembles. It stands right on the banks of the Saryu and from its ramparts we could clearly see that the sacred city of Ayodhya is enclosed in a bend in the river. The breeze blew towards us over the water and an expanse of sandbanks where melons grow during the summer months.

Dr Shastri was dressed in a shining white sari with a blue border. Her black hair was tied in a bun. She was plump and could well have been a prosperous mother of young children, but she was a celibate preacher. Admitting it was still rare to find a woman preacher she said, 'In the past women used to teach kings the Vedas and now look how things changed. We never had purdah here, then it came in medieval times, especially under Muslim influence, and you still find Hindu women observing purdah.'

Dr Shastri's father had been a bank manager and had arranged to be transferred to Varanasi when his guru told him he should educate his two daughters in Sanskrit, not in English, which would have offered better prospects both for a career and in the marriage market. In Varanasi, Dr Shastri had met her first guru and made up her mind to be a good scholar, but at that stage she didn't have any ambition to become a preacher. When I asked how that had come about, she explained, 'It is written in the Ramayana that whatever is in your future your fate takes you there.' Now she travelled all over India telling stories from the Ramayana and drawing morals from them, the traditional way of preaching.

Dr Shastri proved once again how complicated Hinduism is, how difficult for anyone trying to draw lines, to define schools or classify sects. Her guru had brought her up to be a devotee of Shankar or Shiva. Rama, whose devotee she eventually became, is an incarnation of Vishnu. To the outsider both gods seem very different. Vishnu, the preserver, is a god who is greatly concerned with

dharma, with the right ordering of the world, and when there is
disorder he comes down to put it right. Shiva, the destroyer, appears
more remote from the material universe. Traditionally, the followers
of Vishnu are known as Vaishnavas and those of Shiva as Saivas, but
in practice many Hindus find it only natural to worship both deities.
Dr Shastri did acknowledge that there was a difference between the
theologies of the two, but she said, 'We are all like small pots filled
with Saryu water. We appear to be different but when the water is
poured back into the river it all becomes one. You know that there
are four different roads back to Kanak Bhavan, but you also know
each one will take you to the same place. All our traditions accept
this.'

To complicate matters further Dr Shastri said we had been
misinformed, she was not a rasik, but at the same time suggested
that we learn about that sect by reading a book she had edited in
memory of her Vaishnava guru who had been a rasik. In that book
a rasik stated straightforwardly, 'Now I have become the bride
of Rama ... I have begged to experience the joy of the husband
of Sita.'

We also found this poem which describes how emotional a rasik's
relationship with Rama can be.

With swaying enticing movements, after meeting the beloved, after
   giving each other the essence of the joy of lovemaking
Then, you, woman seeking fulfilment, you shall become the necklace
   round your beloved's neck.
You are he and he is you in this union, and there can be no duality.
Just as once the waters of the river meet the ocean, they are no longer two
   in form but one.

In literature, in sculpture, and in worship, Hinduism has often
managed to combine the sacred and the sensual.

For many devotees of Rama, the rasik way is a scandal. Their god
is primarily a moral exemplar. Not surprisingly, this was a Rama
who appealed to the British who ruled India in Victorian times.
F. S. Growse, a British civil servant and devout Roman Catholic,

translated Tulsi Das into English and strongly approved of the poet's 'absolute avoidance of the slightest approach to any prurience of idea'. On the other hand, an unsympathetic modern scholar has described the Rama of Tulsi Das as 'a tiresome prig'.

It's no surprise that the RSS family have jumped on the chariot of Rama, the moral exemplar. For them he is the perfect king, a god but also a man, a historic figure who ruled the whole of India, an inspiration to unite Hindus and re-create a Hindu India. One of Ayodhya's most successful sadhus, Mahant Nritya Gopal Das, is an evangelist of the VHP Rama. He is the founder of a religious order whose property, or cantonment as it is known, spreads over a square kilometre of valuable land near the centre of Ayodhya.

Ajai refused to meet Nritya Gopal Das because he regarded him as a politician rather than a holy man, and wanted nothing to do with any political party. The mahant insisted that although he was the vice-president of the trust established by the VHP to build their Rama temple, he had nothing to do with politics. He was sitting cross-legged on a small square of carpet in the hall of a modern temple, which laid no claim to architectural distinction and could have been anywhere in north India. Broad-shouldered, with the arms of a wrestler, and the torso of a man who no longer exercised with the vigour of his youth, Nritya Gopal Das had the dishevelled appearance most sadhus cultivate. His broad forehead was smeared with orange paste, his oily greying hair, faintly coloured with henna, fell down to his shoulders, his beard was untrimmed, the white cotton robe wrapped round him was creased. But he was a man used to commanding respect. As he ordered us to sit down, the acolytes surrounding him obediently moved aside.

'You must remember,' he scolded me, 'the temple trust is not just VHP, it has other members and we should all work together. That is the Hindu tradition, where there have always been different ways to worship Rama, and everyone is welcome to worship as they like.' Laughing he jabbed me with his finger and said, 'Anyone is welcome to join my sect, the Ramanandis, you can join too.'

As we spoke visitors to the temple came and prostrated themselves at the mahant's feet. He accepted this as nothing more than the respect due to him, continuing our conversation, and casually rewarding each devotee with a handful of sacred tulsi leaves from a bowl by his side. One or two visitors did manage to engage his attention briefly, but when a woman tried to extend her audience a young sadhu asked her abruptly, 'What else do you want to ask? Hurry up.'

I asked the mahant how he counselled those who came to him with their troubles or asked for a blessing or a boon. He replied, 'They ask for things and we say, ask God not us. He alone gives, ask Rama, pray to Rama. But we do give a blessing, satisfaction, peace, we explain things to them.' The beat of the drums and the clashing cymbals – the temple's background music – didn't drown his deep voice.

Nritya Gopal Das was reluctant to say much about the Rama of his sect, the god he believed in. Instead he ordered one of the young sadhus sitting beside him to take us to another member of his sect who was also a scholar. 'But first,' he said, 'I want to show you something. Some people say we sadhus eat all the money we get in donations. Now you'll see that's not true.'

Sitting down, the mahant seemed to be a great bear of a man, but when he rose I saw he was far shorter than I had thought. He led us into another hall where long lines of pilgrims were sitting on the floor eating vegetable curry, daal, chapatis and rice, off plates made of dried leaves. He pointed at the diners and said, 'Now you see who eats the money and you will eat some too.' With that he dismissed us and we were taken to an upstairs room to be given a similar lunch in more privileged company. The sadhus not only served the food, they also did the cooking, and the washing up. Our young guide, dressed like his guru in white cotton, explained that the sadhus even swept the floors – there were no servants in the *math*, or monastery.

Walking down the road to the pilgrim's hostel where the scholar lived, we passed a sadhus' dormitory. Some five hundred beds were arranged in long lines. The dormitory opened on to the road, and so we could see a few sadhus enjoying their post-lunch siesta. Our guide said no check was kept on where the sadhus came from and how long they stayed. A senior police officer had told us that criminals often fled to Ayodhya and donned the saffron robe to escape the law.

The scholar was Acharya Kripa Shankarji Maharaj. *Acharya* means a man distinguished for his learning and *Maharaj* indicates just how distinguished. He started his theological studies in Varanasi at the age of seven but moved to Ayodhya where he had been teaching for many years. Sitting cross-legged on a bed, wearing a saffron robe, with a grey beard flowing down to his chest he didn't seem too pleased to be interrupted. 'You'll need chairs,' he said with obvious disapproval, and didn't soften when we told him we would rather sit at his feet. 'What have you come for? Who sent you?' he asked.

When we told him that Mahant Nritya Gopal Das had sent us to explain the beliefs of the Ramanandi sect, he said that we must first understand who Rama is, and asked, 'Was he born in Ayodhya?'

'There is a tradition,' I replied.

'No, he wasn't. He wasn't born anywhere. He came into the world. Why?'

Like schoolchildren overawed by a particularly strict teacher, we hesitated.

'Hurry up!' he barked. Then, giving up on us, he went on, 'Rama came into the world not just to teach us to kill Ravana, but to establish a model to teach who you are, what are your duties, and what are your rights.'

He compared the example Rama had set with Krishna, another avatar of Vishnu, saying, 'One had one wife, the other had many women. You should do what Rama did. You should do what Krishna said, not what he did. When Krishna was six days old he drank poison. Could you do that?' he asked, leaning towards us and wagging his finger.

Then without waiting for an answer he went on, 'Provided you are inspired by Rama's example you can worship him in many ways. For instance, my own guru worshipped the child Rama. His devotion was so deep, so intense, that he often experienced God playing in his lap.'

When Gilly asked whether that meant you could worship Rama as though you were his lover in the way rasiks do, the Acharya was not amused.

'Man-woman love is dirty, forget it,' he said, but then seemed to have second thoughts and went on, 'well you can say it's good but not in a good sense. Love is a *ghalat paribasha*, a dirty word these days, as you know.'

By now it was clear we were testing the crusty celibate's patience to breaking point, and we took our leave after he'd reluctantly given us a blessing.

Our young guide was much more friendly. He told us he'd left a comparatively prosperous family – his brother was an inspector of police, a much sought after job in India – to join the mahant's math at the age of fifteen. Now only twenty-five, the mahant had already entrusted him with a year-long mission to Thailand where he'd spread the gospel of Tulsi Das. The mission, he said, had been a success: 'Lots of people became Hindus, became interested in Rama.'

Traditionally Hinduism is not an evangelical religion which sets out to convert the world, but the mahant clearly owed some of his theology to the Arya Samaj, a Hindu sect founded in 1875 to combat the efforts of Christian missionaries. Learning from the enemy, the Arya Samaj tried to emulate the discipline and organization of the missionaries and their zeal for souls. As there was no procedure for conversion in Hinduism, the Arya Samaj reinterpreted the ceremony for purifying those who had been polluted by some impurity or by breaking some caste rule as the rite for receiving new recruits into the Hindu fold.

Our guide insisted that we must see the bank Nritya Gopal Das had founded. It was situated on the first floor of yet another building owned by the mahant's trust. The bank turned out to be an institution for storing treasure which moth and rust cannot corrupt and thieves wouldn't bother to steal. The bank manager, a thin, surprisingly dapper sadhu with long white hair, clean and carefully combed, showed us some customers' account books. They were exercise books with pictures of the divine couple and a younger

Nritya Gopal Das on the yellow and red covers. Each page was ruled with 297 small rectangles, and in each of them customers had written 'Siya Rama', that is Sita Rama. Anyone who deposits 125,000 Siya Rama's can open an account. The bank's deposits now amounted to twenty-eight thousand million Siya Ramas.

'What interest accumulates?' I asked.

'The deposits are for welfare in this life and the next,' the manager replied. 'Writing like this is one hundred per cent more profitable than the traditional reciting the name of Rama because you have to concentrate so hard. Your mind can't wander.'

This brought back unpleasant memories to me of impositions, or lines, at school. Nevertheless, there was a queue of customers waiting to have their deposits recorded in their passbooks.

We still had to learn more about the Rama of the VHP, but first we decided to see the image of Rama they wanted to install in their grand new temple. So early the next morning we went back to the entrance of the fortifications surrounding that Rama. Once again we were the only pilgrims there. The police were very polite, providing us with an escort to help us find our way through a maze of passages between fences of steel piping topped by barbed wire. Gilly protested mildly at the third body search, and was assured it was the last. But as we were proceeding on our way we passed a constable who noticed something was still wrong. 'A pen,' he said in horror, 'you are taking a pen inside with you. Hand it to me.' I surrendered my pen, my notebook had already gone.

Eventually we came to a small square surrounded by yet more steel pipes. Inside the barricade women in khaki shirts and trousers, constables of the paramilitary Central Reserve Police Force, were deployed. Walking round the square we came to the side overlooking the site where the mosque had stood. In the distance, on a mound surrounded by sandbags, there was a tent inside which we could see small images of Rama and Sita. A pujari sat by the fence offering *prasad*, consecrated sweets, but there were no temple bells, the air was not laden with incense and there were no *kirtans* or hymns. This was a uniquely silent temple of Rama, a Rama under arrest.

When we got back to Kanak Bhavan, Ajai was there waiting to take us to see the VHP themselves. This was surprising for someone who was so definite in his disapproval of politics and politicians. He declined to join us for breakfast, saying he only ate food he'd cooked himself. Judging by his figure he didn't eat much of that either.

We walked through the grounds of the VHP's headquarters in Ayodhya to the office, a modest, functional, one-storeyed modern building. Inside it was orderly and clean. Cheap coir matting covered the concrete floor. We were told that the 'manager', Prakash Avasthi, would be out when he'd finished his bath. Being a celibate he lived in the office building.

We were discussing a poster of Rama carrying a bow and arrow, towering over the VHP's temple when Prakash Avasthi walked in. He was diffident but not deferential, a man, I felt, who would prefer not to deal with the public but did so because it was his duty. Although only in his fifties, he was partially paralysed down one side, the result of a stroke he was still recovering from. He explained that his previous position in the VHP had put him under great strain and that was why he'd been sent to Ayodhya, which seemed rather strange logic as Ayodhya could hardly be called a peaceful posting. He'd sacrificed his whole life for the RSS and the VHP, working full time for them. When his father negotiated a bride for him, and pleaded with him to come home and take up family life again, he replied, 'You took me to the RSS parades when I was young, you made me mad for the RSS, so now you can't complain when I want to give my life for it.'

I explained that we had been discussing various traditions of Rama and his worship and wanted to find out how the VHP interpreted him. He pointed to the poster of Rama and said, 'That is Rama *vir*, the brave, the warrior. Rama was a perfect man, we certainly believe that, but he was not weak. God does not help the weak.' He then went on to remind me of the story in the Ramayana about the monkey king Sugreev who had been dethroned by his brother and was restored by Rama. 'Sugreev was weak,' he said, 'but when he organized and fought, then Rama came forward to help him, and killed his brother. Rama will never help India if the people don't organize. That's been our trouble in the past, we have been disorganized and weak.' The RSS consistently rubs salt into the wound of those centuries of foreign rule, but the irony is that, in doing so, they demean Hindus, paint a picture of a cowardly race who allowed themselves to be dominated. The story is in fact much more complicated than that.

Avasthi maintained Hindus were still showing their weakness by tolerating Muslims who were traitors to their country, because they rejoiced when Pakistan won test matches. They were deliberately having large families so that they could swamp the Hindu population. They had loyalties 'outside the country', and, he added, so did Christians.

When I suggested that his views might be seen as promoting religious hatred he became quite angry. 'Why shouldn't we react to what has been done to us by Muslims? They ruled us, they destroyed our temples. They react, they react the most to anything done to them. Salman Rushdie writes something true and they want to cut him up.'

I tried to trap him, asking, 'But aren't you proud that Hinduism, unlike Islam and Christianity, is tolerant? I've often heard your leaders claim that.'

'Yes, we are tolerant. We have all gods, not just one god. You needn't even believe in God. We don't just have Rama. It's not like Islam where if you don't believe in the one God you get the sword. We haven't burnt libraries. Ours were burnt.'

'But you did pull down a mosque, and you did shout obscene slogans against Muslims while doing it,' I pointed out.

'Our self-respect had been damaged,' he replied. 'How would you feel if someone insulted your religion, your motherland? But it was young men who shouted the slogans. When you are angry curses come to your tongue. The elderly people did not shout those slogans, and our leaders told the young people not to, but they were carried away and you should understand that.'

Avasthi's Rama was a god who said 'get strong, gain strength'. He was 'a warrior dressed for war' who, if Hindus fought together, would guarantee them victory over Muslims threatening to swamp his motherland, and Christians trying to convert their weaker brethren.

When we got up to go I was surprised that Ajai said, 'I would like to come back and talk to you again. What you say, we should discuss.' I never thought he would be interested in the worship of Rama, the warrior. His love of his Lord seemed so gentle.

When I asked him about this Ajai explained, 'Perhaps he's right, maybe we are too tolerant. We allow them everything, and they just ride over us. On the other hand I need to hear the other side of the story too.'

Ayodhya is a strange town where arch-enemies are the best of friends; Lord Rama is a symbol of love for some and hate for others. It's a Hindu holy place which enjoyed its heyday under Muslim rulers, it's the focal point of a militant religious movement but it elected an atheist former communist as its MP, it's home to thousands of holy men and a refuge for criminals.

On our last day in Ayodhya, we got up early to see the end of the festival. The pilgrims were bobbing up and down in the muddy water of the Saryu river, no one venturing beyond the wooden barriers warning of the fast-flowing current. Pandas, squatting on the steps leading down to the river, provided services to the bathers, looking after their clothes while they were in the river, lending them a comb and a mirror and marking their foreheads with red paste when they came out. They had tethered half-starved calves beside them, hoping they could persuade the pilgrims to make *godaan*, the gift of a sacred cow, but the donations were not even adequate to pay for the panda's scrawny beasts. The pandas complained that they barely made enough money to cover the fee they had to pay for occupying the steps. The wealthy, for the most part, don't take a dip on Ayodhya's annual auspicious day.

By Indian standards it's a small-scale affair, and by eleven o'clock the banks of the Saryu were left to the marigolds, the plastic bags, the paper, and the other detritus of an Indian bathing festival. One panda sat beside his bedraggled calf hoping for some latecomers.

The festival had been entirely peaceful. There had been no tension, no objections from the Muslim community, nothing for the police to do except reunite children with their parents. Tolerant Hinduism had triumphed.

But as we had our last cup of tea on the verandah of Kanak Bhavan's guest house, Ajai returned to the subject of tolerance which was clearly bothering him. 'You know,' he said, 'I bought a Bible and a Qur'an and I found no religion teaches violence, but still I do think Hindus' peaceful nature has always been exploited by fanatics.' I didn't want to argue with him, or remind him that it was Hindus who were threatening the peace of Ayodhya, with their warrior Rama. No one could be less aggressive than Ajai or more peace-loving, yet even he had been influenced by the Rama who seeks revenge. The festival had confirmed our belief that in spite of the destruction of the mosque and the BJP coming to power in Delhi for the first time, Hindu fundamentalism was not sweeping the country; but we had come to realize how insidious creating a sense of grievance could be.

Misplaced Charity

Mirzapur stands on the banks of the Ganges, overshadowed by two neighbours. Varanasi or Benares, Shiva's city, is downriver, and upriver to the west is Allahabad where every twelve years, when the stars come together in a particularly auspicious association, millions and millions of Hindus gather for the Kumbh Mela and bathe at the point where the Ganges meets Delhi's river, the Jamuna. But I believe on the festival of Diwali in the year 2000, Mirzapur outshone both its neighbours.

Diwali is the festival of lights. In northern India it celebrates the joyous return of the warrior king and god Rama after rescuing his wife, Sita, from the demon ruler of Lanka. On the evening of Diwali 2000 in Mirzapur an armada of *diyas*, or traditional lamps, set sail on the Ganges to welcome Rama and Sita home. Standing in the darkness on a cliff high above the river, as one of many guests at a Diwali party, I saw first a pinpoint of light float slowly downstream. It was soon followed by another, and another, until the flames flickering in the clay saucers became a Milky Way on the dark waters of the Ganges. Lamps were still being launched as the vanguard of the armada disappeared round the distant bend in the river.

When the last lamp had sailed past us a torch flashed from the river, and somewhere from the clifftop a reply was sent. Inevitably there followed much shouting from the river and the cliff before fifteen boatmen from the Mallah, or fishermen, caste scrambled up a steep path to join us. They had launched the fleet, but the review had been organized by our host Edward Oakley, chairman of the Mirzapur-based carpet company Obeetee, and for many years a member of the Mirzapur Club on whose lawn we were standing, and from where a regular supply of drinks flowed.

The tall, blonde wife of the American ambassador, carefully

casual in a stylish white kameez patterned with large red flowers in Moghul design, stood out from the rest of Edward's motley guests assembled on the clifftop. The host himself had made no sartorial concessions to his distinguished guests. He was dressed in trousers which fitted loosely round his enormous girth, a shirt, and braces clearly visible to all. Edward was a large man. With his rubicund face, head fringed by just a thin strip of closely clipped grey hair above what can only be called a bull neck, he reminded me of the pictures of Edward VII seen on cigar packets. Speaking basic Hindustani with an almost deliberately English accent, inheritor of a business founded by his father during the Raj, upholder of the British tradition of the burra peg or large whisky, and accompanied usually by his faithful factotum, Bhagwan Das, Edward Oakley could all too easily be taken as a caricature of someone who had 'stayed on', a relic of the Raj. In fact he was an extremely astute businessman who had converted his father's somewhat ramshackle business into what an American carpet designer once told me was the most efficient and quality conscious manufacturer he had ever come across.

The headquarters of Obeetee were just across the road from the club in the spacious compound of what had been Edward's parents' home. We were to dine that night in the burra or big bungalow, now the company guest house. But before we left the river, Edward called for a group photo, and announced that he would sit in front on the ground with the Mallahs.

'Yes,' piped up Bhagwan Das, 'but how will you get up?'

Edward's voice boomed, 'With your help. After all it was you who organized this whole *tamasha*.'

That was certainly true. Edward never tired of acknowledging his dependence on Bhagwan Das, often saying that he should run Obeetee. Between the two men there was what seemed to me the close relationship of a master and a faithful servant. Edward put it differently.

'When Bhagwan Das is not around I get into trouble. When he arrives on the scene he gets me out of trouble, and when he is with me he ensures that I do not get into trouble, and what is more, he thinks for me both at home and in business. He is my thoroughly modern Jeeves.'

As we were assembling for the photo, there was a slight hiccough when I asked the boatmen how many lamps there were. The Hindi word for lamp is very similar to the past participle of the verb to give and the boatmen, thinking I had asked how much money they'd been given said, somewhat aggressively, 'We haven't discussed that yet.' Bhagwan Das rescued me, making my meaning clear, and the Mallahs told me they had launched a thousand lamps from their boats.

Sitting on the verandah of the big bungalow having yet more drinks, the American ambassador explained how his wife's interest in carpets had led to their friendship with Edward. The Diwali party would have been an opportunity for Edward to lobby the ambassador about the threat to his sales in America from a campaign against child labour mounted by the Rugmark Foundation. But Edward considered this would be rather tasteless.

The Foundation was attracting US importers by stating on its website that 'The Rugmark label guarantees the carpet was not made by children' and that 'Through Rugmark's media campaign your company will be highlighted in the national news as an importer of child-labor-free carpets.' Though elsewhere on the website Rugmark's claims for its label were diluted to 'the best assurance that a child's fingers will not weave the carpets you import', Edward felt that the impression was being created that Rugmark was promising something it couldn't deliver. Carpets are a cottage industry, woven in looms scattered over thousands of villages, which makes inspection very difficult. Edward has argued that there isn't an inspection scheme which can guarantee that no child has worked on any labelled carpet. He is afraid that if any Rugmark manufacturers are exposed as using child labour, it could have a disastrous impact on every company whose carpets carry the label. His company had paid a price for rejecting the Rugmark label, losing their market in Germany, the largest European carpet importer. The foundation was launched there with the support of the German government, and had now turned its attention to the United States, Obeetee's main market.

Edward was a natural raconteur of the self-deprecatory tradition nurtured in British public schools. His career at his father's old school, Rossall in the north of England, had apparently 'not been entirely satisfactory' and he'd left as soon as possible to be articled to a chartered accountant. He'd chosen that profession because all the accountants he'd met had seemed to be 'thickies', and so he thought the profession would suit him.

He scraped through his intermediate exam first time, but then, Edward explained, there came a setback in his career. 'For the next two years I considered passing such an achievement that I didn't do any study whatsoever. I gambled on the horses and cards and had a jolly good time. The first time I took the finals I failed.'

Edward guffawed, and we all laughed too, including the ambassador, who, although he gave me the impression of a man who had never failed at anything in his life, was greatly enjoying Edward's story.

'Of course, my father didn't think it was quite so funny,' Edward went on. 'He was out here in Mirzapur and he proceeded to turn my photograph on the mantelpiece around to face the wall and I was in disgrace. But my mother turned the picture round and I took the exam again and passed. I don't know how.'

White uniformed, bare-footed servants, under the ever-watchful eye of Bhagwan Das, ensured no glass was empty. Punkahs turned lazily, more to disturb the flight plans of the mosquitoes than to provide relief from the temperature, which was quite comfortable that night. But there was no sign of dinner. I didn't mind, having reached the stage when I didn't want dinner to interfere with the drinking. Nor did Edward, who continued his story.

Apparently, Edward's joining of his father's business had not been planned. He came to Mirzapur on holiday from the London accountancy firm where he was working. It was the first time he'd been back since he left as a child and he was bowled over by the bungalow and its magnificent, manicured garden. He thought to himself, 'Edward, this is going to be like early retirement to come to Mirzapur, and no more of that ticking trade called accountancy.'

Another Englishman in the party who had stayed on in Mirzapur too, and was still running a small carpet firm, said, 'Come on, Edward, you didn't just sit on your backside. You really gave the old firm a good shaking. What about the day you burnt all the files?'

'Well,' replied Edward laughing again, 'I was a great admirer of my father and he taught me everything about this business. But I was young and I did think there were some rather strange things which could be improved. One was Afaq Ahmad, who was meant to tell me about the progress made on any order. He had a straggly beard, looked like somebody out of the Bible. So rather than a Pharisee, I called him a scribe, because he always had a pen and his fingers were covered with ink. When I asked him what the position was with a carpet he would say with great confidence, six feet had been woven, the next day he would tell me with equal confidence that nothing had been woven. Amusing maybe, but not to our buyer in New York who was wanting to cancel his order.'

One day an infuriated Edward had summoned the scribe and ordered him to hand over all his records to a peon who had dumped them in the boiler. 'After that,' Edward said, 'Mr Afaq had another job and life became a lot easier.'

Edward had also cleared out the design room in the factory where thousands and thousands of old carpet designs were kept suspended precariously in wire netting over the heads of the designers. Edward's father, who apparently was 'not a throw away person', had refused to let him burn the designs, and so he hired four bullock carts to carry them from the factory back to the compound in Mirzapur. 'My father and his partner were quite shocked,' Edward said, 'but that was the end of the designs.'

It was well past ten o'clock and the *diyas* lining the paths of the Obeetee compound were burnt out when Edward finished his stories and led us into the main room of the burra bungalow. Separate tables for four were laid out on the polished wooden floor. The vast room with its sparse, dark, colonial-style furniture, its faded antique rugs, and its fireplace would have changed little since Edward's parents lived there.

The dinner opened with soup followed by fish and chips, but moved from there to tandoori chicken and other Indian dishes. As soon as dinner was over the ambassador and his wife retired to the best bedroom in the bungalow and the rest of the guests dispersed. This was not discourteous but just normal practice in India today – drink hard, eat late and then leave.

Mirzapur had not yet gone to sleep. As we drove back to the Hotel Galaxy, which had none of the old world charm of the bungalow, in fact it had no charm at all, children threw crackers under our car, stalls selling small clay images of Lakshmi and the elephant god Ganesh were still open, and sweet-makers were bawling their bargain prices over loudspeakers. Our driver said, 'They must be duplicate. You can't make pure milk sweets for that money.'

Carpet making is the backbone of the economy of a vast region centred on Mirzapur. It's an industry with a long history. In the late 1830s Emily Eden, travelling up the Ganges with her brother Lord Auckland who was the Governor General, noted in her diary, 'We made an expedition to Mirzapur the great carpet manufactory.' Unfortunately she did not describe the manufacturing process but it seems unlikely that the weaving would have been markedly different from today.

The looms are still heavy wooden beams round which the cotton threads of the warp are stretched. The weavers sit in a pit behind the loom, tying knot after knot, each one marked by a dot on the *naqsha*, or map of the carpet. The ill-lit sheds in which most weavers work have probably not changed that much either. But the finishing processes have. To a first-time observer, it's a miracle that those processes don't finish the carpet.

In the washery, the back of the intricate floor coverings the villagers have toiled so long at their looms to weave are first singed with a blowlamp. As if that wasn't hazardous enough, they are then doused in a series of baths with different strong chemicals which can all too easily discolour them if not applied in correct proportions.

After each bath the sodden wool is pummelled by wooden paddles until most of the water has oozed out. When at last the bathing and bashing is completed the bedraggled carpet is laid out in the sun to dry.

The washing, and the more intricate finishing that takes place afterwards, are labour intensive, a vital employer in one of India's poorest regions. Edward believes that shock publicity, if it leads those in the developed world to believe that all Indian carpets other than those endorsed by Rugmark are the product of child labour, is a threat to this industry, which is one of the very few in India that puts money into the villages. Other traditional manufacturers like potters, cloth weavers, shoe and soap makers have been driven out of business by modern machinery, forcing millions to leave their villages and swell the slums of the large cities.

Before we'd left Delhi, another Englishman involved in the carpet industry, who agreed with Edward's assessment of Rugmark, had come to have lunch with us. Robin Garland had once been chief executive of Scottish Heritage, a group which owned E. Hill and Company, Obeetee's traditional rivals. When he was accused by the British press of employing child weavers, he admitted he didn't know whether that was so and promised to go to India to see for himself. On that visit he decided education was the main problem. Because there were no schools worth the name, children had no alternative but to work on the looms. He founded a nongovernmental organization called Project Mala which had established schools in the carpet belt.

Although Robin now spent all his time on Project Mala, he still looked like a businessman with his pink shirt, and tie – only obligatory in Delhi's business and diplomatic communities – his expensive shining black slip-ons and his neatly cut grey hair. He was a rich man, a millionaire, but he did say, 'only a small one now'.

I asked him, 'How does an efficient businessman like you cope with all the inefficiencies of India?'

His bright blue eyes softened, and he gave one of his rare smiles. 'Sometimes you don't. The other day I told an official of the education ministry that many of the government schools did not have teachers or pupils. He accepted that but when I suggested that Project Mala should take over some of the schools and run them he replied, "Oh, we couldn't possibly abdicate our responsibility for education." That's the bureaucracy for you. Not exactly logical.'

In India words often don't mean quite what they appear to mean, and the carpet industry is no exception. A carpet manufacturer usually has no role in the manufacture of the carpet, the weaving. He gets the orders, supplies the wool and the design, and finishes the carpet when it comes off the loom. But the weavers are employed by a loom owner, often a weaver himself, and most of the manufacturers Rugmark deals with don't have any contact with them. They deal through a middleman, a contractor. So the manufacturer can be two stages removed from the looms yet he is the person who guarantees to Rugmark that no children are working on them.

Robin had seen a recent television documentary on Channel 4 called *Slavery* which had shown the ethical director of B&Q, a major British retailer, advocating Rugmark. Robin said, 'I let him know what I thought of his ethics. I told him, "You are having the wool pulled over your eyes. You are buying Rugmark carpets from an exporter who doesn't have any looms of his own. How can he know whether they are genuinely child-labour-free?" I told the director straight.' He added, 'I'm a blunt Yorkshireman. I'm not known for my tact.'

Perhaps, not surprisingly, Robin Garland's man on the spot, David Rangpal, was not an enthusiast for the labelling scheme. Driving out of Mirzapur to see one of the Mala schools, he told us that he had shocked a United Nations working group on child labour by telling one of their meetings in Geneva, 'Child labour as such is no problem in the carpet industry. The problem is lack of an alternative, and in particular lack of educational opportunities.'

David Rangpal, tall by Indian standards, white haired, soft spoken and sad faced, was a distinguished educationalist himself. A sociologist with an American Ph. D. and post-doctoral work at the School of Oriental and African Studies in London behind him, he had come back to the Punjab to head a Christian college. During the Sikh troubles, the separatist movement led by Sant Jarnail Singh

Bhindranwale in the eighties, he had narrowly escaped an attempt on his life. He and his wife had then both felt called to this educational backwater, to accept a meagre salary, and manage the Mala schools. We soon learned the reason for his sad expression. His wife had been killed in a car accident two years earlier. He said, 'I see in Project Mala my wife.' A devout Christian, he didn't worry what others thought of his work. 'I am not the judge,' he said, 'nor is anyone else. God is the judge, let him decide.'

However, David Rangpal did judge the government's efforts to provide education for the children of the carpet belt. His view was that the government was not competent to provide education or any other services. As we drove past a new large office block, with residential accommodation for staff, he peered out of the window shortsightedly and said, 'Take a look at that. It's a good example of the way the government functions, or doesn't function, I should say.'

He told the driver to stop and reverse so that we could get a better look and went on with remarkable bitterness for such a mild-mannered man: 'This is the new local government headquarters. The public have to come here for everything they want to get done, for all their needs, but they can't get here. It's in the middle of nowhere.' The complex was indeed set in the middle of a treeless, barren wasteland, miles from the nearest town.

A short distance ahead David stopped the car again and insisted that we got out to inspect a local health centre. The only sign of medicine we could see was a datura bush growing out of the dilapidated, deserted, building. There were two charpoys inside, evidence that it was occupied at night, and evidence on the floor that the accommodation was shared by cattle.

From there we proceeded to the small town of Marihan where we drove into a walled compound, with another crumbling concrete building at one side. 'This is the bus station, and that's the ticket office,' David said. 'But as you can see, no buses. They can't be bothered to come in here because it's easier to stop on the road.' We checked with the only government employee we could find, a watchman. He confirmed it was a bus station unvisited by buses.

'Everything is rotting away,' he said. 'This is the arrangement of the government.'

After Marihan, we turned down a road which ran along the banks of a canal, full of green water. The unhealthy colour didn't deter young boys from bathing. We learnt that the canal had been dry until farmers had blocked the road and forced the government to attend to their demand for irrigation – just in time to save the rice crop. At last we found a government school. There was no one to be seen. A notice chalked on a blackboard read 'Going to the Bank'.

When we reached the Project Mala school there was a full staff, classes in Hindi and environmental studies were underway, girls were learning to tailor school uniforms, and boys were sitting behind looms learning to weave. Signs on the wall advocated a mixture of health, hygiene, morality, and commonsense: 'Eat Green Vegetables', 'Weakness is the Biggest Sin', 'There is Strength in Unity', 'Keep Food Covered', 'Strength Without Wisdom is in Vain'. We shared an excellent lunch of *khichri*, spinach, and raw white radishes, with the girls and boys dressed in uniform dark-blue checked shirts worn outside sky-blue trousers. They sat in orderly lines cross-legged on the floor. A brief grace, appropriate to any religion, was said before lunch, 'Oh, God bless this food, and we thank you for this meal.'

After lunch the children poured out of the whitewashed concrete school into the playground at the front surrounded by roses, and purple bougainvilleas. Impromptu games of football and other sports broke out. Gilly persuaded some of the boys to surrender part of their break and be interviewed. Only one said that he did work on a loom at home but maintained his father was very keen that he should continue his education. David explained that much of the confusion about child labour was caused by a failure to differentiate between bonded, or slave labour, children working for wages on looms near their homes, and children who helped their families to weave carpets. 'So much of the publicity,' he said, 'gives the impression that every child working on a loom is a slave.'

Several years earlier we had seen slave children. There were six of them, all seemed about ten years old, weaving on a loom in a village some distance from Mirzapur. Clothes hung on pegs on the wall behind them. Their bedding rolls, and a pile of tin plates showed quite clearly that the boys ate and slept in the shed where they worked. They were too frightened to talk. We were taken to that weaving shed by volunteers working with Champa Devi, a woman who practised what most Indians unfortunately now regard as the outdated virtues of Mahatma Gandhi.

We found Champa Devi again, still wearing a sari woven from hand-spun cotton, the Gandhian material known as *khadi*, and still working from her small house facing a noisy, narrow street in the heart of Mirzapur. The walls of the front room, which doubled as her office, were lined with the legal books of her husband. I remembered him telling us that he never got time to attend to his own practice because he was so busy fighting cases brought by his wife on behalf of slave children or their parents, so I asked whether that was still so. Tears welled up behind the spectacles of the diminutive fighter for children's rights – she must have been well under five feet – the white, blue-bordered sari was adjusted to ensure it covered all her hair – and she replied, 'My husband died just before my daughter's wedding, so we had to have the funeral and the wedding. It was hard to bear. You knew him, he was a good man.'

All we could mumble was, 'Yes.'

Champa Devi had been working for the release and welfare of bonded labour since 1973. All her workers were volunteers, and quite a few of them were crammed into that small room. When we last met her, she had been concentrating on releasing slave children and bringing cases on their behalf against their owners. But now she seemed less confident about that course of action. Staring directly at us, with her lips pursed grimly she said, 'I got two thousand two hundred people released, many of them were adult bonded labourers, but they are not insects that fly against the lights at night and can be swept away dead in the morning.'

One of Champa Devi's volunteers, making full use of tortuous legal terminology, tried to get us to understand how difficult it had been to get the police and the courts to interpret the legislation against child labour in their favour, but Champa Devi stopped him in his tracks. 'Don't start another meeting,' she said sharply, and then went on, 'as I said, I had those children released but now they are bonded again because they have no money. Without the help of the government I got them released but what will they eat if the government doesn't do anything for them after that?'

Champa Devi was also critical of other NGOs, especially those conducting raids to release slave children. 'After twenty years of releasing children I have to say I don't consider raids necessary. Publishing photos in the paper, that is not the answer.'

She would not name the publicity seekers, but we both knew who she meant.

When we came to Rugmark, Champa Devi was prepared to be specific. Pursing her lips even more tightly, and frowning, she launched into a diatribe against the foundation's practice of charging a percentage of the carpet's value from both exporters and importers who use the Rugmark label.

'Rugmark charges two per cent from the carpet people, and then what is the use of it if it can't get to the root cause of the bonded labour? It is certainly not our aim to collect money from the industry. What do they think, that you can stop slavery by centring your attention on money?'

When I pointed out that Rugmark spent much of the money it collected on rehabilitation and education she became even more incensed. 'If there is no rehabilitation for the family of the released boy then what will happen? Everything will be in vain unless the family is rehabilitated in a real sense. By putting twenty-five children in school will tens of millions of people be fed?' she ended scornfully.

We left Champa Devi to her battle with the government, which was refusing to take the problem of rehabilitation seriously, a losing battle, I couldn't help feeling.

As Champa Devi was no longer involved in releasing child slaves, we drove out of Mirzapur early the next morning to find a young man who was. We had been assured that he knew of villages where children were employed on looms. Crossing the bridge over the

Ganges, we drove on to the Grand Trunk Road which connects
Calcutta with Delhi. In the time of Kipling's young hero Kim, the
Grand Trunk Road used to run on to Lahore in what is now Pakistan.
In those days it was 'a broad smiling river of life'. Kim found 'new
people and new sights at every stride ... here and there he met or
was overtaken by the gaily dressed crowds of whole villages turning
out to some local fair'.

We were on the road before the noxious river of modern life
was in full flow. The trucks were still parked outside *dhabas*, the
Indian equivalent of transport cafés, which also supply rudimentary
accommodation. Many of their drivers were still asleep on charpoys,
but the earlier risers were soaping themselves under hand-pumps, or
reading the papers and discussing the news.

We drove for many miles before finding a dhaba with a really long
line of trucks parked outside it – the more the trucks, the better
the dhaba, is a rule of the Indian road. As we were waiting for our
strong, sweet tea we casually enquired how far Meja was. It was the
town where we were to turn off and drive into what is known as 'the
interior'.

'Meja?' came back the surprised reply. 'You are on the wrong side
of the Ganges. It's on the road which runs along the south bank, not
this one.' Several drivers confirmed that we would have to go all the
way back to Mirzapur and cross the river again there.

That wasn't the only delay we suffered. Once we had penetrated the
interior we came across a line of traffic held up by a roadblock. This
was a *chakka* or wheel jam. Redundant workers of a defunct spinning
mill, owned by the Uttar Pradesh government, were protesting. The
magic word 'journalist' didn't help – they weren't letting anyone
pass. So we went in search of the office where negotiations were
taking place.

It was set in a vast campus with spacious bungalows for the more
senior staff. Their gardens were running to seed, and there was no
sign of any industrial activity. Inside the office we found two police
officers negotiating with trade union leaders. Everyone was very
polite. The senior policeman, a short, stout young man from the
elite cadre of the Uttar Pradesh state police, left most of the talking

to his junior who was in charge of the local police station. The union leaders maintained that the commitments made by the government when the mill was closed had not been fulfilled. The final straw had been the visit of an accounts officer from the headquarters of the Uttar Pradesh Spinning Corporation, three of whose four mills were defunct. He had sold off waste from the factory, distributed derisory sums among a few of the workers and driven off with most of the proceeds. On the wall hung the obligatory portrait of Mahatma Gandhi who had warned that nationalization would make 'men moral and intellectual paupers'. Moral paupers had bankrupted the mill by buying cheap cotton at expensive prices and sharing the spoil with the merchants.

Eventually, the senior police officer managed to contact the managing director of the corporation on the phone and he agreed to talk to one of the union leaders. Although the offer made by the managing director – to do what he could to redress their grievances – seemed barely worth the cost of the call, it proved adequate to get the roadblock lifted.

Eventually, several hours late, we arrived at the rehabilitation centre where Rajnath, the young man we had been sent to see, was working. It had just been opened by the Roman Catholic diocese of Allahabad. The buildings were incomplete and there were only seven boys, all said to be former child slaves. They were being supervised by a staff of four nuns and Rajnath, whose duties seemed indeterminate.

He lined the nuns and the boys up to welcome us with flowers and oranges picked from the garden. The boys sang, danced, and raised slogans against child labour. Sanjay Ram, who was aged about ten, had been held for a year, and used to sleep outside on a roof. He looked happy and fit now, but told us he had been 'slapped and caned' if his owner was not satisfied with his work. Nandu Kumar, a big boy with a broken voice who must have been very near the minimum working age of fourteen, had been one of thirteen working for the same loom owner. Six of them had come from his home district. He didn't know where they were now.

Rajnath showed us round the new institution. Although not

particularly tall, he towered over the tiny nun who accompanied him, dressed not in the habit of her order, the Institute of the Blessed Virgin Mary, but in a green and white sari. Standing in an airy dormitory with only six double-decker bunks, he explained that the aim of the institution was to enable the boys to catch up on the school years they had lost.

Inside the institution Rajnath was clearly the boss, but once he got outside his self-confidence evaporated. He had once worked for an organization that swooped down from Delhi to raid villages where children were weaving and then beat a hasty retreat. Now that he was actually living in the carpet-weaving area, he had to be more cautious.

'You can't dial 100 and the police will come like in a big city,' he warned us. 'Anything can happen here if you're not careful. Child labour is a very delicate subject in these villages.'

He even took the precaution of taking us to meet the district magistrate before we left, so that he would be in the clear if there was any violence.

We certainly didn't get a warm welcome from the villagers of Garha. They kept their distance, until Rajnath managed to persuade them that we were journalists who had come to write about the slump in the carpet industry. One loom owner, Mumtaz Ali, was prepared to discuss that. He showed us his six looms, only three had carpets on them. Times were so bad, he said, that Obeetee was the only company which still paid advances to loom owners, and he couldn't get any work from them. Soon the villagers' curiosity got the better of them and a crowd gathered to join our discussions. Slowly, trying to hide my nervousness, I brought the subject round to child labour. This provoked an angry outburst against the NGOs who publicized the problem.

Mumtaz Ali said, 'They don't care that they are ruining our livelihood by all their bad publicity.'

Rajnath hastily assured the villagers that we were not involved in that and nor was he.

As he was speaking, a man with skeins of wool strapped to the back of his bicycle dismounted and stared at us from a distance.

Mumtaz Ali slipped away to whisper urgently to him and he hurriedly remounted his bicycle and pedalled off. When we left the village, Rajnath told us that he suspected the cyclist had some children in his weaving shed. Darkness descended and we had drawn a blank, so we agreed to return a day or two later.

On our next visit Rajnath took us to a small hamlet called Ashoknagar. We had to walk the last kilometre or so down a narrow path between two rice fields. A herd of buffaloes driven by a boy wielding a stick twice as big as he was forced us into the paddy. 'More child labour. What are you going to do about him?' I asked.

'The trouble is the poor can't wait for tomorrow. Today is what matters to them. That is the economic reality of the situation.'

The first weaving shed we came to was built of brick with a rough-and-ready thatched roof. There were four looms but only one carpet and no weavers. An elderly man dressed in a vest and dhoti followed us inside. He was introduced to me as the father of the loom owner. When asked why no one was weaving he replied, in a surly voice, 'Because all the children have gone. They've gone back to Bengal. We had to send them back.' But I did see some clothes hanging from pegs on the wall.

His son made a hurried entry, obviously worried that his father might put his foot in it. I had been told that he had been in jail for fourteen days on a charge of employing child labour, but he was adamant that he wasn't employing children now.

'It isn't worth it,' he said. 'Every contract you get says you mustn't. It's all our responsibility,' he went on bitterly. 'The companies tell us – you have to make sure there is no child labour, you have to weave the carpet right, you have to deliver the carpet on time. There is no responsibility on them, and they make all the money.'

Outside that shed we came across a young boy washing. He admitted that he was a weaver and that he came from Bengal, but he maintained that he was eighteen and there was no way of telling whether that was true or not. He certainly did not have the tiny hands that anti-slavery publicists claim are employed because they are nimble knot-tiers. Nor did the boys working for another loom owner. None of them were knotting carpets because of the Diwali holiday. They mingled quite freely with the crowd that gathered around us in the courtyard of the owner's house. There were six of them, again all from Bengal. I was assured they were over fourteen, and certainly most looked it, although I was a bit suspicious of one who was having difficulty growing his moustache. The boys themselves said they were all earning a wage and could go home whenever they wanted. 'But then,' I thought, 'they would in front of the owner.'

As we were walking back to our car, I met yet another young Bengali, Bishu, from Malda district. A cheerful young man returning from an outing to the teashop on the main road, he was not in the least shy or reticent. In spite of a mouthful of paan, he was able to tell us that he had been working as a weaver for three years, was paid according to the amount of weaving he did, and was free to come and go as he wanted. According to Bishu the loom owners go to his district and offer advances to attract weavers. There used to be younger people he said, but now they were all eighteen and above. I asked him what happened if someone who has taken an advance doesn't like the work and goes home. 'The owner says, "Bad luck. I've lost my money," I suppose,' he quipped and sauntered off.

It was obvious from our first interview that children used to be imported to work on the looms in Ashoknagar, but Rajnath said he was reasonably certain the young man was right, that there was no longer child labour there. The hamlet had been raided no less than ten times by government inspectors since January, there had also been an arrest, and so he felt the loom owners had learnt their lesson. He had no suggestions for any other village where we might expect to find children on looms.

We now needed to have a serious discussion with Edward. He invited us to breakfast in the small modern house he'd built in the compound, more convenient but less beautiful than the burra bungalow. Edward didn't want to spoil his enjoyment of a full English breakfast, and so we didn't discuss business at the table but waited until Bhagwan Das had organized the clearing away of the dishes. Then, still sitting round the table, we started.

I first reminded Edward that he had once admitted to me that he owed a debt to the foreign coverage of the carpet industry he now resented so strongly.

'Yes,' he agreed, 'until this publicity I certainly was not aware of the scale of the problem. When it was brought to our attention that made us do something. It's not a thing to be proud of but there it is. We were an out of touch management. My days of going round the looms had ended many years previously.'

'So why do you feel so strongly about the anti-child labour campaign now?'

'Because they exaggerate, and they are in the hands of NGOs like Rugmark whose business it is to paint as bleak a picture as possible. If they don't, who will support them?'

I knew that Edward's company now took stringent measures to try to ensure that no children were employed on their looms and so I couldn't really understand why Edward refused to cooperate with Rugmark.

But he explained, 'I find their methods and claims unacceptable. And don't think we haven't paid a price, we have, we have suffered because of the propaganda organized by Rugmark.'

We were joined by Vinoo Sharma, a member of an old Mirzapur family who had spent his whole career working with Edward in Obeetee. Edward had wisely left most of the negotiations with Rugmark to Vinoo, who was less excitable and more diplomatic. He explained that Obeetee had been involved in the original negotiations which led to the formation of Rugmark. The negotiations had broken down because Vinoo had argued that inspection of carpet looms had to be done professionally. It couldn't be done by an NGO. He had even suggested two professional companies. One had refused to even consider inspecting such a complicated industry. Vinoo showed us a letter from the other company, SGS India Ltd, the branch of a Swiss company, which did send representatives to Mirzapur. On their return the company wrote, 'It will not be feasible to monitor on a regular basis to ensure that carpets woven at various and far-flung units are meeting the required criteria.'

One of the phrases that always crops up in anti-child slavery campaigns is 'India has the largest number of child labourers', a phrase which ignores the fact that India probably has the largest number of children in the world. China is the only other country which might just have more, and that is unlikely if the claims made for its family planning programme are valid. What is more, there is very little information about child labour in China because the authorities don't exactly welcome investigations into such matters.

When I put those points to Edward he exploded. 'Why do they always target India? I'll tell you why. Because they can get away with it here; it's a soft target because it's an open country. They have no wish apparently to disturb the ayatollahs and they don't wish to join with the victims of Tiananmen Square, so Chinese and Iranian carpets are exempted.'

A video of the Channel 4 film *Slavery*, with the most recent Rugmark publicity, had just arrived in Mirzapur. I suggested that Edward should watch it with us, but that was a mistake.

'I can't bear to see all that exaggeration,' he said. 'It makes me sick.'

We left Edward and set off for the burra bungalow. Edward's golden labrador Tipu, out for his morning walk, bounded towards us. Butterflies, pale blue, black and white with red spots, brown, and peacock-eyed orange, fluttered about lantana bushes. Banana plants were so heavily laden with fruit they had to be held up by stout bamboos. There were dark green-leafed mango trees as well as jackfruit, orange and grapefruit trees. In the distance we could see an extensive vegetable garden. Neat red gravel paths edged by upturned bricks criss-crossed the compound.

We passed under three horseshoes above the door of the bungalow, not a common sight in India where a tulsi bush is the customary auspicious symbol, and took our seats to watch the video with the heads of the last leopards to be shot by the Oakley family before hunting was banned staring down at us.

The section of the television programme which dealt with India was the story of a child slave called Huru and his rescue. He had been located and rescued by volunteers from the South Asian Coalition on Child Servitude, a Delhi-based organization which is the main Indian NGO supporter of Rugmark. The script maintained that as many as 300,000 children were enslaved on India's carpet looms. It suggested SACCS was the only organization looking for child slaves and, as part of the promotion of Rugmark, estimated that 'as many as nine out of ten carpets which don't carry the Rugmark label may have been touched by the small hands of slavery'. This, if true, would inevitably mean that some of the biggest carpet manufacturers who were not supporting the scheme were regularly exporting carpets woven by children. We saw the scene which had enraged Robin Garland – Dr Alan Knight, the ethical trading director of B&Q, standing in front of a pile of the cheapest carpets, promoting Rugmark and suggesting that other carpets might well have been woven by 'a ten-year-old slave in India strapped to his loom making this rug for twenty hours a day'.

Vinoo muttered, 'That's nonsense. Weaving a rug requires concentration and no child could weave for twenty hours a day without producing a botched job which would be rejected by the manufacturer.'

Dr Alan Knight was no fool. When I spoke to him about this film he pointed out that Rugmark had the backing of Christian Aid, Oxfam, and other British NGOs. He saw the label as an answer to the dilemma buyers face when they are expected to find solutions to the ethical issues in the supply chains they buy from. The only other practical way for B&Q to handle the pressure from NGOs would be not to buy Indian carpets, 'and who would that help?' Dr Knight asked me. But he had been put in a false position, led into making an exaggerated claim by overstated campaigns against child labour.

During the scene when the raid took place, Vinoo became even more suspicious. The police seemed remarkably inactive, there was no sign of the senior official of the government who ought to have been there, and the name of the village was not mentioned. 'I wouldn't necessarily say that's a put-up job,' he said, 'but it certainly doesn't seem to be the official raid they claim.'

Vinoo pointed out other strange circumstances in the film. The father had asked SACCS to find his child, but did not have the first idea where the boy was. So how had SACCS located him? If there really were 300,000 slave children spread over thousands of square miles, it would mean they had found a needle in a haystack. The journalists posed as carpet buyers to meet the loom owner, who didn't actually turn up, but sent his representative along. According to Vinoo, importers would not normally deal with a loom owner but with the next step up the ladder, the manufacturer who commissioned the loom owner.

We had already heard of a raid which had been filmed a few months ago in a village near Mirzapur. The district magistrate told us he had no knowledge of that raid, and so we thought perhaps that was the Channel 4 raid and it had been staged by SACCS. But then we found two representatives of the Bachpan Bachao Andolan, the member of the SACCS coalition that conducts raids in the carpet belt. They were hanging around a shop which sold marble. Apparently the proprietor, Rama Shankar Chaurasia, was the general secretary of SACCS. He was away in Delhi where he spent most of his time. His shops – he also owned one which hired out tents for weddings and other functions – as well as the raids were looked after by his son, Rajesh. He was somewhere else in the town 'on business' we were told by a young man wearing a scruffy baseball cap on his shaven head.

'You can speak to me. I am authorized, I'm district coordinator,' Sudhir Varma said, revealing paan-stained teeth. Pointing to another young man leaning against the counter of the shop he went on, 'This is my colleague Dinesh Yadav. He is a volunteer.'

Although of a more humble status, Dinesh Yadav – a self-confident or perhaps I should say cocksure young man – took over as the spokesman. He maintained that the movement made a lot of raids, six, seven or ten a month, sometimes two or three in a day. This year they had released 165 slave children. When we asked for details of the raids in Mirzapur district, Dinesh became a little less confident, 'There were some bonded adults released, I think, on the 3rd of January and some children on the 6th or 7th of January.'

It was by now the end of October.

The coordinator came to his rescue, 'We will have to look at the files and we can't do that because Rajeshji is not here.'

They seemed a little too surprised when asked about the raid which had been filmed near Mirzapur recently. They knew nothing, but nothing, about that, but when we asked about the Channel 4 filming, Dinesh was able to give us the precise location and date – village Vishwanathpur on 28 December 1999.

Although SACCS is closely associated with Rugmark, Dinesh maintained he had found children working on looms which were licensed by the foundation. 'Half their looms are not registered and they check only the registered ones,' he said scornfully.

Pushing his cap to the back of his head, Sudhir sneered, 'The exporters make fools of the Rugmark people. They will write that they are using one loom, and take work from another.'

We asked Sudhir whether he had ever found children on the looms of Obeetee or Hill and Company. Without any sign of reluctance, which surprised us because we knew how bad the relationship between SACCS and Obeetee was, he said, 'Obeetee and Hill don't have child labour. They have their own inspectors.'

That was a claim Edward himself would never make. He would only say that Obeetee did their best to ensure there was no child labour on their looms.

One mystery about the Channel 4 film remained to be cleared up – how had SACCS found a specific child when his father did not have the first idea where he was? I asked Dinesh how they located children.

'Mainly we know the child's address, the child sends a letter home, or there are labourers all from the same village, and one goes home.'

Sudhir interrupted hurriedly, 'Doesn't go home, you mean to say escapes.'

'But,' I insisted, 'supposing you don't have an address at all, how do you find a boy you have been asked to locate?'

'That's a huge problem. We can't do that,' Dinesh admitted.

Just to be absolutely sure about the Channel 4 raid, we drove the next day to Gyanpur where the sub-divisional magistrate – who, we were told, had accompanied the SACCS volunteers – was posted. He had been transferred, as is the way of things in Uttar Pradesh. But we did manage to find a more junior revenue official, naib tehsildar Ganpat Ram, sitting outside the yellow concrete box the government had allocated to him as his quarters in the compound, which separated the administration from the people of Gyanpur. A defunct hand-pump stood in a puddle of stagnant water surrounded by weeds. Here, apparently, the administrators of Uttar Pradesh didn't even seem able to look after themselves. The naib tehsildar was relaxing in a vest and lungi before going to work. When we asked him about the Channel 4 raid he said, 'This raid did take place. It was official because the magistrate gave permission and the labour officer and naib tehsildar went along with them.'

There is an unpleasant side to journalism, and to all journalists, and I have to admit to feeling disappointed that the naib tehsildar had spoilt a 'good story'. Good in that context nearly always means bad for someone else, and it would have been bad news for Channel 4 if there had been no official record of the raid. But that would have only been an incidental bonus. We had not come to Mirzapur to investigate the film, but to tell the story of Edward Oakley and his battle with Rugmark, to discover whether this was another case of a misconceived First World intervention in a Third World problem, or an obstinate expatriate businessman refusing to collaborate in an effective scheme to prevent child labour and save the carpet industry. To tell that story fully we had to see what steps Obeetee were taking to prevent children weaving their carpets.

The factory where the wool is dyed before it's distributed to the weavers, and where the carpets are finished when they come off the loom, is in the town of Gopiganj across the Ganges from the company headquarters. The factory is ancient and modern. Old-fashioned balances, instead of modern scales, weigh wool in the yarn shed. Stokers streaked with coal dust labour to keep a boiler in steam. A brass plate on the boiler reads: Engineers Yates and Thorn, 1921, Blackburn. But just beyond the boiler is a modern plant for treating effluent, and in the office is an air-conditioned room with a battery of computer screens. This is where the records of looms are kept.

Mithilesh Kumar, the dapper senior vice-president accompanying us, punched in a number and on the screen appeared a buyer's code, an order number, a design code, a loom owner's name, details of the progress on a carpet, and a depot code. Obeetee apparently has twenty-five depots spread over fourteen districts. Each depot has loom supervisors and inspectors whose job it is to ensure that no children are weaving Obeetee carpets. Mithilesh Kumar gave the computer another order, and up came more details of the loom owner including the names of every member of the family. This meant that if any children were discovered on the loom, Obeetee would know whether they belonged to the owner's family or not.

Mithilesh Kumar admitted that Obeetee inspectors did sometimes find children, and that was why the company could not give an absolute guarantee.

'It's very rare now, however,' he said. 'People know that Obeetee polices their looms and if they find children the company people rush to the spot, verify, remove the loom owner's card, and they lose work.'

Just down the road from Obeetee's factory was Rugmark's office, from which they monitored 28,000 looms working for 225 exporters. They did not have offices or officials spread throughout the areas where their registered looms were located, although they had to carry out inspections in twenty-nine districts, many more than Obeetee's fourteen. Rugmark's eleven inspectors were based in Gopiganj itself, or in Varanasi. They had a computer, but the day we called on them unexpectedly, the only person who could operate it was on leave. The office itself was on the ground floor of a large house and Rashid Raza, the coordinator of inspection and monitoring, told us the computer was often out of action because the electricity supply was erratic and the landlord wouldn't let them use a noisy generator. The recent records all seemed to have been handwritten.

Rashid Raza was a youngish man who obviously sincerely believed that Rugmark's claims were valid.

'Ninety-nine per cent we can guarantee that no child has worked on a carpet,' he said. 'And I can give a total guarantee that if a child is working he will be caught.'

But he did admit there was a problem with exporters who did not declare all the looms on which their carpets were being woven. The problem was compounded by exporters' reluctance to provide up-to-date lists of their looms. He told us, 'Some unlisted looms we do find, some we don't. The difficulty is that most exporters do not know where their goods are being woven.'

Recent economies had lowered the inspectors' effectiveness. They used to travel by car but now went out in pairs on motorcycles, which had reduced their range and meant the loom inspections were almost entirely concentrated within two circles each with a radius of fifty kilometres from Varanasi or Gopiganj, circles which must have overlapped.

'There is a problem,' Rashid agreed, 'but there are advantages. A car can't go into the interior and people can see in advance a car is coming, with a motorcycle people's suspicions are not aroused.'

Rashid broke off the conversation to take a telephone call from another room. He returned looking very pleased, sat down, and said with a satisfied smile, 'Well you are in luck, one of our teams has found a child labourer.'

We couldn't go straight to the loom because Rashid didn't know its location, and so we had to drive to the home of one of the inspectors and wait for him to return. His house was in the shadow of the tall brick-built chimney of Hill and Company's factory. Some of the company's work was contracted out to people living around the factory. In one house down the road from where the inspector lived artists were colouring maps of carpets and in another I saw a sight I had not seen on the earlier visit to Mirzapur and its surroundings. A young man was hammering what looked like a chisel into a carpet stretched so taut that the weaving appeared to have been pulled apart. Rashid explained that with each tap on the chisel the craftsman moved one knot to straighten what I could see was a very crooked line. As he moved the knots a gap opened up which would apparently close when the carpet was released from its stranglehold. The tool the craftsman was using turned out to have the head of a chisel but with a very fine point, like a needle. Nevertheless, anyone who didn't have the excellent eyesight, the steady hand, and the coordination of the craftsman, would do severe damage to any carpet with that implement.

As we walked on and the tapping of the hammer died away, I said to Rashid, 'The poor guy who wove that carpet must have paid a heavy price for making such a mess of it.'

Eventually the two inspectors returned from their day's work. It turned out that they had not found one, but two looms with children on them. They showed us the inspection reports. On loom listed number 52, in Jigna village, some forty kilometres from Mirzapur, a child had been found weaving a carpet for a listed manufacturer, Madhu Carpets. It was a sad case. The boy's father was handicapped and his elder brother, who was working on the loom beside him, only had one leg. The inspectors said the child labourer himself was about thirteen.

The other child had been working in Mirzapur itself, and so we decided to go to see that loom. As we approached the garage of a house in the centre of the town, we heard what sounded like the clicking of a battery of knitting needles. When we got there, we saw nine young men sitting in front of metal looms jabbing needles into the threads of the wefts. They were mechanical needles which clicked each time they injected and cut a tuft of wool. None of the weavers of these tufted carpets, very much cheaper than the hand-knotted variety, was under age, but standing in one corner, silent and confused, was a boy wearing trousers and a vest, yellow with age, which revealed the ribs sticking out from his chest.

The looms were being supervised by the owner's brother. As soon as he saw the inspectors he started to protest, 'It's not our fault that this boy was working. His father begged us to give him a job because he needed the money.'

Rashid Raza reassured him, 'I am not here to get you arrested. I am here to find out what should be done.'

But he continued to argue, 'The exporter's name on your forms is not the same as the order form we have, so this carpet is not for you to worry about.'

There did appear to be some confusion, because the inspectors thought the looms were weaving for Shukla Brothers, but the carpets had been ordered by another company. While all this was being discussed, other members of the family arrived to plead for the owner. Then he himself arrived, a sullen man, who seemed prepared to let the rest of his family fight his cause.

Eventually, to turn the hearts of the inspectors, Jalil, the father, was produced. A frail man with unkempt white hair, pinched cheeks, and rheumy eyes, wearing a stained white kurta and pajama trousers made from the thinnest cotton, he squatted in front of us, folded his hands and pleaded, 'I am a poor man. For God's sake, please do something for me.'

We asked him to sit on a stool, but wheezing like a badly maintained steam engine, he refused saying, 'No, I am a small man, you are big people. Have pity on me and this boy.'

An embarrassed Rashid Raza eventually persuaded him to get up from the floor.

The old man continued to beg for his family, 'This boy is the only worker we have. My wife is ill and my other son can barely see. You can see that I can't work.'

Emaciated to the point of near starvation, his breath rattling in his chest, that was self-evident. But the Rugmark team insisted that the boy couldn't be allowed to continue on the loom.

Jalil beseeched him, 'So far only God knows how we have survived, now we will be finished.'

The old man swore that his son was born in 1986 which would have made him fourteen, but that did look unlikely. He apparently earned between twenty-five and thirty rupees a day, which his father said was just enough for a couple of kilos of flour a day.

The Rugmark team remained adamant. Then Gilly suggested that the father should be eligible for a state old-age pension which, meagre though it was, would be some help. One of the inspectors pointed out that it would be very difficult to get the government to pay a pension, no matter what the law might say about his eligibility. But in the end it was left that the inspectors would do their best to get him a pension. In the meanwhile no one said as much, but we all knew the boy would have to look for another job.

At the other end of Mirzapur, past the ruins of the Anglican church, and the spacious bungalows occupied by the successors of those British administrators who used to worship in the church, behind high white walls, the Obeetee compound was a different India. With its modern head office, its computer-generated carpet designs, its international consultants, its well-paid staff, Obeetee was not surprisingly the largest contributor to Indian exports among carpet manufacturers, the largest employer of weavers too, paying the best rates according to all the loom owners we met, and one of the few companies which gave orders direct to them, cutting out middlemen. Obeetee was bucking the current slump in the industry too, protecting the livelihood of its weavers; all this was under threat from Rugmark's campaign in America aimed at discouraging the sale of Indian carpets which didn't bear its label. Rugmark had been advertised as coming to America 'to free enslaved children'. Americans had been told that 'Your demand for oriental rugs with the Rugmark label can help stop the horror of child slavery' and that 'Hundreds of thousands of children as young as seven years old worked in slavery to make beautiful hand-crafted carpets for consumers in the United States.'

Before leaving Mirzapur we asked Edward Oakley once again whether he would not be better advised to take the Rugmark label himself. But he was adamant: 'That would be giving into this campaign to blacken the image of an industry I have worked in all my life, a business I'm really committed to, as was my father,' he said angrily.

I was about to interrupt but Edward held up his hand. He was silent for a moment, then, all trace of anger gone from his voice, his eyes downcast, he went on, 'It's heartbreaking when you read frequently, or see the television programmes, which depict the industry as really bad. The allegations they make that not only are children working illegally, but they are working as slaves, bonded labour, are something so atrocious that it is very depressing to find that most people living abroad believe everything they are shown or read. It means they believe that I am working in an industry like that.'

Back in Delhi, in an office in the diplomatic enclave with a German flag flying outside, Dr Kebschull of the Indo-German Export Promotion Project, who was the driving force behind the formation of Rugmark, and still an adviser, was unrepentant. He pointed out that Rugmark had been founded to forestall a threatened boycott of Indian carpets by German retailers, alarmed by vigorous anti-child slavery campaigns. When I suggested that in attempting to promote Rugmark, the foundation was damning all other carpet manufacturers he maintained, 'We have never done anything against the Indian carpet industry. We want the Indian carpet industry to flourish.'

'But surely in order to make everyone take Rugmark labels you are suggesting that those who do not take the labels employ child slave labour.'

'We don't want everyone to be a Rugmark exporter. The Indian government has introduced a rival label, and we have worked with them. Why would we do that if we want everybody to be a member of Rugmark?'

'But that is the impression your publicity gives,' I argued.

'That's not the impression we want to give,' Dr Kebschull replied brusquely.

In a very much more downmarket office in Delhi, we found Kailash Satyarthi, the only Indian NGO representative on the board of Rugmark, and the chairperson of SACCS – the organization which had provided the story for Channel 4. I put it to him that it was outrageous to suggest that nine out of ten carpets which did not have Rugmark labels were made by slave children.

'No, that figure is not correct, I don't believe it, not at all,' he replied hurriedly.

Asked about the figure of 300,000 child slaves in the carpet industry, he admitted that the figure was based on research done in the eighties, and that the figures thrown up by recent research were much lower. He did not believe there had been any good scientific survey on the carpet industry so far in India.

All the evidence we had come across suggested there had been a considerable improvement in the situation since the eighties, and Satyarthi agreed. So I again asked why he still used the figure of 300,000.

After some thought he explained that it was based on 'some sort of assumption'.

'For instance,' he said, 'the number of carpet looms, and the assumption that at least two children are working at each loom. That makes more than three hundred thousand.'

I asked yet again, 'What evidence do you have?'

'There were some studies,' he replied vaguely.

When we'd arrived at the office, we had been given a publication written by Satyarthi himself. On the back pages was a lengthy article 'About the Author' which was first published in the *Far Eastern Economic Review*. The writer exalted him as, 'The leader of the fight against the exploitation of child and bonded labour', and described him as 'a very tall and handsome man in his late thirties, with a rich dark beard, and intelligent soft eyes, masking a hard core of determination within'. Now well into his forties, the years had obviously dealt kindly with Satyarthi, and he had advanced even further on the world stage. Kerry Kennedy Cuomo, Robert Kennedy's daughter, had chosen him as the only Indian to include among fifty human rights activists described in her book, and Satyarthi had just been in America for the launch of the book by President Clinton. In it he was described as 'India's lodestar for the abolition of child labour'.

I asked Satyarthi, 'Does it worry you that there is too much attention on you?'

'In the Global March against Child Labour there has been a lot of attention on many others.'

'But in your own publication you are described as a lone figure.'

By now uncertainty was undermining that hard core of determination. 'It is not my article,' he replied apologetically, 'it's an old booklet too, and I promise you I will remove this article from the next edition.'

I then went on to point out that in the same article, India, his own country, had been described as 'dominated by the politics of opportunism and riven by communalism and caste warfare'.

Satyarthi was very uncomfortable. 'No I don't believe that either,' he said. 'In fact India is the only country which has done a great deal to find answers to the problem of child labour. The best experiments in civil society interventions you will find here. With laws that are much more progressive than any other country, there are schemes that are much more progressive than other countries too.'

I came back at him, 'But in all the publicity this message does not come through.'

'Perhaps not. All the positive things which are happening in India or elsewhere in the world should be highlighted.'

All the positive things, I thought to myself. In that case surely Edward Oakley's efforts to abolish child labour should also be publicized.

Corruption from Top to Tail

For the first time in his life Mathew Samuel walked into a clothes shop in Delhi to buy a coat and tie. It took one hour's practice before he was satisfied with the tie knot. The son of a bank clerk, Mathew Samuel had been educated in a remote Syrian Orthodox Christian college. He would often say, 'I am not one of these city educated boys. I am a country boy from a rural background.' Jovial, and not given to self-deception, he would readily admit he was a 'degree failure', or, as is often said in north India, he was a 'BA plucked'. He'd only come to Delhi five years earlier, and he eked out a precarious existence as a reporter. His career had been limited by his unwillingness to flatter his superiors or play office politics. He disliked 'hi-fi people', and never 'massaged the egos of editors'.

But for all his dislike of dealing with 'hi-fi people', and his unsophisticated background, Mathew had been engaged for some weeks in an investigation of corrupt defence deals during which time he had already managed to convince senior bureaucrats, army officers, and arms dealers that he himself was an arms dealer. By using a hidden camera he had obtained film that showed them discussing and accepting bribes. So far none of this film had been shown, no stories of his exploits had been published, because he still had to capture politicians on film. Hoping to net one, he claimed to represent a fictitious arms company he called West End International, which supposedly sold hand-held thermal cameras, a product about which he knew nothing. He was now preparing for an appointment; the coat and tie were required for a meeting that had been arranged with the defence minister George Fernandes's longstanding friend, Jaya Jaitly, who was also the president of the minister's Samata Party. The meeting was to take place in the minister's official residence.

Mathew was an investigative journalist for a dot-com company called Tehelka, which means 'sensation'. I met him after his story had created a major sensation and threatened the survival of the government. Rumour had it that Mathew had gone underground because of threats to his life, but when he heard that I wanted to interview him he rang very promptly and agreed to have lunch in the coffee shop of the Oberoi, one of Delhi's most prestigious hotels and hardly the place for someone who wants to hide.

Mathew appeared to me more Middle Eastern than southern Indian with his light brown skin, broad nose, and closely curled black hair. He had a sizeable belly but moved with alacrity. He was a natural narrator, speaking idiomatic English with a strong southern Indian accent. We sat down at a table in the coffee shop where you pay a price for the marble floor, the Taj Mahal-style white marble panels inlaid with semi-precious stones on cream-coloured walls, the watercolours of palms as well as the real ones in pots. Mathew already knew that I wanted to hear how he had exposed the Tehelka scandal and was eager to tell his story. He started even before I'd been able to find out what he wanted for lunch, telling me first about that meeting with Jaya Jaitly.

'I'll take that first,' he said, 'because it was the most difficult assignment. We had been warned through a friend that Jaya Jaitly had been told about the camera hidden in a briefcase, which had shot Tehelka's first exposure – allegations of cricket match fixing. Ever since then, so we had been told, she'd refused to allow anyone to meet her carrying a briefcase, so I couldn't use that camera for her. I had to use one I'd never tried before. It was strapped to my side.'

'Wasn't that very dangerous?' I asked.

Mathew laughed and patted his belly. 'This tummy helped. You see, the camera was bulging out under the coat but I don't think they could tell it wasn't my tummy.'

There was one crisis when a switch fell into Mathew's crotch through a hole in his trouser pocket. 'There it was,' he said. 'It throbs when the camera is on to tell you it's working, and now it was throbbing against my penis. I wanted to swipe it or scratch it to move it aside but couldn't. Somehow I was able not to be affected by it.'

I had seen much of Mathews film before our meeting, and had

wondered why this incident had been shot at an odd angle. Mathew explained that the lens of the camera was stitched to his tie, and might well have slipped slightly. I realized he was lucky to have caught the long, lean face of the president of the Samata Party.

The elegant steward in a blue sari who had shown us to our table came back to remind us that we hadn't ordered anything. Mathew chose soup and french fries. I ordered fish and chips. As I had heard that Mathew liked his drink, I offered him a beer, but he said he had work to do later and alcohol would send him to sleep. So we both settled for fresh lime soda.

Reverting to the film, Mathew said, 'You must have seen. I was quite *chaalu*. When I was introduced to Jaya the first thing I said was, "I'm from Kerala." She is too and these things count in India, you know.'

The film had gone on to record a conversation between Jaya Jaitly, Surendra Kumar Sureka, an industrialist, and a recently retired Major General, S. P. Murgai, who had accompanied Mathew. Murgai was a small, foxy-faced man, who had just retired as additional director general in quality assurance, in army headquarters – a key position in the arms purchasing system – and had made a seamless transfer from arms purchaser to arms dealer. General Murgai and Sureka could be heard extolling the virtues of investing in electronics when Mathew suddenly interrupted, pulling out an envelope containing a wad of notes and asking him, 'Can I give it to Madam?'

I hadn't been able to understand why Mathew had brought the subject of money up so abruptly. He explained, 'I was scared. I am in the defence minister's house. If anything happens they will shoot me on the spot. I know that I have a lot of confidence – it's God given – but this time I was scared. There I was sitting at this table with General Murgai and another arms dealer on one side of me, and a senior leader of Jaya's party on the other. My chest was pressed up right against the table and I was trying to point the lens at Jaya opposite me. This was a different camera and so I couldn't be sure how long it would work either. Then there was this throbbing against my penis, and I'd left my normal camera in my briefcase in the outer office and it was not properly locked and anyone might have opened it. So, suddenly, I came to know, this is dangerous. I wanted to bring it to an end.'

I had been surprised by Mathew's abrupt offer of money but it had not surprised the president of the Samata Party. The film showed her saying, 'Please send this to our minister who is hosting the national council.' Mathew kept on muttering nervously 'Okay, okay, okay, okay' as Jaya Jaitly went on to explain the purpose of the national council. She ended by saying, 'So in that process we need some help because he said, "look, I can do fifty per cent of the expenses, you do the rest."'

Mathew laughed, 'We need your blessing also for this our company.'

Then the voice of General Murgai was heard explaining that it was 'proving difficult to get West End's thermal camera past the first hurdle'. The army hadn't even put it on the list of cameras to be tested before a shortlist of competitors was drawn up.

Jaya Jaitly promised to help, saying, 'If they don't we can always say, "Look you mustn't treat anyone unfairly. Give everybody a chance."' She then rambled on, apparently trying to convince herself as much as anyone else that there was nothing wrong in ensuring that a company got a fair chance to have its products considered by the army. 'Yeah, yeah, yeah,' replied Mathew to Jaya Jaitly's every statement. Finally the conversation came round to the defence minister himself, with Jaya Jaitly saying, 'I will not have any direct this thing. I will only request Sahib's office that somebody is not being considered, so please send a word down that if anybody is offering a good quality thing at a good price they should also be considered. It's because we don't have any extra interest in anybody, we have an extra interest in good quality and good price.'

General Murgai said firmly, 'That's true.'

Jaya Jaitly went on, 'It's in the interest of the nation, so that we'll ensure they don't neglect you. After that it's up to you and your product.'

In an attempt to bring the meeting to a close Mathew gabbled, 'That's all we are expecting, that's all.'

General Murgai got the message and suggested they should go.

But before they left, to make doubly sure the deal was on record, Mathew said, 'That's two lakhs, two lakhs.' More by luck, than good judgement, according to Mathew, the film showed Jaya Jaitly nodding as he repeated the sum he had just given for the benefit of the camera.

Mathew was too busy talking to make any progress with his soup and french fries, and so I suggested a break, but he wasn't keen. 'No, I am enjoying this,' he said. 'But maybe I will have a beer after all.' A bottle of ice-cold Kingfisher was brought and presented to Mathew for his approval as though it were a bottle of vintage champagne. He gulped some beer, lit up a cigarette and hurried on with his narrative.

'You know, so many people think this was a well-planned operation, thought out properly by my editor and me, but in a way it was an accident. My editor had been saying that we should do a story on defence procurement. I knew this clerk in the defence ministry who would be a good starting point but I didn't have the confidence to do it on my own. But then it happened over drinks with a man called Anil Malviya who I'd met in Bombay. He'd come to Delhi with me because he was a middleman dealing between suppliers and defence canteens and he knew about corruption there. You think of many ideas when you drink and so we decided that Anil would pose as an arms dealer and I would take him to meet a Keralite I had come to know in the defence ministry, and we would just see where that led.'

Even though the alcohol-inspired enthusiasm wore off the next day, meeting Mathew's contact still seemed a good idea to the two men. The contact was known to Mathew as Sasi Menon, although it later transpired his name was P. Sasi. He was also from Kerala and claimed to be a senior section officer in the defence ministry, which is not as senior as it might sound. 'That didn't matter,' Mathew told me. 'You see, you have to understand how much the army officers and bureaucrats are dependent on the junior people in their offices. After all, they know a lot of what has happened, and they can do a lot for you. Actually this Sasi Menon, who I had only met casually, was the cornerstone of the whole operation.'

'But Menon knew you were a journalist, he'd met you before, wasn't he surprised that you were involved in arms dealing?' I asked.

Mathew looked at me as though I was born yesterday, 'Don't you know that many journalists are involved in rackets? Sasi Menon certainly did.'

Mathew delighted in telling me how he'd nearly been caught out on several occasions. He'd told General Murgai that Thomas Cook was his company's banker. He'd told an arms dealer that when he was in Britain he stayed at the hotel 'Manchester United'. But neither seemed to smell a rat. He'd nearly fallen at the first fence because he'd been unable to think of any products when Sasi Menon asked what his company wanted to sell and so he'd blurted out, 'Anything from pins to tanks.' 'Pins to tanks' was lost in great waves of laughter and I had to ask him to repeat the words three times before I got them down in my notebook.

Sasi Menon's suspicion was not aroused by this impressive product list and, for a consideration, he agreed to introduce the two men to his boss.

'What was the bribe?' I asked.

'Oh, nothing, five thousand rupees,' replied Mathew. Then he started laughing again. 'Whenever I paid money to Sasi Menon I made him pay me ten per cent. I thought he would expect me to do that if I was a crook like he was, it would improve my credibility and come in useful paying for Anil's stay in Delhi.'

Sasi Menon's boss was Colonel Anil Sehgal, director in the directorate general of ordnance and supply. Sasi, negotiating on his behalf, asked for three lakhs for the information he had to offer about the equipment the army was looking to buy, but Mathew got away with twenty thousand as a starter. He handed that over in one hundred-, not five hundred-, rupee notes to ensure that the parcel was large enough to be seen on film.

Sehgal's willingness to cooperate increased. He told Sasi Menon to open a cupboard and hand over papers relating to the equipment the army was seeking to purchase. These papers excited the interest of Mathew's editor, Aniruddha Bahal. He and Mathew selected thermal cameras as the product they would go for, and Tehelka's design department produced a brochure for the fictitious company – West End International, based in London.

Tehelka also set up call-girls in a hotel for Sehgal and a fellow officer. 'It wasn't one of the most expensive five-star hotels,' Mathew said. 'I didn't know how much more bribing I had to do and I'd been given a budget of eleven lakhs, so I wanted to save wherever I could. That's why I bought the drinks for this occasion from outside too. I didn't want to pay expensive hotel prices.'

Mathew sat back in his chair, stretched, and lit another cigarette. Then without any encouragement from me he went on, 'After the call-girls came one of the occasions when we could have been in trouble. I needed more information about equipment from Sehgal and contacts too, senior officers we should meet, and he was demanding more money. So I went to see him and paid him another twenty thousand rupees. We had paid twenty before the call-girls. But he kept on insisting that I open my briefcase. Somehow I got away and I went back to tell my editor. He thought our cover was bust and wanted to break the story there and then, but I persuaded him to give me another two days. We thought about how to put their suspicion to rest. Finally we told Sasi that the briefcase had been full of porn magazines, pictures of gods and goddesses and money. So we couldn't open it in front of Sehgal, or what would he have thought of us? Luckily that worked.'

By now it was becoming expensive to fly Mathew's partner Anil Malviya to and from Bombay every time they met a contact so he was pulled out, leaving Mathew to represent the fictitious West End on his own. The suspicious Colonel Sehgal was getting too dangerous so he needed to open what he called 'a second front'.

That front was Lieutenant-Colonel Sayal, a retired officer who had also served in the directorate general of ordnance and supply and was now a middleman. He gave Mathew a hard time.

'Oh, that Sayal,' sighed Mathew, 'he was a money-eater. He also had the habit of doubting my credibility. He would say this card is nothing, this brochure is nothing, I want to know more about you. I want to know where you live.'

Fortunately, Mathew had been prepared for that and gave him

the address of a vacant first-floor flat, near where he lived in west Delhi. The ground floor was occupied by an eccentric old man with a pack of dogs who saw off anyone trying to get into the building. Mathew came to know that Sayal had twice tried to get past the guard dogs and failed. Sayal was somewhat mollified by an assurance that he would get a job with West End and that a company car would come with it, an Opel, near the top of the range.

'These Delhi wallahs are always very particular about their conveyance, they always ask what sort of car they will get,' said Mathew with all the scorn of a southerner who regards northerners as crude, conspicuous consumers.

By now the buffet lunch had been removed from the brass-railed sideboards and only a few stragglers were left in the coffee shop. The Kingfisher bottle was empty so I ordered another.

It was through Sayal that Mathew met Major General Murgai and another general I'd been particularly interested in when I saw the film, Major General Manjit Singh Ahluwalia, director general of ordnance and supply. He was slim and smart, very much a military man and he used military language too. I was amazed that an officer in such an important position could talk so carelessly to someone he had never met before. I'd seen him warning Mathew, 'You have to create a network, and let me tell you, because the carrot at the other end is big for everyone, you need very deep pockets, let's be clear about that. So if you want it, if you have that type of a thing, only then venture into it.'

General Ahluwalia never asked for any money, nor did he take any, but the festival of Diwali was coming up, and he did seem to expect Mathew to follow the tradition of bringing him a present on that occasion, so he barked, 'Sala [bastard], if you come to my house to meet me on Diwali you can't talk without bringing Johnny Walker Blue Label. If you are talking about bloody making a couple of crores of rupees you can't give me bloody Black Label also. Isn't it? Let's be very clear about that.' A crore is no less than 10 million rupees.

Although the government's policy is that there should be no middlemen in arms deals, the general made no secret of his contacts with them, nor of the low esteem in which he held them. 'I've been here now two years, I must have met at least thirty-five to forty people. Every other fucker knows bloody Putin. Everybody knows George Fernandes, everybody knows bloody Putin,' he raved. 'Everybody knows bloody Saddam, then they say get this done for me now.'

The general admitted his own limitations too, warning Mathew, 'If you give me ten lakh rupees, I don't know whether you will get the order or not. I have done my bit and there are twenty people in a chain like this. There is a man who has to go and do a certain evaluation. You have to feed him there. If he doesn't do it, if he writes no, he screws up the whole bloody deal. He screws up everything that has happened up till now.'

I told Mathew that remark reminded me of an American industrialist of Indian origin who told me, 'I want to invest in my own country but I go to south-east Asia. There you pay a bribe but you know you'll get what you paid for. In India people come out of the woodwork demanding money, one after another, and there's no end to it, and no one, not even the minister, can guarantee that your investment will be cleared.'

Mathew swung back in his chair. His flaying arms knocked over a bottle of beer, his face contorted with anger. 'He's so right!' he exclaimed. 'These bastards, it's a disgrace, they are ruining the country. Wherever you go here it's a jungle, with everyone wanting to eat money and everyone saying if you don't give it they can stop your project.'

A waiter politely asked us to move tables so that the bottle could be swept up and I ordered a third beer. Mathew recovered his sense of humour and continued with the story, telling me that by this time the competition between Sayal and Murgai was hotting up, with Murgai urging Mathew to cut the colonel out and suggesting yet another front – the additional director general, weapons and equipment, General P. S. K. Choudary. Mathew had been led to believe that he would issue the 'evaluation letter' which would allow West End to have their thermal camera tested. General Choudary, who was tall, lean and very much a military figure from south India, was reluctant to be seen in a five-star hotel because military intelligence was keeping an eye on him, but he did agree to meet Mathew in Murgai's house, and later in his own house. He was filmed warning Mathew that the army had already purchased some thermal cameras from Israel and some from France. According to the general the French purchase was 'a hiccough because of bargaining'. He had already put his foot down, preventing other companies from having their products tested. Nevertheless he promised to see what he could do, and Mathew managed to film him stuffing a lakh of rupees into his trouser pocket.

I was surprised by the comparatively small sums generals were paid for parting with information, but Mathew explained to me: Army officers, politicians and middlemen did ask for lakhs just for arranging this meeting but somehow, through God's grace, and my convincing power, I managed to keep it down. If we had gone on to do the business it would have been much more.'

The credit Mathew gave to God regularly during our conversation was genuine. He told me he'd gone into churches to pray for help before some of his riskier assignments.

General Choudary had told Mathew that he would need clearance from the bureaucracy who sat over the army officers in the defence ministry, before he could go back on his decision to close the field for thermal cameras and allow West End's product to be tested. General Murgai was able to help here too, taking Mathew to meet one of the most senior bureaucrats in the ministry, the additional secretary, L. M. Mehta. The filming didn't show him doing anything more heinous than accepting a gift of a gold chain, with much protestation. In fact, it's far from clear that he accepted the chain, but Mathew said he did.

Mathew had not been impressed by Mehta. 'I gave myself away again,' he told me, 'but Mehta didn't see anything wrong. He had been a joint secretary in ordnance and now he was at the top but he didn't show any surprise when I told him we had some very typical type of bombs. I am sure a genuine arms dealer would never have described a product as vaguely as that, but Mehta didn't pick it up.'

We still hadn't come to Mathew's biggest coup of all, getting to the highest echelons of the prime minister's party, the right-wing BJP, but by this time we'd been talking for more than three hours and I was getting a little tired. Mathew was not always easy to understand, my hearing wasn't helped by the water splashing from the marble fountain just behind me, my writing was getting worse and worse and I had serious fears about its legibility, and keeping the sequence of events clear was becoming harder and harder. So I suggested to Mathew that we break and meet another day to finish the story. His enthusiasm was undimmed and he said, 'No, let's finish it up today. But you can order another beer if you like.'

So Mathew's glass was replenished and I ordered my third coffee.

Mathew took up the story again. 'There were a lot of people offering help to get to the BJP, and some were asking a hell of a lot of money. You must have seen some of them on the film but in the end I got to the party president, Bangaru Laxman, through his private secretary, T. Satya Murthy. I negotiated a price with him for a meeting with his boss – ten lakhs – but I only gave him a gold chain on the spot. He was not happy, and complained, "Why are you being mean? All other companies pay money," but he did arrange the meeting.'

Just before that meeting there was another of Mathew's narrow misses when he passed through the garden gate of Bangaru Laxman's bungalow in Lutyens's Delhi and saw two or three journalists he used to drink with sitting in the outer office waiting to meet the BJP president. Luckily he was able to withdraw before they saw him, ring Satya Murthy on his mobile, and persuade him to take him to his boss without passing through the outer office. 'That was the first meeting,' Mathew explained. 'During that meeting I asked him for political help because two companies were already supplying the thermal cameras and it was difficult to persuade the bureaucrats that there was any need for a third company. No money changed hands at this meeting but I understood clearly that an advance was expected. It was at the second meeting that I got the shot which came on everyone's television screens time after time.'

The shot was of the BJP president accepting cash from Mathew.

The film had shown Bangaru Laxman, wearing a cream waistcoat and white kurta which contrasted with his dark, pudgy face, and dyed black, thinning hair, barely looking up from the papers he was perusing as Mathew sat down on the other side of his desk and tried to establish his credibility. The only time Bangaru Laxman showed any interest was when Mathew mentioned a middleman who had claimed that he was a trustee of the RSS, the Hindu sect the prime minister and many other BJP leaders belonged to, as one of his guarantors. Bangaru Laxman said, 'Leave him out, you have come directly.' Apparently he wanted to cut the middleman out of the deal.

Mathew was then heard saying his boss had arrived in Delhi and wanted a meeting. That didn't appear to interest Bangaru Laxman much, he just grunted, 'Accha.'

Mathew asked nervously, 'So he will come and meet you?' Then, without waiting for an answer, he stammered, 'So will you, er ... what I told to Mr Satya Murthy?'

Bangaru Laxman was no help, he just muttered 'Hmm', still peering through his steel-framed spectacles at his papers and making an occasional note on them.

'For the party fund,' continued Mathew.

'Hmm,' said Bangaru Laxman.

'And today I will give you one lakh rupees for the beginning – a New Year gift.'

Bangaru Laxman remained unmoved.

So in desperation Mathew held a wad of one-hundred rupee notes in front of the camera and flipped through them so that it was clear beyond all doubt that he was holding cash in his hand. The film then jerked as Mathew yanked his briefcase round to focus on Bangaru Laxman, who was seen holding out his hand lethargically, taking the notes and, without looking up from his papers, putting the money into a drawer in his desk as though this was all part of the daily routine.

Mathew made doubly certain the transaction was recorded by saying, 'New Year party fund, yes? One lakh rupee, yes?'

There was still no reaction and so Mathew went on to arrange for his boss to come to the office the next day to make the big payment. He asked whether it should be in dollars or rupees. Bangaru Laxman preferred dollars. Mathew assured him the company could provide dollars and added 'We need your blessing' to make absolutely clear that he was paying for Bangaru Laxman to intervene in the defence deal. Bangaru acknowledged that with just the one word, 'Okay.'

It was a hot, sticky, monsoon day outside but the Oberoi was almost too cool and I was beginning to wish I'd put on a waistcoat over my kurta. Perhaps it was the cold which made Mathew suddenly regret that he'd neglected the french fries, now beyond redemption, on the plate in front of him. He summoned one of the waiters hovering around and ordered chicken kebabs. Then, looking round the coffee shop, he said, 'Do you know I met General Murgai here once? We also booked my editor, Aniruddha, into this hotel in the name of Alwyn de Souza so that he could play the role as the boss of West End. The Oberoi gave him credibility. The day after he booked in I took him, as promised, to meet Bangaru Laxman who was expecting to be given some twenty-five thousand dollars in cash.'

'That was way beyond your budget, wasn't it?' I asked

'Oh yes,' Mathew agreed readily, 'we only spent ten lakhs on bribes altogether. They are all listed in the transcript of my films.'

'So what did you say to Bangaru Laxman?'

'We managed because he had demanded dollars. My editor explained to him, "We were supposed to convey some money today and as you can understand, getting dollars was a little hassly, and we didn't get it the way we want. So is it possible that I could come tomorrow with the dollars?" Bangaru Laxman did not suspect anything.

'By now we were in real trouble,' Mathew went on. 'I had created such a *hangama* about my boss coming, that all the people we had promised money to were hearing about this and asking to meet him to collect money. After our visit, Bangaru kept on ringing me on my mobile asking where is the money, so did others. I was really fed up, how many times can I answer them, more than two or three times? No, it's not possible, so I switched my mobile off and I had seventy-four missed calls in the two days after that meeting.'

'Seventy-four?'

'Yes, seventy-four.'

'You say you were fed up. Were you frightened too?'

'No, you see, as I said, I was given this confidence by God, and when I say "fed up" I was really still enjoying playing around with these idiots. It was a great game.'

In the film I had seen one of those who did manage to meet Aniruddha Bahal and Mathew in the Oberoi. He was R. K. Jain, the treasurer of the Samata Party. A businessman not a politician, Jain had clearly not done any homework on West End because he thought it was a major arms manufacturing company and had come to offer interviews with several ministers who would be interested in its products. He was filmed with what looked like a glass of whisky in his hand, relaxing on a sofa beside Mathew's editor. A glib talker, unlike Mathew obviously at home in a well-cut suit, Jain bragged with unbelievable indiscretion of his role in deals for jet trainers, fighters, artillery, and a naval missile system. Although only treasurer for two years, Jain claimed to have raised more than fifty crores for the Samata Party. He named ministers with whom he could 'do work', told the two journalists about the huge sums of money involved in defence deals, discussed the commissions to be earned, and even described the way those commissions were paid. He boasted, 'I am basically the front of George Fernandes and Jaya Jaitly.' Jain provided no corroboration for his claims, nor was any asked for by Mathew or his editor. But this interview and Mathew's meeting with Jaya Jaitly were enough to bring about the defence minister's resignation.

When I asked Mathew about the meeting with Jain, his head fell to one side, he looked down at the white marble floor, and for once he thought for a moment before replying.

'Well, it produced good stuff but I reckon it bust my cover, and that was a pity. When Jain didn't get any money from it, and I didn't answer his calls he realized there was some dirt in the daal.'

Then he related how four or five days later in the Tehelka office he saw three unwelcome visitors enquiring at reception. One he recognized as R. K. Jain's nephew. He darted upstairs and two journalists were sent to deal with the visitors. On being told that Mathew was not there, one of the visitors said, 'I know he's here. I know how to contact him. Now we are going away.' Jain had managed to trace Mathew through his mobile number.

Tarun Tejpal, the head of Tehelka, sent Mathew to his home in Kerala. But a few days later he was back in Delhi to help with the transcription of the films. Even though he knew his cover was blown, he couldn't resist playing the game again. 'The third day I did go to Murgai's house but when I saw the cars of General Choudary and one of the arms dealers there I realized the game was up.'

'You don't still feel in danger?' I asked.

'No, I wouldn't be sitting in this place, with my mobile on if I felt threatened.'

It was by now half-past four, and the story was complete. I felt in need of a beer and I was sure Mathew would welcome another one, but he had other places to go to. Perhaps that was no bad thing, as I needed a fresh memory and a clear mind to transcribe my notes. We walked through the long lobby with its red granite floor, past the receptionists in black suits and the sari-clad guest relations officer sitting at her desk, through the doors, out of the air-conditioning into the humidity of a monsoon late afternoon. A Sikh doorman in colourful uniform summoned Mathew's car. As it drew up we shook hands and I embarrassed Mathew with my profuse thanks.

'No, no,' he said, 'I have enjoyed this first opportunity to tell my story. But before you go, I don't want to take the credit for this. I must tell you I am sincerely grateful to Aniruddha and his boss. They trusted me and had full faith in me so that I could complete the project.' With that he drove off.

The editing and transcribing of Mathew's films had started after Aniruddha Bahal returned to his desk from the Oberoi hotel, but they took almost a month. On the day of the well-planned release on 13 March 2001, extracts from films reached television networks by twelve-thirty in the afternoon. Amitabh Bachchan, Tehelka's most high-profile director, had been warned that there would be a sensation. By a quarter to two, a large audience had assembled in the Imperial Hotel to watch an edited four hours of the films. A former chief of the army staff and a former vice-chief, neither of whom were in any way involved in this scandal or in any other scandal, sat side by side watching senior officers being taken for a ride by Mathew. The former vice-chief, Lieutenant-General Nambiar, later said to me, 'When I saw chaps pocketing money, stuffing wads of notes into their pockets, I was sickened, and the language they used too. I was always proud of my uniform and I still am, but I was disgusted by what I saw on the screen.' General Nambiar went on to criticize the stupidity of the officers filmed by Mathew. 'They were just so idiotic, so naive, why didn't they check on this manufacturer? Having served as the military attaché in the High Commission in London, my first reaction would have been to send an e-mail to confirm their authenticity. I can only put it down to sheer greed.' But when I suggested that the Tehelka revelations would undermine the morale of the army as a whole, he did not agree. 'This is a malaise, it's a cancer, but it's not across the board. Our system still has a lot to recommend it. There are so many officers and men I still personally know, and they are great chaps. All that the serviceman will demand is that the persons caught red-handed should be dealt with, and given the maximum punishment.' He reminded me of the gallantry young officers had shown only two years earlier in the battle to recapture territory on the Indian side of the Line of Control in Kashmir which Pakistan had occupied – the so-called Kargil war. The general was delighted that his own son was an officer and had chosen to join his infantry regiment.

By three o'clock television viewers were watching Bangaru Laxman, calmly putting wads of notes into his desk drawer and continuing with his work, as well as Jaya Jaitly trying to convince herself there was really nothing wrong in accepting money from an arms dealer to pay for her party's conference.

The resulting political scandal centred on Bangaru Laxman, the BJP president, and George Fernandes, the defence minister. Bearing in mind the all-pervading corruption in Indian politics it was, I felt, a little unfortunate that they were the politicians who happened to be exposed. They were by no means the worst offenders.

Bangaru Laxman was the first Dalit president of the BJP, and there are still far too few prominent Dalits in both the BJP and the other national party, the Congress. A comparatively unknown politician who had never held high office before, he always gave the impression of an innocent abroad, a man finding it difficult to swim in the murky waters of political Delhi. He was having difficulties within the BJP because of his background and because he was seen as the prime minister's nominee rather than the party's choice.

George Fernandes is one of the most charismatic Indian politicians, and one of India's most persuasive orators. The only leading opposition politician who managed to avoid arrest and go underground when Indira Gandhi declared a State of Emergency, he was eventually caught and, in the election which brought the Emergency to an end, he campaigned from jail, winning a larger majority than any other candidate. A one-time Roman Catholic seminarian, he entered politics as a socialist through the trade union movement. His career in the fissiparous politics of India involved him in the making and breaking of several parties and alliances, but he didn't lose his socialist credentials until he agreed to an alliance between the Samata Party, which he had helped to found, and the right-wing BJP. Eyebrows were raised then, and Fernandes had difficulty in defending himself against charges of opportunism. But even when the BJP prime minister rewarded him with high office, I could never believe that Fernandes had lost all his convictions. Others have not been so charitable. The writer Amitav Ghosh said of him, 'A lifetime in politics and the system had spun him around until what he did and what he believed in no longer had the remotest connection.' Whatever he might have been doing in the defence ministry, the minister himself continued to maintain the image of a self-sacrificing socialist. He continued to dress in a crumpled kurta and pajamas, only occupied one room in his official bungalow, leaving the rest for refugees from Tibet and Myanmar or others who had fallen on hard times. This is not necessarily hypocrisy. Although it is very difficult to believe that Fernandes could have survived at the top of Indian politics on an MP's or minister's salary, and it's certain that his Samata Party hasn't been kept afloat by open and audited donations, there is no evidence I have come across that he has the sort of personal wealth so many leading Indian politicians accrue.

Having said all that in mitigation, I have to admit that neither Bangaru Laxman nor George Fernandes was repentant. The BJP president at first refused to resign, maintaining that he had been receiving a donation for the party and saw nothing wrong in that, but the pictures on the television screen were too embarrassing for his party and he had to go. When Bangaru Laxman reached his home city of Hyderabad, he was greeted by a large crowd of supporters and he gave an interview in which he repeated his contention that he had been taking a donation for the party, and claimed the very fact that it had been filmed showed he hadn't taken it secretly. At the same time he suggested there might have been a conspiracy against him within his own party after an appeal he'd made for Dalits, Tribals, and Muslims to play a bigger role in the predominantly upper-caste BJP. When asked whether he thought that his being a Dalit had been the reason for his being 'fixed', Bangaru Laxman replied, 'It may not be the main reason but it could be one of the reasons also. As the head of the party I was trying to give entirely a new social look to the organization, which it richly deserves. There was a positive response to my efforts which certainly might have caused eyesore to many.'

When George Fernandes resigned he was given time on the government-controlled television service to justify himself. He told viewers, 'When I came to the defence ministry on 19 March 1998, I came with the determination to run a clean and transparent ministry.' He had installed complaint boxes at many places in defence ministry offices and had taken action on the complaints which 'poured in'. He gave his version of the deals which had been described by his party treasurer and claimed that the government 'had taken many steps to eradicate and eliminate the role of middlemen and agents'. But there was no explanation for Mathew's conversation in the minister's official residence with his longstanding friend and party president, Jaya Jaitly.

The government did the bare minimum required to survive. Although George Fernandes's resignation was accepted, he was kept on in the important office of convenor of the National Democratic Alliance, the rickety governing coalition. He was promised his job back in the defence ministry if cleared by the inquiry the government set up. Inquiries are the standard response to any allegations of corruption and their analysis, which usually takes an inordinately long time, rarely leads to action. On first reading, the terms under which this one was set up seemed par for the course, but then lawyers noticed a sting in the tail. The last clause called on the retired judge conducting the inquiry to look into 'all aspects relating to the making and publication of the allegations'. In other words, the judge was to inquire into Mathew and Tehelka. One of India's most distinguished legal commentators, A. G. Noorani, pointed out that this was the first time an inquiry had been asked to look into the credentials of those who had made the allegations under investigation. He commented, 'If this move is allowed to pass muster, the press will be effectively muzzled. Any time it publishes an exposé, the government will retaliate by setting up inquiries, not only into the truth of the charges, but also into motives, finances, and sources of the journal which published them.' The *Hindustan Times*, in an editorial, was even more outspoken, accusing the government of trying to tarnish Tehelka's name to 'erase some of the black marks on the image of the ruling parties'. Continuing in the antique, didactic English of Indian editorials the paper went on, 'Such an attitude is both vindictive and grossly cynical. While such a casual resort to minatory tactics can be expected from parties under pressure, to involve a judicial commission in such an intimidatory task on their behalf is outrageous.'

It wasn't just the judicial commission the government employed to tarnish Tehelka's name. They wheeled out the standard weapon used against those who displease governments, the income tax act. Tehelka's accountant was grilled for two weeks by tax inspectors. But that wasn't the end of the matter. The government knew that Tehelka needed to raise further funds, so it decided to warn off future investors by making an example of two people who had already invested in the dot-com company. Shankar Sharma and Devina Mehra were the founders of First Global, a broking and investment banking company holding 14.5 per cent of the shares in the company which owned Tehelka dot-com. First Global was an unusual Indian stockbroker because, in addition to trading at home, it had also passed all the stringent tests required to become a member of the London Stock Exchange. It had never had a serious brush with the Indian income tax authorities or any of the other financial regulators. But after the Tehelka revelations, First Global was hounded out of business. Its licence to trade was suspended by the stock exchange regulator and it had to close all but one of its offices. The property of Shankar Sharma and Devina Mehra was attached, and their bank accounts sealed. Summonses fluttered down on them like autumn leaves, two hundred of them at least. Their houses and their offices were raided, their passports impounded, and they themselves detained on several occasions. Shankar Sharma spent two and a half months in Delhi's notorious Tihar Jail before he could get bail. He was arrested under a law which parliament had already repealed because it was outdated and provided draconian powers that officials were prone to misuse. After eighteen months of 'investigation' neither Shankar nor Devina were charged with any offence or ordered to pay any arrears of income tax.

While harassing the partners of First Global to warn off other investors in Tehelka the government was also trying to prove that the Tehelka investigation had been part of a plot to rig the stock market. Government lawyers filed an affidavit before the commission of inquiry accusing First Global and the dot-com company of publishing the investigation to cause a stock market crash. In fact, First Global bought more than they sold in the days before Tehelka revealed the scam. Had First Global been planning to bring the price of shares tumbling down it would have been selling as hard as it could. What's more, Tehelka only caused a minor blip on the stockbrokers' screens. A major collapse followed nine days later when a scandal broke in which First Global was in no way involved.

The opposition did not defend Tehelka and First Global, nor were they able to make political capital out of the government's embarrassment. The Congress Party announced that it would hold meetings in towns and cities throughout the country to 'expose' the government, but very few meetings materialized, and those that did had little or no impact. Instead of exercising their debating skills to embarrass the government in parliament, an unruly mob of opposition members shouting slogans and demanding the government's resignation brought the proceedings to a halt day after day. The session ended with a personal slanging match between the prime minister and the leader of the opposition, Sonia Gandhi. The prime minister accused the opposition of defaming him, saying, 'I was abused in this very house, no one intervened to say this was unparliamentary and this type of words should not be used.'

Sonia Gandhi, forgetting her usual reticence in parliament, responded by attacking the prime minister for 'sermonizing' to the Congress Party, reducing the whole debate to a family quarrel. 'My husband was abused and crucified, he [the prime minister] didn't lift a finger. My mother-in-law was rubbished when all of you were in the opposition. Hurling abuses began with you. Even now me and my children are being called thieves. I am not scared but I will not put up with this any more.'

In India, what goes up usually comes down quite rapidly and, true to form, it wasn't long before the tempers aroused by the Tehelka scandal cooled, the excitement diminished, and the nation realized the revelations were not going to lead to any meaningful measures to curb corruption, let alone reforms of the administration which had been shown to be so porous. George Fernandes returned to the defence ministry although the inquiry was still rumbling on.

Tehelka exposed corruption at the top. A month later, villagers who would be turned away from the doors of a five-star hotel, who would not even receive a hearing from Bangaru Laxman's private secretary, who may well have served in the ranks of the army but would never have got near a general, exposed corruption at the bottom, the economic cancer which has spread throughout rural India. The cancer is so debilitating that Rajiv Gandhi, when he was prime minister, admitted that only fifteen per cent of the money the government allocated for rural development reached its target. More than ten years later, the planning commission found that only ten or fifteen rupees out of every one hundred spent on rural development reached the poor.

The corruption was exposed in the western state of Rajasthan, renowned for its Rajput warriors, in the village of Janawad, where a public hearing was held to identify those who had misused government funds, and put pressure on the government to punish them. One of the organizers of this unoffical hearing was a woman who knew the ways of the government all too well. Aruna Roy started her career as a bureaucrat in the Indian Administrative Service, or IAS, the elite cadre of the civil service. She joined because she believed it was dedicated to building a more just India, but within a week she realized that the IAS wasn't implementing the letter, let alone the spirit, of the law.

In 1950 the people of India gave themselves a constitution which resolved to secure for all citizens, among other things, 'justice social, economic, and political' and 'equality of status and of opportunity'. But Aruna found that the only Indians she was serving were the elite, whether they were those who wielded power and commanded influence in villages, in small towns, or in cities.

After seven frustrating years, she left the prestigious service to join her husband, Bunker, who had founded a community in the Rajasthani village of Tilonia, helping villagers to help themselves. Tilonia became recognized as an outstanding example of rural development, but Aruna came to feel that it was only benefiting a limited number of villages and was not challenging the system she had once administered. Having travelled widely and seen in village after village money allocated for development by the government dissipated because the power politics of rural India went unchallenged, she decided to fight for changes in the laws and the rules of the administration, which would give those dispossessed of power a voice in the planning and implementation of the schemes that were meant, on paper, to benefit them.

She moved to a small village, with a few colleagues, where they lived as the villagers did, and started a battle with the administration to ensure that labourers were paid the minimum legal wage. After three years, several hundred villagers who had taken part in this struggle came together with Aruna and her colleagues to form the Mazdoor Kisan Shakti Sangathan, or the Organization of Labourer and Peasant Power, always known as the MKSS.

The public hearing in Janawad was part of a campaign launched by the MKSS to secure the right to information about government transactions. Aruna has said that the decision to concentrate on the right to information was not taken by her, nor by intellectuals, or graduate social activists, but by villagers who insisted that corruption could only be curbed if the records of government expenditure were made public. Aruna herself has said, 'Inevitably as we try to break the power centres which have come to be, we will have to break through the walls which have facilitated years of arbitrary decision making and acts of corruption in the safe haven of secrecy.' By forcing their way into that haven, the villagers of Janawad, with the help of the MKSS, were able to expose a number of 'ghost projects' at the public hearing – ghost because while on paper the projects had been completed, on the ground there was nothing. A veterinary hospital had been paid for but was nowhere to be seen, credit had been claimed for constructing a health centre in 1998 although the building was more than thirty years old, there were dams which stored no water, and roads leading from nowhere to nowhere. The results of the hearing were almost unprecedented. The former *sarpanch*, or head of the village council, and its secretary, and a government engineer were all arrested and charged with corruption. Normally, the maximum sentence the few officials caught with their hands in the till receive is a transfer to a post where opportunities to make money are limited.

The MKSS had started organizing public hearings seven years earlier. They were so effective that junior officials threatened by the possibility that details of their transactions would be revealed went on strike, but despite this the public pressure was so strong that the chief minister of Rajasthan was obliged to react. He announced that he would grant the right to information, though no orders were passed. A year later the MKSS organized a sit-in outside the district headquarters in the town of Beawar. At first the townspeople were sceptical, writing off the protesters as 'the skirt platoon' and 'twits'. A sympathetic but pessimistic lawyer asked, 'How can you ever succeed when you are asking a completely rotten system to expose its innards?' But the protesters were not daunted, and after forty days the government of Rajasthan did promise that a committee would be set up to examine methods of implementing the chief minister's assurance, a convoluted bureaucratic means of delaying action. It took more demonstrations outside the state assembly in Jaipur to get the committee to meet, and when it finally produced a report it was marked 'secret'. The MKSS, with its village supporters, refused to surrender and eventually the government of Rajasthan did pass its own Right to Information Act, which a large number of officials throughout the state proceeded to ignore.

The sarpanch and local officials did all they could to avoid villagers' requests for documents showing how the panchayat's money had been misspent in order to sabotage that public hearing at Janawad. A junior official refused to hand over the papers detailing the 'ghost projects' and, even when ordered to do so by his superior officer, fell back on time-honoured methods of procrastinating. He made promises which he failed to keep, maintained there were loopholes in the law, disputed the procedures that villagers with the MKSS had followed, and eventually claimed that the documents were being audited. He hoped that the villagers and the MKSS would give up in despair. When he sensed defeat on that front, the official, in conjunction with the former sarpanch, changed tactics, claiming that handing over the information would disturb the peace of the village. When that fear was dismissed by the government, he arranged for a committee consisting of three local officials likely to have colluded in the ghost projects to investigate the allegations. The collector, the head of the district administration, insisted that the papers should be handed over, and so the junior official turned to the last resort of the corrupt, the courts, which all too often provide temporary shelter and sometimes long-term protection to those who have stolen government funds. Although the chief minister was by now taking an interest, because events in Janawad were damaging his claim that the new right to information act was a major achievement, the village official took the papers to Jaipur and didn't return until he had an order from the high court allowing him to withhold the information until the case he had filed was decided.

By the time the court eventually pronounced against the village official it had taken one year of ceaseless pressure at all levels of the administration, right up to the chief minister, to obtain what was the villagers' right under the new act. If the MKSS had not supported and advised the villagers, they would not have had the perseverence to pursue the case nor the skill either – there is no one more cunning than a lowly village official, no one more knowledgeable in the ways of obstructing justice. During the year the records were delayed, the sarpanch and corrupt officials had all the time they could ask for to put pressure on the village panchayat and so muddy the water that without the public hearing, it is more than likely no action would have been taken against anyone, except perhaps the transfer of an official or two.

At least there was a law in Rajasthan, and it was eventually implemented in the case of the Janawad hearing. In Delhi, the central government was still dragging its feet, sheltering behind the Official Secrets Act passed by the British in 1923. The secrecy of a colonial regime is one of the many legacies of the British Raj that survived independence. A distinguished Indian lawyer has accused the democratic administration of 'guarding information as zealously as gold in Fort Knox', so it's hardly surprising that neither bureaucrats nor politicians have been in any hurry to repeal the act which they find so convenient. The central government came under pressure from the Supreme Court which found that 'the right to know seemed to be implicit in the free speech and expression guaranteed under the constitution', but it took another sixteen years

for a bill reforming the Official Secrets Act and providing for freedom
of information to be introduced in parliament. Three years after that
the bill was still not law.

Janawad had been a very impressive affair for a village meeting,
with thousands of men, women and children sitting out in the
open only protected from the summer sun by a colourful canvas
awning, and a panel of distinguished guests, including senior
government officials, sitting behind trestle tables, listening to the
evidence like judges. The evidence took all day to give, with dozens
of villagers stepping up one by one to bear witness to the money
they had never received, though falsified records said they had, and
works never carried out. To liven up the proceedings there were
some entertaining songs. 'We don't want,' chorused a group of
MKSS supporters at the top of their voices, 'we don't want – a big
bungalow, a verandah with plant pots, a dog with a collar, a big
smart car, chicken curry, mutton curry, Pepsi-Cola, mineral water!
We want facts and figures, account ledgers, receipts and vouchers!
We want the right to information!'

A few weeks later, the vigilance commissioner for Rajasthan
and the deputy inspector general of police in charge of eradicating
corruption found themselves up in front of another MKSS hearing.
This was a more select affair, held in an adult education centre
in the state capital of Jaipur with less than one hundred villagers
attending, selected for the roles they played in local movements
fighting corruption. Gilly and I sat with the villagers on the floor
of the bare-walled conference room, with only sheets to cushion us
from the rough concrete floor. Aruna, her iron-grey hair pulled back
tightly in a bun, her finely shaped features hidden behind a pair of
spectacles, and a round red *bindi* on her forehead, was perched on a
pile of cushions. She would not normally have excepted herself from
any hardship suffered by those she led, but a surgical belt strapped
round her wine-red cotton sari revealed that she was suffering from
a back problem. In deference to my age and infirmity Aruna insisted
that I should be given a chair, which while embarrassing was, I have
to say, something of a relief. Neither the vigilance commissioner nor
the police officer were granted that privilege.

Aruna presided over the hearing with an authority accepted by the villagers and the officials alike. The first villager she called on to speak was a young man from the Jat caste. They are by tradition farmers who usually go in for macho, short haircuts, and clothes cut from coarse cloth, but Ram Karan Saran was a lawyer and there was something of the dandy about him. His neat black hair shone in the sunlight, his clothes were made from expensive cotton and fitted him well, and there was a gold stud in each ear. In spite of the presence of the police officer, he explained how he had taken the law into his own hands to punish corrupt officials.

'Every month one hundred and fifty of us will go to an officer who has taken a bribe and tell him to either give the money back or we will strip you naked and parade you outside. We bring witnesses to the bribe-taking but we don't bother with any police stations. If you want to get justice you have to get it for yourself, the courts are useless.'

Ram Karan Saran went on to relate the story of the first people's court he held, at which a bank manager who had taken a bribe for sanctioning a loan was forced to pay the sum back with interest. Apparently the villagers, who were judges, jury, and witnesses, sat in the manager's office for two days before he accepted his sentence.

Aruna got up, took the microphone from the lawyer, and handed it to a villager who told a lengthy story about muster rolls, the lists of people who have been paid for working on government construction works. Apparently some of those listed on muster rolls in his village could not have worked because they were dead, others came from prosperous families and would never have demeaned themselves by doing manual work. He had complained but the collector had dismissed the whole matter as merely a family quarrel between the villager and the sarpanch. The collector maintained they were brothers when in fact they were only distantly related.

'The sarpanch is still not willing to hand us the muster rolls,' the villager complained. 'He is still sitting in his house and preparing them, and tells us "Nothing will happen to me because I now enjoy the protection of a political leader." In the current two muster rolls, out of one hundred and fifty names sixty-five are false, and their wages are being shared by the sarpanch and the officials.'

Aruna intervened, looking in the direction of the police officer. 'There's a pattern with these muster rolls. The sarpanch says, "We won't give the information." Then when forced to do so, they say they haven't got it, it's with a local official, and that official says it is with another official and so you move from pillar to post all the time. They don't give information because the muster rolls and bill vouchers are all false and the money goes into their pockets.'

The officer, wearing a blue, branded shirt with the sleeves fashionably rolled up just above his wrists instead of his khaki, quasi-military uniform, did not comment on Aruna's allegation. He didn't even say anything when a villager complained he'd been assaulted in a police station after complaining about the sub-standard materials being used in building a school. He said, 'The station house officer, instead of registering my complaint, booked me for a breach of the peace. I refused to sign the statement he had written so he beat me with his fists and his belt and in the end I signed and was locked up.'

The complaints continued with Aruna urging the villagers to be concise to leave time for the officials to reply. When the scheduled tea-break came she announced, 'Tea is available downstairs, but how many of you want to forget that and continue with the meeting?' There was a rumble of assent and Aruna said, 'Hold up your hands anyone who wants to have tea.' Somewhat to my dismay, because I would have loved a cup of hot strong tea, only one courageous hand went up and the break was forgotten.

More stories followed. One sarpanch regularly demanded a thousand rupees before recommending anyone for government housing. Another threatened to break a villager's bones when he complained about an official who had paid workers half the wages they were due and then demanded they sign for the full amount. No action was taken against the sarpanch because he was 'the man' of the local Member of the Legislative Assembly, or MLA. A villager chipped in, 'There are many places where no work is done and the money goes into their pockets.'

Eventually Aruna summed up the proceedings so far saying, 'The question before us is how to get the information and what to do to stop this corruption. We have to get the information out, but what about after that? We are not against the sarpanches but against this whole system which allows this corruption.' She then called on the police officer to speak.

The deputy inspector general of police had little to say beyond recommending the 'tarep' as the best method of ensuring that charges would be brought against corrupt officials. It took me a bit of time to work out that 'tarep' was what the English word trap became in Hindi. The police officer was recommending catching the guilty in the act of receiving a bribe. 'Tareps,' he said, 'I believe in tareps. Try to tarep. There are many irregularities and illegalities and the anti-corruption department can't deal with them all but with tarep there is concrete proof and the stigma too. It is a big disgrace for an official to be caught with his hand held out.'

Villagers pointed out that trapping was easier said than done, and required the help of the police. The DIG admitted that there was a shortage of officers trained in trapping, and so that didn't take the discussion much further.

The dialogue with the vigilance commissioner was more lively. R. D. Nair doubled as the home secretary, one of the most important posts in the state bureaucracy, which put him in charge of the department that controlled the police. A small man with thinning grey hair plastered across his head and a bushy, military moustache, he spoke slowly and deliberately, not unlike a colonel giving orders to his troops. Admitting that the right to information act was 'only fifty per cent effective so far', he said there was a need to ensure that officials were better informed about it. 'They will be in the next few months,' he added firmly.

But Aruna was not satisfied, 'I want one assurance. If there is proof, then something should happen. If it doesn't, it gives a free signal to all those sat at every level who want to be corrupt and do bad work.'

The vigilance commissioner argued that it wasn't possible to give an assurance that all cases would be dealt with in a fixed time because of possible delays in the investigations, delays which might be caused by handwriting tests, post-mortem results, investigation of documents, or many other causes. But the commissioner did accept that there should be 'no unnecessary delays', and went on to assure Aruna 'there will be effective and timely investigations'.

Aruna was not assured. 'There is an attitude among the bureaucracy to protect officials,' she insisted.

The commissioner shot back, 'Change your attitude about government servants being treated softly, that is not true.'

But one of Aruna's colleagues maintained there were many cases when the MKSS had provided proof of corruption and nothing happened to the officials because the inquiry was not independent.

The commissioner had no answer to that and so just grunted, 'It must be.'

Aruna then took up the argument again, 'You are telling us to swear by the system but we can't. Your system isn't foolproof and yet you are giving assurances on the basis of that system. Look at the state of the courts where so many cases end up.'

Nair refused to take any responsibility for the courts, excusing himself on the grounds that he might be held up for contempt, but he accepted that the situation in the administration was far from satisfactory. 'I do agree,' he told Aruna, 'new thought, new initiatives are necessary, there is a need for new solutions. Surprise spot inspections of muster rolls might be one answer. Now people who complain are more afraid than those who are corrupt. I do want to see those who complain, and may be endangered, protected, but I am not in a position to provide protection. However, I hope in future such a system can be in place.'

So in the end even one of the most senior bureaucrats in the state administration could offer little hope of improvements in a system which he admitted could not even protect complainants. But Aruna was not downhearted. She told the villagers, 'We will just have to set up more of our own watchdog committees.'

Aruna and Mathew Samuel, in their very different ways, are

watchdogs over those who should themselves be watching the interests of the people of India. It all comes back to that one crucial constitutional conundrum – *quis custodiet ipsos custodes.*

Altered Altars

I first went to Goa before the tourists got there. It was in 1967, just six years after what is officially known as the liberation, when the Indian army marched into Goa, ended four hundred and fifty years of Portuguese colonial rule and declared a shotgun marriage between the 700,000 citizens of the tiny enclave on the Konkan coast and the rest of the vast republic. Although Goa had become part of India and the Portuguese had gone, the church, which had always been an arm of the colonial administration, was still very much a presence.

White cassocks were as regular a sight on the streets of the capital, newly renamed Panaji, as black suits and dog collars used to be in Dublin. Congregations on Sunday spilt out of church doors. The saints and the sacred heart of Jesus looked down from the walls of shops and bars. Goans' enthusiasm for their church is perhaps surprising because it was fear not faith which originally converted them. Father Alexander Valignano, a sixteenth-century Jesuit, who served as Visitor of the Province of the East Indies admitted, 'Conversions were not commonly done by preaching and doctrine but by right methods, as for example preventing idolatry or punishing by merciful rigour those who practised it, denying them such favours as could rightly be denied and conferring such favours on the new converts, honouring, helping, and protecting them, so that the others might be converted with this.'

It was only when threatened by the independence movement across the border in India that the Portuguese government sought allies among the Hindu community by giving them opportunities which had been almost entirely restricted to Christians.

Over the next twenty-odd years after my first visit, the cassocks disappeared as the priests shed their traditional uniform, but the congregations didn't seem to diminish and neither did the sacred heart nor the saints. So in the year the Pope had declared holy, the first year, he maintained, of the new millennium, Gilly and I decided to go again to Goa to discover how the church, which had been one of the pillars upholding a colonial regime, could now be a progressive political force in a Goa which was part of independent India.

It's easy to be misled into thinking that the church still survives and flourishes because four hundred and fifty years of colonial rule turned Goa into a European outpost. Goa was the capital of the Portuguese empire in the east, the seat of one of only six Roman Catholic patriarchs, the longest and the last survivor of Western colonialism in the sub-continent. Those long years have left their imprint, particularly on coastal Goa which was colonized two hundred years before the interior. The white churches, the chapels, the wayside crosses still seen in every coastal village, are the most obvious legacy of the Portuguese. After they left Goa became India's first international beach tourist resort. It was sold to the charter flight operators as a home away from home, a tiny European enclave in a vast and, for many tourists, all too Indian, India. An Air India calendar even described Goans as people of Portuguese descent, while one tourist brochure claimed that Goa was 'a small replica of Europe's Latin culture'.

But Goa has a history that stretches back long before 1510 when Afonso de Albuquerque ordered a church to be built on the battlefield where he had won his second and decisive victory against the Muslim rulers of that time. Under Portuguese rule Goa was the headquarters of the mission to convert the Orient, and was often described as the Rome of the East, but earlier it was renowned as the Kashi, or Benares, of the Konkan because it was so sacred to Hindus.

The city which sprang up on the site of Afonso's victory is now known as Old Goa because the Portuguese moved their capital to Panaji on the coast. The road from the new capital to the old runs alongside the mouth of the Mandovi, crossing a causeway built by the Portuguese. When we drove along the causeway the monsoon rains had swollen the river and the water, coloured dull red by the ore-rich soil of Goa, was seeping into the mangrove swamps and rice fields. In the distance we could see the Western Ghats, the mountains which run for hundreds of miles down the western side of India. It wasn't long before we entered Old Goa and I was appalled to see that the magnificent sixteenth-century Se cathedral was no longer white but a hideous utility yellow. So was the church of St Francis which stands so close to the cathedral that as you approach Old Goa they seem to be one and the same building.

Old Goa is now little more than an ecclesiastical museum, a place of pilgrimage and a tourist destination. The hillside is dotted with churches. Below them, near the banks of the river stands the Viceroys' Arch, the Portuguese version of the British Gateway of India in Bombay, and the jetty on the River Mandovi where the imperial grandees used to disembark. Opposite the jetty, in the middle of the river, is the small island of Diva dominated by a white church set on a hilltop. Perhaps the Portuguese wanted to demonstrate that they had captured even the smallest of places for Christendom. With churches almost everywhere in coastal Goa, it is easy to forget that throughout Portuguese rule, the majority of Goans remained Hindu and now Hindus were laying claim to a share of the island of Diva, building a temple just below the church to commemorate an ancient image of the elephant god Ganesh. Legend says the image used to stand on that hilltop, until it was removed to safety during the Portuguese war against idolatry.

Loyalty to Portugal never went very deep either. At the height of the decolonizing period, when the Portuguese were condemned by the United Nations and the Non-Aligned Movement for continuing to hold on to Goa, they replied that Goans were not colonial subjects but fully fledged citizens of the motherland, and claimed they were so proud of their citizenship they would die fighting if India invaded. When the Indian army did eventually cross the border in 1961, the Portuguese surrendered without a fight and there was no Goan resistance. But Goan Christians have not cast away their entire Portuguese heritage.

We had gone to Old Goa on a Sunday to attend a mass in the Basilica of Bom Jesus, the shrine of St Francis Xavier, revered by the Roman Catholic church as the Apostle of the Indies and Japan, and the Patron of Foreign Missions. One of the small group who joined St Ignatius Loyola to found the Society of Jesus, he became what I suppose might now be called a religious imperialist, credited by his order with making 700,000 converts. He regarded the Portuguese government as the secular arm of the church, invited the king to establish the Inquisition in Goa, and was renowned for having no interest in Indian religions or indeed any religion except his own. But attendance at the mass confirmed that he is still Goa's most popular saint.

When we entered his elaborately carved, brown laterite shrine, we found there was standing room only for the eight o'clock mass. Old Goa now has a very small population and the cathedral is their parish church, and so this congregation must have come from far and wide especially to worship in Bom Jesus. A few elderly ladies covered their heads with black lace, and some of the young girls were dressed up in party frocks with lace-trimmed socks. There was a fair sprinkling of nuns in their habits too. But many of the worshippers had adopted today's Western informal style of church-going. A letter I had read in a parish magazine suggested this had gone too far. The writer complained of 'modern Goan bimbeties' coming to mass 'clad in an all-to-dare-and-bare variety of sexy clothes – tank tops with their midriffs showcased, revealing blouses, hot pants, skimpiest of skirts, sleeveless blouses, baggy jeans etc' But in front of us a young woman in jeans, which neither bagged nor clung, and a long-sleeved blouse knelt on the stone floor during the consecration.

After the service we joined the long line of worshippers waiting to pay their respects to St Francis Xavier. The queue moved very slowly and so it took some time for us to reach his chapel just below the high altar with its golden reredos, dominated by the figure, not of St Francis Xavier himself, but of his friend St Ignatius Loyola. The marble mausoleum of St Francis took the Florentine sculptor Giovanni Battista Foggini ten years to finish. The mortal remains of the saint are contained in an elaborately carved silver casket, crowned with a cross and placed well out of reach of the faithful, but some did kiss the stone of the mausoleum, while others stood with hands folded staring at the casket, as Hindus do when they have a darshan, standing before an image of one of their gods, gazing in awe, believing they are in the presence of the divine.

After our darshan, we walked through an arch in the south wall, past the sacristy where we could see a priest robing for the next mass, and out into the cloisters where an elderly father dressed in a white cassock sat selling books and pamphlets. He seemed more interested in talking to those who passed by than promoting business, and when he saw us asked the inevitable question, 'Where are you from?'

After satisfying himself on that point, he took our guide book and opened it at the entry on the Se Cathedral. His face, which bore the marks of a haphazard encounter with a razor, broke into a satisfied smile. He carefully bracketed the words 'built by the Dominicans', wrote 'wrong' by them, and then handed the book back saying, 'Everyone makes that mistake. Actually the Dominicans only established themselves here much later, although there were four on Albuquerque's ships whose job it was to sing Te Deums.'

Having dismissed the Dominicans and their contribution to Goan Christianity, he went on to say proudly, 'I am a Jesuit. It's our society which is in charge of this church because St Francis Xavier was one of us.'

I told him a story about his society I'd heard many years ago from an Irish secular priest. There had been a great convocation of all the orders held on the top of Mount Sinai to try to resolve the rivalry between them. The Superiors of the orders knelt in a circle and prayed, asking God to let them know which of them he regarded most highly. After long hours of prayer a dove descended and dropped a message from her beak. The Jesuit General managed to pick it up first and read out, 'You are all equal in my sight. Signed God, Society of Jesus.'

The old priest roared with laughter. 'Yes, the other clergy here do say that we are arrogant, but the people love St Francis Xavier you know and, as I told you, he was a Jesuit, and so we are popular with them. You can see they come here in large numbers to make their confessions to us.' He paused for a moment to make sure that the nun sitting next to him wasn't listening, leaned forward and in a conspiratorial stage whisper, said, 'Mind you, I do sometimes think many come because they have something they want to confess to a strange priest rather than the parish priest who knows them.'

To bring the subject round to the Portuguese influence on the church, I asked how much still survived. 'Sometimes you do still find someone confessing to you in Portuguese. But most of the priests can't understand the language any more. The only foreign language they know is English. We have exchanged Portuguese colonialism for yours.'

The Roman Catholic church is now trying to shake off all colonial influences and become manifestly an Indian church. This movement is known by the rather ugly word – enculturalization. The elderly Goan Jesuit thought it was all a bit overdone. 'What do we need enculturalization for?' he asked scornfully. 'We have always had a lot of Hinduism, if that's what you mean by it, in Goan Catholicism. Many customs which still go on, and have gone on for long before I can remember, are very Indian. Take for instance at this time of the year – because there is no work in the fields, whole villages of Hindus are making pilgrimages to temples and Christians are, in the same way, making pilgrimages here to Bom Jesus. Then again, young couples bring their children here to cut off a lock of their hair just like Hindu children are taken to river banks or the seashore to have their heads shaved.'

The Portuguese did their best to dig up those Indian roots. An edict of the Inquisition published in 1736, more than two hundred years after the Portuguese established Christianity in Goa, prohibited specific Hindu practices creeping into Catholicism. Anointing brides and bridegrooms with a mixture of milk and coconut oil, or touching their foreheads with grains of raw rice were banned from marriage rites. After a death the walls of a house were not to be plastered with cow dung, and the clothes of the dead person were not to be thrown into a river or the sea, which are sacred to Hindus. If it were necessary to destroy them to avoid contagion they should be burnt. The living were strictly prohibited from wearing 'Hindu clothes'.

Even when the Portuguese left it took the Vatican a long time to accept that the Goan church must be Indian. The Portuguese Patriarch who had written to his clergy on some sixty occasions urging them to remember that it was their duty to obey the Portuguese administration, didn't leave with the governor general. He stayed on until Vatican Two made his position well-nigh impossible. Even then Rome did not feel able to trust Goans fully. A Goan, Francisco Xavier da Piedade Rebello, who was a safe choice as he was closely identified with the Portuguese church due to his years of service in the Patriarchal Curia, was consecrated bishop but only appointed administrator apostolic. The See of Goa was kept vacant. It wasn't until 1978 that Goans once again had an archbishop, and the titles Primate of the East and Patriarch of the East Indies were restored.

The Vatican feared that Goans, if they were given full charge of their own church, would allow Hinduism, with its long history of syncretism, to seep into the orthodox faith the Portuguese had preserved. From Rome it was not possible to see that a measure of syncretism was essential if the church was to flourish in its new surroundings. But that was clear to the Society of Pilar, a society of priests founded in Goa which does not have its headquarters in Rome, as the Jesuits do.

The headquarters of the Society of Pilar, some ten kilometres inland from Old Goa, is approached by a road winding up a hill, past a school of music, an industrial training school and other buildings indicating the extent of the Pilar fathers' activities. The road ends at another white Portuguese church. Beyond it stands a modern office block known, rather formidably, as the Generalate, and at the very top of the hill is the seminary overlooking the mouth of Goa's other great river, the Zuari, and the port of Marmagao. The older fathers remember going up to the roof to watch Indian planes bombing shipping during the 'liberation', which must have been something of an overkill bearing in mind the Portuguese lack of resistance.

We arrived at the Generalate without warning and without introduction, we didn't even know who we wanted to meet. The shy young girl at the reception desk didn't know what to do with us and so she sent us up to the seminary to see the museum, and rang the curator to warn him that foreign journalists were on the way.

We didn't have to wait long before the curator, Father Cosme José Costa, arrived with a younger priest. It was soon clear that the white-bearded Father Cosme was a gentle, guileless scholar and an enthusiast for his museum. I suspected that the younger priest, Father Sebi Mascerenas, who was thoroughly pulled together, had come along as his minder, to ensure no indiscretions slipped out, nothing was said which would embarrass the Society of Pilar with the religious or the secular authorities.

Many of the exhibits in the museum had been excavated from the area surrounding the Pilar fathers' headquarters. Father Cosme showed us a badly damaged torso of the elephant god Ganesh, and a statue of the Buddha, explaining that they showed that the hill had once been a city called Godavri, the capital of the Shilapara dynasty. Below the hill, in the mouth of the River Zuari there had been an even earlier port, called Gopakapattam. Father Cosme was particularly pleased with two exhibits from the port, a Roman coin from 100 AD and a fragment of a Roman amphora. 'These,' he explained, 'prove that there was trade with Rome, which just shows that it's not merely a legend about the Apostle Thomas coming to India. He could quite easily have done so. You see, we are probably one of the earliest parts of the universal church.'

'Father Cosme is not just a church historian,' explained his colleague, 'he is a part of history himself. Just tell them about that quickly before you go.'

'Do you think I should?' the curator asked doubtfully.

Father Sebi thought he should and so we heard the story of a miraculous birth. Father Cosme's mother had lost her first son within six hours of his birth, then she had three miscarriages and when pregnant with Cosme himself was told by a doctor there was only a one per cent chance either of them could be saved. The family had prayed to Joseph Vaz, a seventeenth-century Goan priest. Apparently, the prayers were effective. On the eve of a Caesarean operation which the doctor was approaching without any hope, Cosme was born naturally. His mother also survived and lived on until the age of ninety-five. The Vatican had accepted this answer to the family's prayers as the miracle required for the beatification of Joseph Vaz. As Father Cosme put it, 'Blessed Joseph Vaz gave me a miracle and I reciprocated by giving him one.'

When the curator left, Father Sebi took us into what looked like a staff common room. There we explained that we were writing about the modern church in Goa, and were interested in learning more about the Pilar fathers because they were a Goan order.

'Yes, we are very much a Goan order,' said the young priest with determination. 'We are known as the Society of the Missionaries of St Francis Xavier, but we have nothing to do with the Portuguese. We never sided with them, we were always nationalists, and that is one reason why we are prospering. Looking at the rest of the world, we'd thought we'd be short of vocations, but, actually, when I was ordained there were only one hundred and twenty Pilar fathers. Now there are two hundred and fifty-nine and twenty more will be ordained this year.'

'How are you doing so well?' I asked.

'Because in Goa we were the path breakers. We were the first people to throw open the seminary doors to everyone, and the high castes didn't like that. It meant we had a tradition since the thirties of getting vocations from a far wider field than elsewhere in the church, and that tradition appears to be surviving better than we'd expected. Perhaps we should have had more faith in God,' he said with a laugh.

Pilar is a society of apostolic life, which is different from a religious order and does not entitle its members to call themselves 'religious'. But Father Sebi was not worried about the niceties of ecclesiastical pecking orders.

'I always tell novices they shouldn't worry either,' he told us. 'After all, we take the same three vows as the religious orders and you can't be half chaste, or half obedient, so we are no less than them. The only difference is that we come under the discipline of the Archbishop of Goa, while the Jesuits and others have a direct line to Rome; they bypass the archbishop.'

Very sure of his vocation, which he had tried sorely by living for twelve years in a hut among some of the poorest people in India, Father Sebi agreed with the Jesuit from Bom Jesus that, in spite of all its efforts, the Inquisition was never able to eradicate the Hindu influence on Goan Christianity. When he was working among the tribals of Nagar Haveli, north of Goa on the western coast, Father Sebi would always celebrate mass sitting cross-legged on the floor with the villagers. He didn't wear a cassock or any vestments, only a shawl round his shoulders. Mind you, none of the Pilar fathers seemed to wear their cassocks very often. Father Sebi himself was sporting a very bright pink, white and blue bush shirt.

'We have to accept that our people and, indeed, we clergy too have very Hindu hearts,' he explained. 'In Goa there are so many crosses and saints everywhere. You must have seen them. But what do the saints mean? When we were converted we all had a family god and we found it easy to replace them with Saint Antony or someone like that, so in some ways devotion to saints has its roots in Hinduism. It is Latin influence but very Indian.'

Some Goan Catholics still also worshipped in temples. Father Sebi told us a story of a priest who had gone to a temple dressed in kurta and pajamas to look like a Hindu. He and some friends watched the devotees going in with their gifts for the deity and coming out again with *tikas* on their foreheads. Eventually they saw a father and son who were wearing crosses round their necks. The priest adopted a Hindu accent – there is a difference in the way that Hindus and Christians speak in Goa – and said how pleased he was that Christians felt welcome in the temple, but then asked, 'Does the Christian religion allow you to worship a Hindu God?' The Christian replied nervously, 'Our priests shouldn't know we've been here.' The priest put them at ease: 'Don't worry, we won't tell anyone. We understand you because we Hindus also like to go to Christian churches, but you are allowed to take our prasad and you won't let us take yours.' That did shock the Christians. 'Ours is the body and blood of Christ, it would be a sin for you to take it. Even we can't take it if we've sinned.'

When the priest asked, 'Have you sinned by coming to the temple?' it was too much for the Christian. He took his son's hand and walked away.

Father Sebi had seen the state of Western Christendom when he was sent to Germany for further studies in theology. He knew all about the shortage of priests and perhaps secretly rejoiced (although he never said as much) in the opportunity the Pilar fathers now had to reverse history by sending missionaries to Europe and America. He told us with some pride that Pilar fathers had taken over the parish of Deptford in south London.

'That's a remarkable turn round,' I said, 'but why isn't the church on the decline here? How is it that your mass-attendances are keeping up as well as all those vocations?'

Father Sebi rubbed his black-bearded chin and thought before answering, 'Well, I don't know whether I should go on about our Hindu hearts, but at least I can say that, for all the Western trappings you see in the church here, and those centuries of Portuguese influence, we remain oriental. There isn't that Western separation of God and us humans, God is in a sense within us. Here also it's taken for granted that you believe in God, it's not like in the West, you don't question. God belongs to your life, God is in you.'

After lunch in the refectory of crispy Goan-style fried fish, fish and vegetable curries too, and plenty of rice – far less spartan than I'd feared – we went to the top of the seminary to see the chapel.

It was a plain rectangular room, with a dome over the marble altar and stained glass windows in the far wall. Father Sebi pointed to the depiction of the Virgin Mary in one of the windows and said, 'We wanted Mary to be wearing a sari, but when the windows came back from the stained-glass makers in Cologne, she was in the robes of a Western Mother of God. That's the problem. We want to acknowledge the Indian in our church, but the West won't go away. Next week the Pilar fathers will be celebrating a public mass on Indian independence day, and it will include Hindu rituals like *aarti* and smearing *kumkum* on the forehead. Our people will take that provided it's just once in a while, but basically, Christians here outwardly still want to be Westernized. We must become an Indian church, and we must be seen to become one, otherwise the rest of the country will not accept us, but we mustn't go too fast or else the passengers will get off the bus.'

There is one Indian tradition, though, that the Goan church of today does want to eliminate – caste. Throughout more than four hundred years of missionary activity, the church, sometimes reluctantly sometimes less so, accepted caste divisions in Indian Christianity. The seventeenth-century Jesuit Robert de Nobili, who is reputed to have converted some 100,000 south Indians, advised missionaries 'to see which of the customs of the place is not sinful and can be used to further God's religion. After having decided then he must follow those customs himself.' Having judged that caste was not sinful, de Nobili set about living like a Brahmin himself, because he believed this was the only way to convert them. He even avoided any contacts with castes the Brahmins regarded as impure. De Nobili was summoned to Goa to explain himself, but in the end it was decided that he could continue living as a Brahmin.

Pope Alexander II was concerned about the impact of caste on the clergy. In 1658 he decreed, 'The schools should be open to all, although to avoid fighting the low-caste children should be separated from the rest. But those of the low caste and the ignorant should on no account be excluded from holy communion. The sick should be visited and the viaticum should be taken to them no matter how miserable be their huts.' In the nineteenth century, Pope Benedict XIV had to make it clear that high- and low-caste Christians should hear mass in the same church at the same time. The Jesuit missionaries of that century were divided, with the French believing that caste divisions should be accepted, the Irish opposing them, and the Italians being split on the issue.

In Portuguese Goa the church lived with caste. The higher castes were members of the confrarias, or committees, which controlled the village churches. They sat in the front pews at mass, and they organized and played the prominent roles in annual festivals. Upper-caste families had a tradition of sending one son into the church so that they dominated the diocesan clergy too. In democratic India the lower-caste Christians became assertive and the hierarchy came under pressure to ensure that there were no longer any second-class citizens of the kingdom of God here on earth.

In the rector's hall of the Diocesan Seminary, which stands on a hillock that was once the site of an important fortress, a massive white building, looking not entirely unmilitary itself, we were told of a recent caste crisis in the church. The rector of the seminary, whose name we could barely believe was Father Tommas d'Aquino, said he'd had to agree to his professor of moral theology taking charge of the parish of Cuncolim because no other priest was willing to go there after a dispute over membership of the committee which controlled the church properties. The lower castes had insisted that the upper castes' monopoly of the committee should be broken. They had also demanded a role in the patronal festival and, when this had been refused, they had boycotted the village celebrations and gone to a shrine near Panaji to commemorate their patron saint. But Father Tommas was confident the upper castes had now learnt their lesson. 'They are frightened,' he said, 'because the whole voice of the church has been raised.'

Father Tommas was under fifty, younger than I had expected, the rector of the seminary to be, and seemed very anxious to convince us that he was no narrow-minded traditionalist, but he did tell us with some pride that he came from a traditional family, which I assumed meant upper caste. 'My generation arrived with some baggage from home,' he said, 'respect for elders, home education, and all that. Now we get seminarians from the rural areas and from families which never had priests before and they don't have that baggage.'

He also seemed to regret what he saw as a lack of rigour in the seminary. In his days as a seminarian, teachers had been venerable figures, awe inspiring, like the portraits of past archbishops, and indeed the present one, staring severely from the walls of the bleak hall. Now, according to the rector all the students were 'his pals'. I couldn't quite square this with his admission that last year the dropout rate was thirty-five per cent which included several seminarians expelled for 'intellectual or moral deficiency'. But Father Tommas maintained that was exceptional.

When pressed on the quality of the vocations, Father Tommas said, 'They are different, they are not what they used to be, but that's good because they don't carry the same subculture with them.' Decoded, that meant they came from the lower castes. I could not help wondering whether Father Tommas really felt that was good.

A friend living in the nearby village of Loutulim had suggested that after the seminary we should call on his parish priest, a man who didn't carry the same baggage as the rector. Our taxi driver had the greatest difficulty in picking his way through the puddled potholes, fast being turned into floods by the monsoon rains. His task was not helped by his only wiper's inability to cope with the waterfall flowing down the windscreen, but we did eventually reach the clergy house of Loutulim, which was as usual built on to the church. We made our way up a path, the rain beating down on our umbrellas, and found a servant, or he may have been the verger, waiting for us at the door. We followed him along a dark, dank passage, and up a dimly lit flight of well-trodden stairs. The house was more like an institution than a home, an institution that was distinctly down at heel, and very short on inmates, but the parish priest, Father Joseph Cajetan d'Costa, had managed to make the one room he lived in bright and cheerful. Although he was off-duty, watching television with a friend, he welcomed us intruders warmly.

This was our first meeting with a parish priest, one of the foot soldiers of the church. Father. d'Costa must have been in his forties but, although his hair had turned grey in the service of the church, he still had a young, unlined face, and did not seem to be oppressed by any of the cares that weigh heavily on clergy in the Western church – loneliness, lack of response, doubt and depression – living, as they do, in a world where Mammon is triumphant and God on the retreat. In Loutulim half the eight thousand parishioners still come to mass every Sunday. Father d'Costa confirmed that he did not come from one of those high-caste families who had once dominated the church – his father was a farmer in a predominantly

Hindu village that had never produced a priest before. This had caused some problems in his earlier parishes.

'The influential people did not always show me proper respect,' Father d'Costa admitted. 'They didn't like it when I opposed their selfish interests. They wanted to grab church properties and if you didn't let them they talked against you. And they gave privileges undue importance, and if you didn't give them, then they turned against you.'

'What do you mean by privileges?' I asked.

'Brahmins, you know, they think themselves superior. They want all privileges for themselves. For instance they say only they can carry the cross on Good Friday. This they maintain has always been their tradition and should remain so.'

'So did this discourage you, make you wonder about a church which has upheld such unfair, unChristian privileges?'

'No, I felt happy to suffer for a good cause, to identify with Christ through suffering.'

'What about this parish, has it been easier here?'

Father d'Costa replied hurriedly, as if anxious to reassure me, 'No, no, there are no disruptive elements here, here people are cooperative and loving.' He paused before adding, 'But I am of course new here,' and for the first time he looked crestfallen. It was clear he feared there might be more suffering ahead.

The narrow road back from Loutulim to Panaji runs along the southern bank of the mouth of the River Zuari. On the day we travelled, there seemed to be an inordinate amount of heavy vehicles on what was a comparatively minor road. Our driver explained that the traffic had been diverted because the bridge on the main north–south road was in urgent need of repair and had been closed to heavy vehicles. When the Portuguese left Goa, there were no bridges over the Zuari or over the Mandovi. The capital Panaji was still effectively an island. Even when the Indian administration did build a bridge over the Mandovi it collapsed after a few years, and had to be rebuilt. Now the Zuari bridge appeared to be in danger of suffering the same fate. Inevitably, the shortcomings in the construction of the bridges were attributed to corruption with the connivance of politicians – contractors paying bribes so that substandard material and short cuts went officially unnoticed. The church in Goa, which had once lent on the state for support, now felt so self-confident that it was not afraid to oppose the government, especially on this issue of corruption. But corruption wasn't the first issue which brought the church into politics.

After 'liberation', Goan Christians feared their tiny enclave would be submerged in the vast ocean of India. That fear became very real with the formation of a party which was overtly Hindu, and determined to merge Goa with its neighbour to the north, the vast state of Maharashtra, and its capital Bombay, that was more than twelve hours away by road and twenty-two by sea. The Maharashtra Gomantak Party wanted to destroy Goa's separate identity in order to undermine the church's influence and to diminish the value of the Christian vote, which was approximately thirty-two per cent in Goa but would have been a drop in the ocean of Maharashtra. It aimed to ensure that government perks and privileges, especially jobs, now went to Hindus. Although the position of the church was delicate, it took the risk and plunged into politics to fight for Goa's separate existence.

Wherever we went we were told, 'You should go and see Willy if you want to know about the church and politics.' Willy, or Dr Wilfred de Souza, is also known as 'double FRCS' because he returned home in 1962 after passing the exams set by the Royal College of Surgeons in London, and appearing successfully before the surgeons of Edinburgh too. When he returned to Goa he found there was no other surgeon and so, with the double FRCS to boost his reputation, he soon found plenty of work. His bungalow, set in a well-tended garden, was in a village to the north of Panaji. He'd not only brought an English wife back with him from his days in training but also a passion for dogs. His dachshund was the largest Gilly or I had ever seen, and there was a friendly Labrador, and a spaniel too.

Willy himself was a small, round, white-haired Pickwickian figure. He was wearing the uniform of a successful doctor, shining white trousers and an equally white bush shirt. I asked why, after spending all those years in training and passing such difficult exams, he'd deserted medicine for politics.

'I was dragged into politics,' he said, leaning back in his elaborately carved Goan baroque chair. 'It was a matter of life and death, we had to defend our identity. But I never gave up medicine. I was operating even when I was Chief Minister.'

'Was Christianity under threat?' I asked.

'Well, I wouldn't go as far as that,' replied Dr Willy, 'but the church felt it necessary to play a big role. Basically the lower standard of Christians was influenced by the church.'

'What do you mean by lower standard?'

Dr Willy was embarrassed. 'Well, you know, the less well educated, the less well off.'

'The lower caste?'

As a good politician he didn't answer that one but went on, 'The priests, who usually guide lay people, were all against the merger. They supported our United Goan Party because it was a Christian party.'

'But wasn't that bringing politics into religion?' I asked.

Dr Willy wasn't having any of that. 'They were playing very dirty,' he shot back. 'A very prominent politician from Maharashtra came here and called Christians "black Portuguese". When people use tactics like that, what do you expect us to do, lie down and be trodden all over?'

In the end it was a division in the Hindu community that saved the day for Goa. The Maharashtrian party had become so closely identified with the lower castes, that the upper-caste Hindus voted against them when a referendum on the merger was held, and Goa retained its separate identity.

Two more issues had to be fought before Dr Willy was satisfied. The merger had been defeated but that didn't mean Goa could administer itself, it was still controlled by the central government in Delhi. Dr Willy believed Goa would not be safe until it became a fully-fledged state of the Indian Union governed by its own assembly. Then there was the question of the state language. The Maharashtrian lobby wanted their language Marathi, while the language of Christians, and indeed of many Hindus, was Goa's own Konkani.

Dr Willy sought the help of the church to fight those battles too, and once again together they won. An independent state did come into existence with Konkani as its official language. The language decision was not as clear cut as the church would have liked, as it also allowed Marathi to be used for official business. The church, in its Pastoral Review, described the compromise as bigamy, but decided to live with this sin.

That, according to Dr Willy, was the end of the church's involvement in politics. 'The church doesn't take part in the political scene any more,' he said in such a determined manner it appeared he'd ordered it to clear off his political patch. 'In fact religion should be removed from politics altogether. I am a Catholic in so far as I go to church on Sundays and say my prayers, but I am not a Catholic politician.'

I didn't care to remind Dr Willy that he was once a Catholic politician by his own admission, fighting alongside the church, and it was his politics which helped the church get over its Portuguese hangover. Just when it needed a new identity, it was given the opportunity to do battle as a defender of Goan culture. Because the church needed the support of the Hindu elite it didn't fall into the trap of presenting that culture as Christian. So from being a colonial church it became a church of what I suppose one would call Goan sub-nationalism. To have claimed to be nationalist would have offended the Indian government, and the church was too astute to do that.

Not all politicians agree with Dr Willy that the church is no longer involved in politics, nor indeed do all priests. Father José Dias, for instance, the priest of a parish a few miles down the road from Dr Willy's village is renowned for his political activities. Although his church, St Alex Calangute, was built by Franciscans, whom historians of Goan architecture have described as more sober in their habits than some of the other church-building orders, it nevertheless has ornate towers on both sides of the façade and between them is a dome with a turret and a cross on top of it.

Flanked by palm trees, the church used to stand on its own, an imposing white landmark dominating the flat countryside, but now a line of identical apartments painted a hideous pink which clashes with the emerald-green paddy fields, stands just the other side of the road, destroying St Alex's isolation. No attempt, either architectural or horticultural, has been made to disguise this scar on the landscape.

When we met Father José in his house, which was also built on to the church, he was wearing his white cassock because he hadn't had time to change after celebrating mass at six o'clock in the morning. It was by now nearly midday and a young couple were still waiting outside his room to discuss arrangements for their wedding. Although Father José is renowned for his involvement in environmental issues – he had been arrested three times during the protest movement which failed to prevent the government building a railway line across coastal Goa – he was still first and foremost a priest. 'I've been ordained for twenty years and I'm very happy with my ministry,' he told us speaking fast and earnestly. 'I feel I have a vocation, and I am quite clear about my identity. Those priests who have problems do so because they have identity crises.'

Slight, with gold-rimmed glasses, Father José seemed the last person you'd expect to come from a family in such a robust profession as the merchant navy, but his home was St Stephen's island in the Mandovi river renowned for its 'shippies'. His father and all his brothers sailed with P&O. When I asked whether as officers or men he replied very firmly, 'Men.'

He is one of those priests who have taken up what is known in the church as 'the option for the poor'. In Goa, as elsewhere in the world, that is a political option, and although many of the issues he has been involved in are environmental, they also involve politics and economics. Father José's own parish was little more than a fishing village thirty years ago, but then the hippy movement discovered the seven kilometres of Calangute beach. The hippies paved the way for both package tours and five-star tourism. Now behind the beach stands a jumble of hotels, hostels, and holiday homes, restaurants and bars, shacks, stalls, and shops. To add to the ugliness, this monsoon the rough seas had washed a sizeable freighter on to the beach. No one seemed to know what to do with it. The manager of the five-star resort whose beach the ship was parked on said he'd protested but nothing had happened. He could only hope that something would happen before the start of the tourist season.

Father José was currently campaigning against the corruption which has made a mockery of every effort to control the development of Calangute. He showed us an article in the latest edition of his parish magazine blaming the greed and corruption of his own parishioners. The writer complained, 'We, the people of Calangute, are now ever willing to buy favours. We want the authorities to legalize our irregularities and regularize our irregularities. We want to cut a tree without permission, build our houses in violation of zoning and building laws, construct an illegal hotel and block people's access to some villagers' traditional pathway, pay the public health officer to look the other way, produce false certificates, alter land records.'

Father José laughed when I told him that Dr Willy described one former chief minister as the second St Francis Xavier because he was so successful at converting – converting agricultural land into land for building construction.

The parish priest was also involved in attempting to prevent a company called Meta Strips manufacturing brass strips from the copper in disused cables. Copper is officially classed as hazardous waste and 70 per cent of the imported cables would have been coated with PVC, a plastic notoriously difficult to dispose of. Furthermore, the process of converting copper into brass would have required vast amounts of fresh water, a resource that Goa was chronically short of.

Father José was very anxious to impress on us that this was 'a people's campaign' involving Goans of all religions. 'We didn't want the church to give the lead,' he said. 'We only wanted, and we got, its support.' But the church had still played a very prominent role, so much so that it's been the target of an apparently orchestrated campaign of legal threats. The church's spokesman had received a series of nearly identical lawyers' letters from aggrieved shareholders, claiming that the campaign against Meta Strips had prevented the factory starting production and thus robbed them of their dividend. The letters accused the church of 'misguiding the innocent, poor and illiterate people of the villages surrounding the factory and inciting and abetting them to indulge in large-scale unlawful agitation against the factory by resorting to violent means'. The church was also charged with 'arm-twisting' the government to order an 'illegal' closure of the factory. The shareholders all threatened legal action unless the church paid substantial sums of money in compensation.

There have been efforts to turn the public against the church by accusing it of communal politics – of mixing religion with politics. That failed because, as Father José explained, 'We had earlier opposed a nylon plant which businessmen wanted to put up in a Hindu area of the state, and so we had already demonstrated that we were not interested in environmental issues for communal reasons. There never was a communal issue in Goa, and still is only when politicians manipulate it.'

Father José maintains that political corruption is at the root of all the issues he has been involved in. 'These projects,' he explained, 'are taken up by the rich against the poor. The poor elect the politicians, but once elected they don't care for the poor, only for the multimillionaires and multinationals who can pay them for their services. If they didn't pay the politicians would have no interest in bending the environment laws, and all the laws in fact.'

Father José took notes of what he was saying when he got excited. Attacking a plan to build a new airport, which he maintained was quite unnecessary, he spelt out verbally and on paper, 'Four thousand crores, ten per cent commission – four hundred crores.'

He went on to say, 'Politicians are no better than the British or the Portuguese colonialists – they only differed in colour. We are now waiting for the second liberation, and I am not very keen on celebrating the first one.'

That was fighting talk in a state where it's not always wise to cast doubt on your loyalty to India. But Father José is not a lone voice in the church. When we went to call on the spokesman of the archdiocese of Goa, to get the official view about the church and politics, he said, 'It is our Christian duty to attack political corruption. In our sermons we preach about corruption. Nothing is done, everything is delayed because the politicians and officials wait for bribes.'

Surprised that the official spokesman for a traditionally conservative organization, whose relations with the government were always delicate, should be so outspoken, I asked, 'Are you sure you want to be quoted on that?'

'Why not? The politicians themselves admit there is corruption everywhere.'

The spokesman then produced a book by Luizinho Falero, a former chief minister of Goa, and showed me that he'd written, 'Corruption breeds corruption and it is a price tag the citizen is willing to pay and the politician is eager to take.'

The church would not have remained a powerful political force in Goa, able to challenge corrupt politicians, bureaucrats, and businessmen, the nexus which holds India in thrall, if it hadn't retained the loyalty of its own people. Fortunately, just at the time the church in Goa needed to change if it was not to be identified with an era that had passed, the Second Vatican Council forced change on it. A priest-ridden, authoritative church, with a clergy educated in a foreign tongue, a Latin liturgy and mystical rituals, was told by the Council that it had to involve the laity. So the priest celebrating mass moved down from the distant, dark, high altar where he was dwarfed by the Portuguese baroque reredos, to the chancel steps. The preacher moved out of the ornate pulpit set in one of the walls of the nave, high above the congregation, and spoke from the floor of the church. The laity took on the readings from the Old Testament and the Epistles. The priest who had been set apart as the representative of a majestic God, became one with his parishioners worshipping a personal God, more a friend than a king.

Not all the changes came as rapidly as they should and some have still not been completed. Although the liturgy was now celebrated in Konkani, the translation of the New Testament was not finished until 1973 and there was still work to be done on the Old Testament. The changes that were made did not go far enough for some. In the 1970s Catholics started deserting the church for charismatic sects. 'Believers' as they are known in Goa.

On the outskirts of the town of Margao there is a Coca-Cola bottling plant and right next to it a new red-brick building which looks not unlike a Swiss chalet. It's the headquarters of the Good News Church. Ranjeet Rodrigues, the young leader of the church and his assistant, Sharmila de Souza, had both been Roman Catholics and confirmed that most of their members had come from the church too. The leader said, 'They come for the message that Jesus forgives sin. I was a Roman Catholic, I kept all their rules and rituals, but there was nothing there to deal with my knowledge that I was a sinner. It didn't touch my life.'

'Did you speak to a priest before leaving the church?' I asked.

'Yes, I told priests that penance was not a Bible concept, that nowhere in the Bible did it talk of the structure of the church, and so many other things they were doing were not biblical. They tried to dissuade me, but all they could say was, "That's the way it's been for the last five hundred years and that's the way it will always be," which doesn't satisfy anyone.'

The Roman Catholic church did some research of its own on why people were leaving to become Believers. Eighty per cent said it was for 'the God experience'. Their second reason was 'the primacy given to the word of God'. The third was 'fellowship and personalized pastoral care'. To combat this, in 1974 the church imported the Catholic charismatic movement which had started in America.

We were told there was a Catholic charismatic service every Friday in the parish church of Mandur. The Friday we chose to go there the monsoon was in spate again and we wondered whether our journey would be in vain, whether the service would be washed out. But when we lost our way in the narrow country lanes and asked directions from a somewhat bedraggled man who, it turned out, had just come from the service, he was able to assure us there was a full congregation, and several hours still to go. Following his directions we came to a village green on which the white church of Our Lady of Refuge stood. Rows of cars and scooters were parked outside and the church was packed with not even standing room for some worshippers who had to shelter from the rain under a makeshift corrugated iron porch. The leader of the Good News Church said that he had about one hundred and thirty people coming to his meetings on a Sunday. There must have been more than one thousand at this Catholic charismatic service held on a working day, so as not to interfere with the normal Sunday worship.

The service was called a retreat, but the congregation certainly hadn't come for the peace and quiet of a normal Christian retreat. The worshippers had been fasting since the night before and were now three hours into the service but their enthusiasm was undiminished. We squeezed into the church through a side door, and stood squashed against the wall. The short break had just ended and a young man wearing an open-necked shirt with a guitar strapped over his shoulder had taken up position on one side of the altar on which two red candles flickered. Between the candles the blessed sacrament was exposed in a monstrance looking like a golden sun with rays shooting out of it.

The evangelist waited until the excited murmuring died down and silence settled on the church, then raising his arms he cried, 'Hallelujah, hallelujah, hallelujah!' Hundreds of hands clapped and hundreds of voices responded, 'Hallelujah, hallelujah, hallelujah!' The evangelist cried out again, 'Jesus I come to praise you, I need you! You have been so good to us. You have done such wonders in our life.' Then strumming on his guitar he sang, 'We are here to praise you, Lord Jesus, let us praise you and sing. We are here to give you the best we can bring.' The congregation listened with rapt attention, some hands were folded in the traditional Christian pose for prayer, some were held palms up, and some were cupped. The evangelist started to speak again, urgently, pleading, beseeching, 'Sweet Jesus, I want to walk in your footsteps. Oh Jesus, I need you. Sweet Jesus, it all comes from you. Show me the way I want to tread on your footpath.'

He spoke sometimes in Konkani and sometimes in English. A woman next to us with a cross tattooed at the base of her thumb and wearing a mangalsutra, like the necklace worn by married Hindu women, threw her arms in the air and shouted 'Hallelujah!' The evangelist moved on to country and western style singing 'One day at a time, sweet Jesus, that's all I'm asking of you.' This time the congregation joined in. The excitement mounted. Pinpoints of light from electric candles glittered in the golden reredos. The figure of the Virgin Mary, surrounded by glowing bulbs, looked down on the congregation. All the colours of the rainbow brightened the dimly lit church – mauve, blue, bright green, rose red, canary-yellow saris, skirts, blouses. They were offset by some traditional black churchgoing dresses. The men were less colourful and fewer in number.

The frenzied evangelist cried, 'Wash us, keep us clean, we pray to you, Lord Jesus, hallelujah, hallelujah, hallelujah!' His voice boomed louder and louder, and the congregation joined him in a great crescendo. Then the diminuendo started, the hallelujahs grew softer and softer until they died away in a last whisper. The evangelist proclaimed, 'You are healed,' and a young bearded priest, wearing a simple white vestment with just a plain cross on it, sprinkled holy water on some worshippers crowded round the altar. I assumed they were sick but from our vantage, or disadvantage point, it was impossible to tell.

A healer, a slight, elderly woman with a headscarf tied firmly underneath her chin, took over the microphone and called on members of the congregation to confirm reports of past miracles. She asked a woman to confirm that her backache had been cured. Someone else had been cured of 'a white discharge', but when the healer announced that a patient suffering from blood cancer had been healed there was no confirmation from the congregation. Eventually a woman stood up and said, 'She can't be here today.'

The evangelist took charge again, leading the singing of 'Jesus loves me, that's enough …' All around us, young and old, clapped and swayed in time with the music. They sang, 'I am happy today in Jesus, I am clapping today in Jesus, I am singing today in Jesus.' The priest lifted the monstrance above his head in a triumphant gesture, not unlike a tennis champion holding a trophy on high. The clapping, the singing, the hallelujahs, it seemed would never end, but eventually the priest put the monstrance down, moved to the centre of the altar and started the celebration of the mass. The traditional hushed reverence of the church was restored until after the epistle when a gospel hymn aroused another frenzy of hallelujahs and the priest was lost in a forest of clapping hands. But as he opened the prayer book to read the Gospel those hands fluttered across chests in the sign of the cross and the singing ceased.

The priest preached an unemotional sermon in Konkani warning the congregation that they must bear witness to Christ in their lives. It was no good being humble only inside church, they had to render service to others, to forgive others, to be humble when they walked outside. That was witnessing to Christ. After the sermon the priest asked whether anyone had any sins to confess. One woman we couldn't see properly raised her hand and said, 'I am not applying the word of God in my own life and I am sorry.' A penitent standing right by the altar had failed to bear witness because of his own weaknesses. After each confession the priest said, 'We have acknowledged our faults, we want to come back to you, please forgive us.' The bread and the wine were then consecrated, the communion distributed and a strangely subdued congregation left the church.

We went to find the priest, Father Agnelo Fernandes, who turned out to be a Pilar father standing in for the parish priest who was in Britain on a preaching tour. Father Agnelo had been hearing confessions since eight in the morning and had only joined the service towards the end. When I suggested that the service had been a little unorthodox, he replied, 'We cannot just go on the old way, that will be the end of the church because this is what the people want, and if we don't give it, they will go to the Believers.'

'So what is the difference between what you are doing and the Believers? You are both charismatics surely?'

'Ours is Catholic, you saw for yourself the mass, and I am

here, a priest, to ensure it's Catholic. All the people are Catholic charismatics.'

The next day I found myself in much more sober surroundings – the Archbishop's Palace, which was built on the highest point in Panaji to signify the status of the archbishop in Portuguese Goa. Even now the chief minister's official residence is lower down the hillside. I was met in the courtyard of the long, white, two-storeyed building by a priest who showed me inside. The grandeur of the spacious entrance hall was marred by a bucket in the middle of the floor catching drips from the leaking ceiling. Obviously the church was having difficulty in keeping the archbishop in the style his Portuguese predecessors had enjoyed. The priest accompanied me to the archbishop's study on the first floor, knocked on the door and left me to enter on my own as soon as he heard 'Come in.'

I had seen the photo of the archbishop in our well-thumbed directory of his archdiocese. He looked very much the prelate, with purple buttons on his white cassock and a purple skullcap covering his grey hair. When I entered his office he was sitting at his desk with a large crucifix behind him. The windows were open, there was no stuffy air-conditioning. I had expected an awe-inspiring figure, but he was shorter than I'd imagined and instead of the severe face scowling from the cover of the directory I was greeted with a broad smile and escorted to a comfortable chair. Mediterranean hospitality had survived in his palace, and although it was well before lunch I was offered a drink and a choice of prawn patties or beef sausage rolls. The archbishop was surprised, and perhaps even a little disappointed, when I settled for coffee and a piece of sweet Goan cake known as bebinca. The archbishop drank coffee too.

He wore a silver crucifix round his neck but that was the only sign of his high office. The buttons on his cassock were mother-of-pearl and his curly grey hair was uncovered. Educated in Portuguese throughout his days in the minor seminary, he spoke English with a trace of a Portuguese accent.

He was gratified by the results of his twenty-eight years in charge of the archdiocese, but did not take credit for this himself. When I asked how the church in Goa was flourishing, when in the West it seemed to be in decline, he replied, 'The finger of God.'

'Nothing more?' I asked.

'Well, yes. The people's participation is much better. Then also we used to be very keen on Eucharistic devotion. Of course we still are, but we are also keen on the Bible now.'

'Is it true that St Francis Xavier never carried a Bible with him during all those years of missionary activity?'

'Maybe, maybe, but those were different days. The church has even changed greatly in my short life, and I am very pleased about the laity's participation. You know the small Christian communities we are setting up, they now take it in turns to prepare the mass on Sundays, decide the hymns and the theme and the readings. That would have been impossible when we priests ran everything.'

But when I told him that I had been very impressed by the charismatic service, I could see we were moving on to less sure ground.

'Where was the service?' he asked.

'In the parish church at Mandur.'

'Ah now, I'm not at all sure that is one that our diocesan charismatic service team has approved. I think it's still under review. We have set the team up to control the movement. There is a danger that it will undermine the parish churches, draw people away from their own churches. That's why I have said the charismatic retreats can't be held on Sundays. Your service wasn't on Sunday?' he asked anxiously.

'No, on Friday,' I assured him and he nodded saying, 'Good, good.'

The archbishop was particularly concerned about the healing at charismatic services. 'We don't want people to go to these services and ask for things. We want them to bear witness to God's will,' he said. 'What's particularly worrying is the misuse of the sacrament in healing. There have even been reports of people being force-fed with the sacrament.'

At that stage, I didn't think I would tell him about the use of the monstrance in Mandur, and so I moved the conversation forward, suggesting that the charismatic movement might become so strong it could dictate its own terms for remaining within the church.

'Oh, no, no, no, no,' he replied hurriedly. 'No one can tell where the spirit will blow, and the church must be open to the spirit. But if you read history you will see that there have been many such movements in the past and the church has contained them. Take St Francis, even the Pope didn't quite know whether he should approve of him. He did and now we have Franciscans everywhere including here, and they are doing very good work and are not a worry to me.'

'Well, I hear that you will be getting rid of the worries you have soon, because you are retiring in two years' time. Is that true?'

He leant back in his chair and smiled, 'I will be seventy-five and so I will have done enough, won't I?'

'Yes, I'm sure you will have.'

'As I told you, I have seen many changes and they haven't all been easy for me, educated as I was in a very different tradition. So it is time for a rest, or maybe a change would be a better word because I want to remain active in some way.'

I came away with the impression that the charismatic movement was one change too many for the archbishop, and that he would be very glad to hand that problem over to someone else.

On the last Sunday we met another priest who had not found change easy. When we were sitting in a pew waiting for mass to start in Old Goa's Se Cathedral, a small, elderly but remarkably spry priest came up to us wearing not the usual white cassock but an old-fashioned, tight-fitting black one with a traditional high dog-collar. He asked whether I was a Portuguese speaker and when I told him I didn't know a word of the language he said, 'I usually ask foreigners that because I love speaking Portuguese but I don't get much chance nowadays.'

I asked why the exterior of his cathedral was now yellow instead of the traditional Goan white and this provoked a diatribe against the

Archaeological Survey of India which had taken over responsibility from the church for the monuments of Old Goa. 'We can't do anything to our own cathedral now,' he fumed, hopping from one foot to the other in his anger. 'We even have to get permission to put up a new collection box, and what do they do to preserve the church? Nothing.' As evidence he took me to the west end and showed me piles of rubble where the plaster was peeling from the pillars.

I had noticed that his cassock had purple piping and purple buttons so I asked, 'Does the purple mean you are a monsignor?'

'No. But I am Father Adolpho Joviano Castro Viegas, a canon of the cathedral and the parish priest and that is just as senior.'

Having been put straight about that, I went on to ask, 'In the cathedral, do you keep up the old traditions of worship?'

'Of course I try to, but what can we do? We don't have money to pay for the choirs and all that you need for proper ritual, and the bishop doesn't care either. The Portuguese bishop used to come here regularly with full pomp and devotion. The present one only comes about four times a year. I love the full ritual and singing, it lifts your heart.'

The peppery priest then left me to robe for the chapter mass.

The vast cathedral was far from full when Father Adolpho and six other equally elderly canons entered through the south aisle. Robed in splendid green copes they walked in a solemn procession, accompanied by just one server, to the altar at the top of the chancel steps. Six of the canons including Adolpho took their seats in high-backed chairs behind the altar and one stood at the altar to celebrate the mass with dignity and solemnity. He was accompanied by a small choir in the organ loft.

Looking at the magnificent gilded reredos crowned by the figure of Christ on the cross just below the white-barrelled ceiling of the sanctuary, I couldn't help but think of the Portuguese who had built this monument to impress Goans with the majesty of a God who lived on high. I knew that the church had to change, to bring God down to earth, if it was to survive in independent India, but I also acknowledged that I came from the old tradition, the tradition

Father Adolpho was preserving. I found it easier to worship God in majesty, rather than God the social worker who battles for the poor, or God the personal pal of the charismatics.

Creating Cyberabad

I had been allowed past the security barrier into the outer waiting room of the official residence of the chief minister of Andhra Pradesh, set in the hills above the lake at the heart of the state capital, Hyderabad, but it didn't look as if I would get any further. An hour had passed. A grizzled politician, built like an ox, had moved, with his hangers-on, into the residence itself. I was now the lone visitor in the waiting room. A woman who seemed to have some ill-defined security role was offering sweets to all and sundry to celebrate the birth of a grandson. I accepted one. It was now nearing a quarter to eleven, and I had been told I must be at the residence by ten o'clock if I was to fly in the chief minister's helicopter to the election meetings he was addressing that day.

I had come to meet Chandrababu Naidu because he was the idol of the World Bank and other institutions that were pressing for better governance, for less government, for modernization of the administration, and eradication of corruption. I was worried that I'd missed him. After all, someone who prided himself on his efficiency couldn't be late. He had to be that rare exception, a politician who arrives at election meetings on time rather than making the crowds suffer in the sun, waiting on his convenience. But, at the same time, I thought that if he were so efficient, surely he couldn't forget to take me with him. I was, as so often happens to me, paralysed by indecision. What start out as conversations, or polite requests, to Indian security officials, all too often end up in shouting matches, and so I didn't want to go back to the gate only to be infuriated by a blank refusal to find out what was happening inside the residence. On the other hand, I feared I would miss the helicopter if someone inside was not reminded that I was waiting. Another fifteen minutes passed and no one showed any concern about me, and so I finally made up my mind to act. At the gate I was relieved to find a mild-mannered Muslim police officer who immediately put down the lunch he was eating from a tiffin carrier, contacted the residence on a walkie-talkie, and gave permission for me to pass the second security gate.

Eventually we took off, an hour and a half after what I had been told was the scheduled time. I was squashed beside the chief minister in the four-seater French helicopter. On my other side were the official photographer and the chief minister's security officer, who at first I thought looked on me with disapproval. The helicopter had been hired from a company called Million Air Executive Jet Services because the chief minister could not use an aircraft owned by the state for party purposes. Outside, on each side of the windscreen, if that's what it's called on a helicopter, fluttered a flag with a bicycle on a canary yellow background. The chief minister himself was wearing a canary yellow bush shirt to match his Telugu Desam Party's flags. The bicycle is the party's election symbol.

Fifty-one-year-old Chandrababu Naidu was not known for small talk. He greeted me with barely more than a grunt, and then got stuck into the papers his security officer handed him. I needed to reassure myself and so I asked, 'We will be able to talk, won't we?'

'After the last meeting,' he replied, and went back to studying the details of the development activities in the district we were heading for.

I looked over the shoulders of the two pilots and tried to read the instruments on the dashboard. To me they seemed to say our speed was one hundred nautical miles an hour and our altitude a thousand feet. I later discovered that we were in fact flying at two hundred and forty kilometres an hour at three thousand feet. So much for my aeronautical capabilities.

After about forty minutes we started to descend, circling over the meeting below. I could see the ground was not covered with a carpet of people, there were gaping holes in the crowd. Some, who had the sense to wait for the sound of the helicopter, were hurrying towards the meeting. When we were hovering just above the ground, Chandrababu Naidu looked out of the window and gave the crowd the Churchillian 'V for victory' sign but, as we were enveloped in a cloud of dust, I doubt whether anyone saw him. Once the whirling blades were stilled, he climbed out of the helicopter to be surrounded by a crowd of party leaders and police. Commanding rather than charismatic, he quickly dealt with the reception committee and strode towards the meeting, his right hand raised once again in the victory sign.

After mercifully short speeches by the local leaders, the chief minister himself rose to speak. These were elections for local bodies called mandais, but Chandrababu Naidu was taking them as seriously as elections to the state assembly, and so were his enemies. They both knew that, if the elections went badly, there could be trouble within the Telugu Desam Party. Naidu ruled with a rod of iron. He had gathered all power to himself, and there was considerable chafing under his harsh yoke. One of his senior colleagues had already broken away and, if it was shown that his remarkable power to win votes was diminishing, others might go too.

I was surprised to see that the only picture of the charismatic founder of the Telugu Desam Party, the film star N. T. Rama Rao, or NTR as he was always known, was stacked away in a corner of the dais. He was Chandrababu Naidu's father-in-law. But then I remembered the history of the Telugu Desam and its founding family.

Telugu is the language of Andhra Pradesh and NTR was the most popular star of the Telugu film industry. He entered politics in the early eighties when Indira Gandhi was introducing her son Rajiv into politics as her successor, and dismissing and appointing Congress chief ministers at her will. T. Anjaiah, a man of humble background and very little English, was her chief minister for Andhra Pradesh, when Rajiv first visited Hyderabad. To give Rajiv an impressive welcome when he visited the state, he brought a crowd of enthusiastic supporters to the airport. Rajiv, a former airline pilot, had been invited into the cockpit and was in the co-pilot's seat when the plane came to land. Having been a pilot for much longer than he had been a politician, he was horrified to see Congress supporters on the tarmac in violation of airport rules and, as he disembarked, gave Anjaiah such a dressing down, in English, that the hapless and uncomprehending politician could only fold his hands and weep. The photographers' cameras clicked, and the humiliation of Anjaiah became national news.

NTR, by then in his sixties, saw this as an opportunity to follow the example of the film star chief minister of the neighbouring state of Tamil Nadu, M. G. Ramachandran. He reckoned that if the heroic roles MGR had played could transfigure him from a screen to a real-life hero, his own heroic roles in more than 320 films could launch his political career. To gain the most from his advantages, NTR dressed in the saffron robes of a hero of the Hindu epics, and campaigned in a vehicle got up like the chariots heroes of old drove. His one-point programme was 'Restore Telugu pride', pointing out, with considerable justification, the hurt that the Gandhis' imperious handling of their party in Andhra Pradesh had inflicted.

'The leader of sixty million Telugu people,' he thundered, 'was publicly humiliated by a man whose only claim to fame is that he was born to a certain woman, and has managed to learn how to fly an aeroplane!'

So effective was the charisma of the stocky film star, with his still handsome, square face and broad forehead, and so well timed was his appeal to Telugu pride that, within nine months of its formation, his party became the first ever to defeat the Congress in elections to the Andhra Pradesh state assembly.

Chandrababu Naidu, who had been a minister in the Congress state government, remained loyal to that party in the election which first swept his father-in-law to power. He lost his seat and decided to start a new career as a businessman, but NTR persuaded him to join his party. Rajiv Gandhi had not learnt his lesson, and the year after his party's humiliation played the 'toppling game' he and his mother were so fond of. Choosing a moment when NTR was abroad for medical treatment, he encouraged some of the Telugu Desam legislators to defect and the government fell.

This was Chandrababu Naidu's chance to demonstrate his political skills. He carted all the remaining Telugu Desam legislators to

Delhi to demonstrate that his father-in-law still commanded a majority, and then packed them off to the neighbouring state of Karnataka where the friendly chief minister kept them out of temptation's way in a hill resort some forty kilometres from Bangalore. Left in Hyderabad they would certainly have been offered money and other inducements. NTR returned, mounted his chariot again, and whipped up such a sense of outrage among the citizens of the state that even Governor Ram Lal, a former Congress chief minister from the Himalayas, couldn't brazen it out any longer and NTR was restored to his throne.

NTR acknowledged his debt to Chandrababu Naidu, crediting him with the 'rebirth' of the Telugu Desam Party, and promising 'never to forget his services'. But gratitude is not a stable currency in Indian politics, and when NTR shocked his family by marrying a singer far younger than he was, Chandrababu Naidu found himself replaced as the man behind the party leader by a woman – the new wife. There was a major political row and Chandrababu Naidu walked off with most of his father-in-law's legislators. Shortly after that NTR died, and Chandrababu Naidu was able to ward off a challenge from his widow to become undisputed leader of the Telugu Desam Party. But, with that background, he was always cautious about claiming to have inherited the mantle of NTR, for fear that the charge of disloyalty levied by his widow would be revived.

Naidu made no attempt to imitate his histrionic father-in-law. Far from donning robes, he was even more low-key than the normal politician, not bothering to wear their uniform – traditional dress. Only that bright yellow bush shirt distinguished his apparel from that of any modern Indian bureaucrat or businessman. Neatly combed black hair and a trimmed beard whitening at the chin did little to differentiate him too.

When Naidu started to speak, it became absolutely clear that he'd decided there was no point in even trying to match NTR's flamboyance. He did line up his party's candidates on the platform and asked whether anyone objected to them. When no one spoke, Naidu led the applause. But that was the only time he tried to work the crowd. After getting the candidates to repeat the oath of loyalty to the party and its principles, he did briefly appeal to the memory of NTR before starting a mundane attack on the Congress Party and its promises. He accused them of 'indulging in bad propaganda against the Telugu Desam', and asked how they could be promising free electricity to farmers in Andhra Pradesh when they weren't giving it away in the states they ruled. Playing on the rivalry within the Congress Party, he said, 'One leader tells you one thing and another tells you another thing.' Then becoming more animated he declared, 'You have to teach a lesson to the opposition by defeating them in this election. Don't let Congress get a single vote.' That would have been a fitting climax but the chief minister went on to catalogue the achievements of his government – more money spent on development, more irrigation, more doctors, more teachers, and still more funds to come, some from the World Bank. But I noticed that Naidu didn't mount his favourite hobby-horses, good governance and the benefits of information technology.

We nearly missed our next meeting. As I was finishing the delicious curd-rice which was the chief minister's normal lunch, I noticed the pilots scanning their map and then peering down at the ground below. The helicopter descended but there was no meeting in sight. There were anxious conversations over the intercom between the pilots and the security officer. Then we turned and flew low over a railway line until we came to a station. We hovered to read the sign on the platform. Discovering that it was one station away from our destination, we flew above the railway line until we reached the meeting. The pilots later told me that they had been given the wrong coordinates.

I nearly didn't make it to the helicopter after the last meeting. When the chief minister had finished speaking, there was a frantic rush to get him away because it was getting late and darkness would impose limits on the helicopter. The chief minister was bundled into an Ambassador which shot off at a great speed. I tried to get into one of the cars in his cavalcade but was pushed out by a policeman. Fortunately the deputy inspector general of police saw this and dragged me into his car, which was already moving. A woman, one of the many trying desperately to get to the helipad to see the chief minister off, almost managed to get on to the front seat before being thrown out by the driver's sudden braking. The cavalcade careered down the road, bumper to bumper, horns blowing and sirens screeching, scattering the crowds leaving the meeting like frightened chickens. Someone should have been mowed down, cars should have collided, but no damage was done. It was one of those Indian miracles of order within chaos.

As we took off for Hyderabad, Naidu was given some newspapers to read. I was getting nervous again. Would my day be wasted? I wondered. The chief minister hardly needed reminding of my presence as I was almost sitting on top of him in the cramped cockpit. Was he deliberately ignoring me? No he wasn't. It was just a case of first things first.

After scanning the papers to see what was being said about him and his government, he turned to me as the least important item on the day's agenda, and without any of the usual polite preliminaries asked, 'What do you want to know?'

I replied with an equal lack of subtlety, 'Why is India so badly governed?'

That was enough to spark Naidu off. 'Because people are illiterate, the leaders don't feel it necessary to give proper direction to the nation. The main problem is poverty and ignorance and they are not interested in doing anything about it.'

'So you believe what is often said that the leaders of India have deliberately kept the people ignorant so that they won't know how badly they are governed?'

'I wouldn't say that,' he replied. 'But you have to answer the question – why, if Indians are so capable and intelligent, as they show around the world, why are they not doing better here? IT has shown how intelligent they are, but we politicians must create the right atmosphere in which they can flourish. We only started to liberalize our economy in 1991, a long time after China, so we have a lot of catching up to do.'

Chandrababu Naidu went on to say it was easier for China too because it was a totalitarian state and didn't have to bother about what the people thought, while India, as a democracy, did. 'In India, to win elections, we have not been going for priorities but for populism,' he explained. 'Politicians have been misleading rather than educating, making tall promises they are not fulfilling. In government they say one thing, in opposition another. As I said at the meetings, how can Congress promise free electricity here, where it's in opposition, and not give it in the neighbouring states where it is the government?'

However, he still insisted that democracy was the only answer for India. What were required were reforms to make government function efficiently. He wanted reforms in the legal system so that government decisions were not forever being challenged in the courts, and he wanted the discretionary powers of bureaucrats to be curbed because they were the means used to do favours and bend the law. He believed the people should become stakeholders so that they could act as 'watch dogs', and he agreed that they should have the right to information about government activities to fulfil that role. He was trying to change his government's role from controlling to facilitating, and he wanted greater freedom to do that.

'I have been saying from the beginning,' he complained, 'that the states should have more power. There'll be coalition governments in the centre for some time now, so this is the time for decentralization, but nothing is happening. Even for small things we are dependent on Delhi and Delhi does nothing. We must decentralize at the national level, but we must also decentralize at the state level. That's what I mean by stakeholders. I don't want everything done by the government. I want people to have a role as well as a voice.'

Naidu had called in perhaps the best known of all international management consultants, McKinsey's, to draw up a document called Vision 2020 – a vision of Andhra Pradesh twenty years on. The buzz word in that document was SMART – simple, moral, accountable, responsive, transparent – government. IT was allocated a major role in achieving SMART government. This enthusiasm put Hyderabad, once considered one of India's sleepiest capitals, on the IT map. Bangalore had been the unrivalled IT capital of India, but when President Clinton visited India he chose to come to

Hyderabad to see the IT industry. While we were in Hyderabad, the chief minister presided over the opening ceremony of a new business school affiliated to the Wharton, Kellogg, and London business schools. It would be difficult to have a better pedigree than that. The board of governors of the school hadn't even considered Hyderabad as a location, but Naidu put such pressure on them they couldn't refuse to visit his capital. He greeted them personally and, with the help of McKinsey's, gave such an impressive presentation that Hyderabad won over much more obvious locations like Bangalore, Mumbai and Chennai.

Naidu was already using IT to deliver some government services but had much more ambitious plans. 'I want to put all information about government activities, contracts issued and work in progress, on an Andhra Pradesh portal,' he told me. 'We will even take video photos of the buildings and show them on the portal. So if you say, where is the school that the records say has been built, or how well has it been built, we will show it to you on the screen.'

'Many are dismissing your enthusiasm for IT as a tamasha, just a gimmick,' I pointed out.

'If you say anything in this country people are sceptical, there is so much pessimism everywhere. You must establish credibility, you must implement successfully. I will work twenty-four hours a day, round the clock, to achieve that.'

'Do you have an ideology?' I asked.

'When people ask what "ism" I subscribe to, I say society is my temple, the common man is my God. I work for that God. Now everyone is talking about reforms with a human face but I don't want only talk, I want to take e-mail to every village.'

By now it was dark and we were approaching the lights lining the runway of Hyderabad's international airport. I still had some questions to ask, but Naidu, who had been so silent earlier, was unstoppable on the benefits e-mail could bring to villagers in Andhra Pradesh. Eventually I butted in, 'If e-mail is going to do so much for rural voters, why didn't it feature in your speeches today?'

'You've given the answer,' he replied. 'Everyone says it's just a tamasha. Until I have proved it is not I don't want to speak about it, because people will only get disheartened and ask what is all this e-mail about? You have to make sure it happens first then let them see the results. You have to supervise the implementation at interim stages; if you don't, nothing will happen. It will all be on paper.'

As we dropped down towards the runway, I asked the inevitable journalistic question, 'Do you have any ambitions to be prime minister of India?'

That would not have been an unrealistic ambition, because in the last three elections no party had won an absolute majority and coalition governments had twice been headed by politicians from small parties. But Naidu shot back, 'I don't have any such ambitions. I want to make AP a role model state. I am doing that and it's giving me great satisfaction.'

'How much time do you need?'

'Ten years. If I lose power before that, all my reforms will go, but over a time a culture will be established and there will be no going back.'

When we landed Naidu returned to his former brusque self. After ensuring that there was an official car to take me back to my hotel, he climbed into his Ambassador, wasting no time in acknowledging my thank you and customary expression of the hope that we would meet again. As we drove off the tarmac and through the security gate, I thought of Rajiv Gandhi, the only other Indian politician I have known who put good governance so high on his agenda, and was obsessed with the potential of IT. The two men were very different. Rajiv had all the charm in the world. Naidu was a hard, humourless man. Rajiv had been thwarted by the politicians in his own party and the bureaucrats who knew that good governance was bad news for them. Naidu seemed to have a firmer grip on his own party and the bureaucracy. Rajiv took on the vested interests opposed to administrative reforms throughout India, Naidu only had to manage them in one state. But Naidu, I knew, was no more certain of success than Rajiv. It wasn't just the vested interests who could derail him. He had to create a demand for change, persuade his people that things could get better, and fight the pervasive cynicism which said they couldn't. That would be no easy task.

Mahatma Gandhi, whose understanding of India and patriotism cannot be challenged, did once describe it as a country of 'self-suppression and timidity'. I would never use such harsh words, nor can I accept the frequent and facile diagnosis of fatalism as the cause of all India's ailments, but two often repeated words 'chalne do', 'let it be' have characterized the country's response to the manifest failures of its system of governance since independence.

Debunking change, known colloquially as 'leg pulling' – pulling people down when they are trying to make progress – is also part of the politics of Indian democracy. Whatever new initiative the party in power proposes, the opposition will inevitably rubbish. The Congress in Andhra Pradesh was no exception, as I found when I visited one of their most senior leaders, K. Rosaiah. His substantial house in Hyderabad was still being constructed, and I couldn't help wondering what Mahatma Gandhi, represented by a brass figurine on Rosaiah's desk, would think of the whirling marble cutters which from time to time disturbed our conversation. Rosaiah was as hard a man as the chief minister. Burly, bald, with eyes set so deep they almost disappeared under his jutting forehead and grey eyebrows, there was menace in his demolition of the chief minister.

Naidu had bankrupted the state, Naidu hadn't started any new irrigation schemes, Naidu's reform of the corrupt state electricity board had increased not decreased losses, Naidu had sold off nationalized companies for a song, and as for e-mail, well, that was – 'just a tamasha'.

He complained, 'If communication has improved, why don't I get a reply when I write to the chief minister? I don't even get an acknowledgement. When I write to a central government minister an acknowledgement will come promptly. They call the new government SMART, but in practice I should get a reply.'

When I told the disgruntled politician that we had a reply within two days when we e-mailed the chief minister about our visit, he replied sullenly, 'I suppose he thinks you are more important than I am.'

Rosaiah dismissed the triumph over the Clinton visit and the new business school as window dressing. 'Where is the new investment we are meant to be getting after all this tamasha and all the money he has spent on creating the image of the IT capital of India?' he asked. 'Why even the boys who went to America to work in IT are coming back now because of the dot-com companies' problems.'

'Is that anything to be happy about?' I asked.

'It just shows that this IT business is a lot of hype,' he replied. Then realizing that he'd perhaps gone too far he hurriedly reassured me, 'I am not against e-government, but it shouldn't just be publicity with nothing happening. My son went to the registration office where Naidu boasts that a new system has been installed and it was the same old system.'

The time had come to press him a little harder, and so I asked how he could complain about the finances of Andhra Pradesh when almost every other state, including those run by his party, was in the red.

'I want to keep my health perfect. I don't want to compare my health to my neighbour's. That's no answer.'

His reply when I asked what his party had done about good governance when they were in power was also no answer.

'We set up an administrative reforms committee.'

The experience of Rosaiah's son with computerized, or reportedly computerized, government services didn't match with reports we had heard, and so we visited the offices of TWINS, another of Naidu's acronyms standing for Twin Cities Integrated Network Services.

Hyderabad, the capital of the Nizam, the Muslim ruler who refused to merge his state with independent India and so was deposed by force, is twinned with Secunderabad where the British had their cantonment. Since the end of the Nizam's rule, the two have become Siamese twins joined in one sprawling megalopolis.

TWINS was situated in Banjara Hills, the smart area of Hyderabad. Unlike a normal dirty and decrepit government office, the premises were immaculately clean. There were no crowds pushing and shoving to get to the front of what should be a queue. Instead some twenty people were sitting on chairs waiting for the electronic queuing system to come up with their token numbers. Clerks sat behind computer terminals. Each was able to offer eighteen services, among them payment of electricity and other bills, registration of births and deaths, renewal of driving licences, and the encumbrance certificate Rosaiah's son had been looking for. Not all the clerical drudgery had been eliminated. We noticed a clerk writing the number of a water bill on each of the five hundred rupee notes he'd received in payment so that the notes could be traced if they were found to be forged. But an ophthalmologist who had worked in Britain's National Health Service was more than satisfied with the plastic driving licence he'd received. A woman sheathed in a burqa and her husband were given their vehicle registration certificate with remarkable rapidity. Only a few weeks earlier the dealer who sold us a second-hand car in Delhi had advised us to pay an agent to get it registered rather than face the ordeal of the Road Transport Office there. The agent turned out to be an employee of that department. It struck me that TWINS might not work so well in more crowded and less orderly parts of the city. I couldn't test my theory because this was a 'pilot project' and the only office open so far. But nine more were opened a few weeks after we left and another eight the next month.

In Indian politics, the enemy within is often more dangerous than the enemy without. In the local body elections, Naidu was not just facing a challenge from his traditional foe, the Congress, but also from a politician who had for many years been one of his lieutenants. From being an avid advocate of economic reforms, Chandrashekhar Rao had become a bitter critic, forming his own party to oppose his leader. To justify his revolt, he had revived an old demand for a separate state for the region known as Telengana, which was basically the old kingdom of the Nizam of Hyderabad. There were some Indian princes who were forward looking, providing better education and other services than the British Raj ever did, but the Nizam was not one of them. The coastal regions of what is now Andhra Pradesh had prospered because of the education provided by Christian missionaries and canals dug by the British, while inland feudalism had held Telengana in a time warp. Chandrashekhar Rao was telling the Telengana electorate that Andhraites, with their superior education, were dominating the state, while Telengana was suffering from discrimination particularly in the matter of water. It is true to say that most of the catchment areas of the Rivers Krishna and Godavari are in Telengana, yet most of the water is used by the Andhraites. There is no major irrigation system in Telengana.

Chandrashekhar Rao had only formed his Telengana Rashtra Samiti, or State of Telengana Committee, three months ago, and he was fighting these elections from the new house he was building in Jubilee Hills, an area now being colonized by the rich who couldn't find space in Banjara Hills. We climbed gingerly up an exterior brick staircase, still not plastered and with no rails to prevent us being pushed off by others trying to gain entry to the upper floor where Chandrashekhar Rao was living – the party workers, political pimps and genuine supplicants who mill around anyone worthy of the title of *neta*, or political leader, in India, especially at election time. The pressure mounted as some of the favoured few inside opened the glass door, but somehow they managed to let us in without allowing any of the less favoured in with us.

We were shown into a marble-floored room where, inevitably, we had to wait for the leader. But it wasn't long before Chandrashekhar Rao walked in. I was immediately struck by the difference between this tall, thin figure and the other two other politicians I had met. They were like Esau to this smooth Jacob, elegant in his shining white shirt and lungi with a narrow purple and gold border. There was a gold pen in his top pocket and on his wrist a gold watch studded with what looked like diamonds. A side parting divided his wavy black hair and a neat red dot between his eyebrows was a delicate acceptance of the need to appear devout. He had charm too, and enjoyed exercising it, not being in the least perturbed when I suggested he'd formed his new party out of pique, not principle, when Naidu had not made him a minister, after the last election.

'That's what you journalists would say,' he said with a smile, 'but history will eventually tell you were wrong. I have no ambition to be chief minister of Telengana and when we get the state you will see. In fact one of my fights is against the tyranny of chief ministers. This is meant to be a democracy but India is under untold autocracy, no minister can dissent with the chief minister. That's why I call it a tyranny.'

Chandrashekhar Rao agreed with his former leader that administrative reforms were essential. Indian politics, he said, had become 'a vote-hunting experience'. Members of parliament and of state assemblies had no training and so fell prey to *babus* or bureaucrats pursuing their own interests. Legislators didn't even take an interest in budget debates and most of the discussions were guillotined.

'Why do we always talk about the ruling party?' he asked. 'How is it possible to rule in a democracy? It's only possible in an autocracy. It ought to be the serving party. This country is under a tyranny of netas and babus.'

'Is that why you fell out with Chandrababu Naidu?' I asked.

He laughed. 'Well, you know Hindi, so you know he's a neta, not a babu, but he is a tyrant.'

'He certainly seems to have an iron grip on the party, delegation isn't exactly the name of the game, but at least he's trying to do something, unlike most netas.'

'Don't be deceived by all this e-government. Naidu has just created hype. You need administrative reforms first. It's not right to do reforms from the top, structural arrangements are needed. In Andhra Pradesh there is no structure.'

That hype word again. We were to hear it almost everywhere we went in Hyderabad. But the IT advisor to the government of Andhra Pradesh, Dr T. Hanuman Chowdary, was anxious to convince us there was more to Naidu's reforms than that. On the wall by the lift, which took us to his office in the secretariat, was one of those exhortations which are substitutes for action in Indian government premises. Described as 'A Divine Thought for the Day', it read, 'A good clean minded person sees the good points in others. A dirty minded person is always looking for dirt.'

I suppose that makes all journalists dirty minded, I thought to myself. But this time I didn't have to look for the dirt, Dr Chowdary exposed it for me. Elderly and eccentric, a non-stop talker with a sense of humour all of his own, during his life he had moved from being an atheist communist to what he called an Aryan, which in his case meant supporting the Hindu nationalist sect the RSS. He had become disillusioned with communism because it provided no reason for a man to be good. 'That reason is explained by spiritualism,' he said. 'Materialism can never make man good.'

He had no illusions about the evil of corruption in modern India. Transparency International's recent finding that India was one of the most corrupt nations provoked a caustic comment from him. 'We must be grateful to Transparency International because they have recognized that. We are a tolerant people so we tolerate corruption. We keep on exposing corruption but, because we are tolerant, we don't convict the corrupt. God and corruption are everywhere. Paupers come into politics and become rich, so poverty must be permanent to keep politics going.'

'But is it just the politicians who are to blame?' I asked.

'Oh no. One of India's most distinguished lawyers once said, "It requires superhuman effort to keep India poor," and I added, "That effort is provided by the government servants."'

Dr Chowdary regarded his own chief minister as an exception to the politicians who wanted to keep poverty going. He praised his 'leadership qualities' and his vision, his willingness to listen, and ability to persuade, his commitment to hard work, and his perseverance. He maintained that the chief minister had now overcome one of the highest hurdles in his way, he had convinced ninety per cent of government servants that e-government would work. 'Now there is no obstruction,' he said, 'just some non-involvement because people are old and sceptical.'

'So in spite of your scepticism about government servants, you think they will allow e-government to work?'

'They tried to stop us,' Dr Chowdary admitted. 'That was when we wanted to deliver the TWINS service through a private agency. They said, "It is our duty to serve the public, it is our privilege" –

which means, of course, "corruption is our birthright".' Looking at me to make sure I'd got the joke, he went on, 'Discretion is the better part of valour and so we withdrew, and thought again. Now we have made government servants the operators of TWINS, although the hardware and the software are provided and managed by a private firm, and TWINS is up and running.'

It was the Andhra Pradesh Non-Gazetted Officers' – or junior officials – Association which had forced Chandrababu Naidu to go back on his plan to get a private company to take over the entire responsibility for delivering the TWINS services. The association strongly opposed the proposal, and made their disapproval clear just before an election. The chief minister was well aware of the essential roles junior officials play during the voting and the counting, roles which can influence the outcome. That was the reason discretion became the better part of valour.

The offices of the Non-Gazetted Officers' Association are in a sprawling concrete building with no architectural merit, no horticulture to relieve the drab construction, designed for no fixed purpose, and dumped on valuable land in the middle of the city which could have been put to far more profitable use. The government had handed over the whole building to the NGOs, as they are known. The NGOs themselves were no more energetic, enthusiastic, or efficient when they were working for their own association than they were when on government service. Notices on the walls announced that there was to be a major convention of NGOs the next day, but you wouldn't have thought so if you'd visited their office. Three or four clerks, lost in a large ground-floor room barely broke off from their conversation to point us up a flight of stairs. There we did find one man at what I suppose would now be called his work station. He was sitting behind a desk, leaning on an ancient typewriter, chatting to two of his colleagues. When we asked for the official who had given us an appointment, he replied, with no trace of concern, 'He's gone out.' Then without bothering to find out what our business was or whether the president was free, the stenographer, for that I presumed was his position in the hierarchy, told us to go and see him instead.

The president peered rather anxiously over his gold-rimmed glasses as we walked unannounced through the open door of his office, but was too polite to ask who we were, or what we were doing. A name board behind his desk identified him as G. Purnachandra Rao, B.A. A mild man, short with untidy thinning hair, his views on e-governance were a little muddled. He admitted, 'We cannot totally oppose computerization,' but went on to say, 'It must go hand in hand with manual work. There should be no reduction in manpower. If one computer can do the work of five, then the other four should not be taken away.'

I suggested that would be inefficient, uneconomic, and defeat the whole purpose of computerization.

He disagreed, insisting, 'The present number of government staff is required. Now we can't satisfy the public because of overwork. If a government servant has fewer duties assigned to him, then he will have time to serve the common man. He does not serve because he is overburdened.'

'But you say that you still want manual work to continue, and that creates the burden.'

'Manual work must continue but the system must change. The rules we work under were laid down by the British, we did not bring in administrative reforms. The system has to be updated, it's not efficiency which is lacking but political will.'

'So do you support computerization,' I asked confused and slightly frustrated.

'As I said we want computers and manual work,' came back the reply.

I could see that Chandrababu Naidu had a long way to go before he won the battle with his junior employees. But he had taken on and defeated the power workers to reform that industry and was managing to reduce the government workforce by four per cent per year.

The current stage in the battle was being fought by a team from an Indian firm, Tata Consultancy Services, which claims to be the largest global software services provider in Asia. The team was working on a project, which, of course, had an acronym – SKIMS or Secretariat Knowledge and Information Management System. They were planning to rid the secretariat, the heart of the government of Andhra Pradesh, of all those brown files lovingly tied up with fading red tape, and to put all the information they contained on a network. The leader of their team was Ravi Prakash Nandivada, a young man who looked barely out of university but had already acquired a self-confidence which left no room for doubt. He told us, 'Our speciality is walking the talk.' This didn't mean much to me, and so he explained, 'We don't just walk away from the project when we've designed it, we get involved in the implementation too.'

So how was he dealing with the recalcitrant NGOs, and indeed the gazetted officers, so many of whom would be unhappy with the disappearance of the files they laboriously made notes on?

'We try to understand the dynamics of a situation first,' he explained.

'But I thought the problem in government administration was a lack of dynamics.'

Ravi was not to be deflected by my rather poor joke and went on, 'We have to consider how people feel threatened by the new technology, what they think they might lose, for instance, their jobs, and we have to involve the people who would resist us most.'

The young team had adopted several methods to overcome this resistance. They had chosen 'department champions' who understood what the team was trying to do, were natural leaders and, because they felt part of the project, regarded it as their own. They automated the most boring jobs first to reduce drudgery and make work more enjoyable for clerks and junior officials, before going on to more difficult procedures. 'Slow poisoning,' Ravi called it, adding hurriedly, 'in a positive sense.' They talked to the junior level employees separately from their bosses so that they felt free to talk, and found many were delighted that someone was at last taking an interest in their work. Ravi claimed that most consultants failed because they treated their 'users' as unintelligent. The Tata team even took an interest in the lowly *tappal*, the clerk who carries the files from office to office. But there was a certain deceit in all this, as Ravi himself admitted when he said, 'The government is reassuring everyone they won't lose their jobs but they will have to. They are planning redeployment but they haven't announced it yet.'

Not surprisingly, the problems with the senior staff, especially the members of the elite Indian Administrative Service were mainly to do with saving face. They were worried that they might actually have to do some typing themselves, and might lose their batteries of stenographers and clerks.

'It's an ego problem,' Ravi explained. 'Senior officers are not used to typing. They're used to having lots of subordinates around them – they're even used to people opening the car door for them.'

One of the project managers, Priya Shankaran, had problems of her own. A young woman who didn't go in for the power-dressing adopted so often by women executives, but wore a demure white sari with a pink border, and allowed her hair to flow over her shoulders in the traditional manner, she had found many of the secretariat staff didn't want to speak to her. 'If a man from my team was with me, I would ask the question, and they would look at the man and answer,' she told us.

'What about youth?' I asked. 'After all, the government is very hierarchical and seniority counts for a lot, and you must all be very junior in their eyes.'

'Our age is a mixed blessing,' she replied. 'We are all young, there is a big age difference, but a lot of the people here have kids of our age, and that can help to form a rapport. On the other hand it can be difficult to get an appointment with a senior official because they like to meet senior people.'

The Tata team had one irrefutable argument on their side. No one would deny that reform was necessary. They had discovered that a standard file had to go through twenty-one stages before any action was taken. Each stage in that process had to be entered manually in a register. A monthly payroll took between seven and ten days to draw up. There was a two-month gap between money being spent and the expenditure being reconciled in the accounts. There was no inventory management to ensure that health centres were stocked with medicines, or ration shops with food. As for management of development projects, Rakesh, the third member of the team, said, 'No one has a clue what is the state of them.'

Bureaucrats and politicians, the beneficiaries of the antique, easily corrupted, administrative system were not the only opposition Chandrababu Naidu was facing. The press in India, like the press anywhere, looks for what is going wrong, not what is going right, undermines innovation, and hence contributes to the 'chalne do' factor, the belief that nothing can be done, that life has to go on as it does now. Dr Chowdary had arranged for us to meet the journalists of Hyderabad for breakfast at the Press Club. Sitting in the garden under a tamarind tree, I was bombarded with criticism of Naidu's e-government. Journalists told me, 'It's just being talked about, it hasn't made inroads except in headlines'; 'Even the urban population is not benefiting, let alone the rural'; 'There are still touts with cards describing themselves as consultants outside government offices.' And so it went on. One journalist did make a very relevant point when he said, 'The core issue is that we are not out of a system which is obsolete and anti-people and so e-government will only help a little.'

Dr Chowdary chimed in, 'We need business process engineering.' I am not sure how many of the journalists knew what that meant. I only understood that it was management consultancy-speak for wholesale reform of the system because Dr Chowdary had explained the phrase when I met him earlier.

But the chief minister had one very powerful ally in the media. We had to drive to Ramoji Film City, forty kilometres out of Hyderabad, to meet him. Ramoji Rao, the proprietor of the Eenadu chain of newspapers which had separate editions for every district of Andhra Pradesh, and the owner of television channels in four different languages, was now concentrating on his new venture, a vast location providing sets for almost every imaginable scene a film director could want to shoot.

We entered Film City through the outer gate, where on average two thousand five hundred visitors are received every day. Fortunately, as guests of Ramoji, we didn't have to pay two hundred rupees to get in. A private road, providing plenty of mileage for the hair-raising, high-speed chase scenes which are almost obligatory in Indian films, ended abruptly at a polyester factory surrounded by a small township. Each lamp-post in the township carried a placard advertising the paper which is the main rival to Eenadu. When I asked how this had come about I was told that the factory owner had put up the placards because he was involved in a land dispute with Ramoji Rao. After passing through the township we entered Film City proper. The first set we saw was a Mughal garden incongruously dominated by a huge statue of Apollo in his chariot trying to control wild, rearing horses. The classical theme was maintained by bare-breasted Aphrodites lining the road leading to two hotels, one very luxurious for the stars, producers, directors, and wealthy tourists who wanted to say they had mixed with the stars, one less luxurious for the bit-part actors and the technicians. Tea plantations are frequent romantic film settings, and so a garden of chandni shrubs shaved like tea bushes was provided. There were golden bougainvilleas on a hillside too, and cacti for depicting not so lush scenes. Heroes frequently find themselves in jail, and there were several different types of prison for their incarceration. There was a railway station with a not entirely convincing steam engine on rubber tyres, and an airport building too, as well as a court, a college, temples, mosques, village and town streets, and a wooden stockade entered through a gateway with 'The Wild West' written above it. With its white fibreglass stallion, its Black Cat warehouse, Flying Fish Beach Pub, and souvenir stores, the Wild West is mainly intended for tourists, who, incidentally, are always told the one thing they won't see is any film-shooting. We too were not allowed to interrupt any filming. We noticed bare scaffolding frames and were told they were for directors who found none of the buildings fitted their requirements and wanted to construct their own, which could be done within twenty-four hours. The entire city, apart from the hotels and office blocks, was built of fibreglass and plaster of Paris.

Ramoji was staying in the five-star hotel but we found him in his wood-panelled office in the administrative building, behind a desk with only a bouquet of flowers still wrapped in cellophane on it, looking as though he had just been waiting for us. Grey, bald, and bespectacled, he sat like a rotund Buddha, still and calm, smiling with a slight air of superiority. Yes, he agreed, he had been one of the original supporters of the film star chief minister NTR. No, Eenadu was not a Telugu Desam Party paper. It had 'blasted' Chandrababu Naidu when he raised the price of electricity.

'Who else should I support? Congress?' the proprietor asked scornfully. 'We give issue-based support. If someone is doing a good job then he should be appreciated. What is wrong?'

'Nothing,' I muttered over the cup of tea which had just been placed before me, and asked whether that meant Naidu was doing a good job.

Ramoji felt the chief minister had lots of problems but, taking them into consideration, he was doing a good job. His biggest problem was the bureaucracy.

'In my opinion,' Ramoji explained, 'they are the bane of the country. Their concern is for power and money. They are corrupt from top to bottom. Chief ministers come and go but the bureaucrats stay on, nobody can touch them. Some people now even feel that the British rule was better. At least they only had limited purposes. Now the bureaucracy are bothered about everything. Nothing can be done without them, and they know nothing about the things they have to decide on.'

Ramoji had just returned from a sales trip to Hollywood where he'd met the chairman of Warner Brothers among others. Four American films – *Nightfall, Crocodile II, Quicksand* and *Shadow of the Condor* – had already been shot at Film City and had demonstrated the economics of the cheaper manpower Ramoji had at his disposal. But his sales pitch wasn't helped when he had to tell producers that their scripts would need to be approved by an official of the Information and Broadcasting Ministry, and they would have to 'excise anything found objectionable'. To ensure they didn't cheat, a minor functionary of the ministry would watch every shot they took. Then there was the problem of getting visas too.

'Charles Sobhraj can be comfortable here,' Ramoji exclaimed, 'but film actors have to be cleared by the Home Ministry. I would scrap the whole bureaucratic system.' Sobhraj was a high-profile international criminal who preferred Indian jails to the hangman in Thailand.

Returning to Chandrababu Naidu, I asked Ramoji about e-government.

'It should be good,' he said slowly, 'and I certainly hope it will mean more open government, but I don't rule out the possibility of these bureaucrats putting their fingers in there too.'

Ramoji didn't allow his feelings about the bureaucracy to disturb him. He never raised his voice, and there was no gesticulation, his hands remained firmly under the desk-top. When we rose to go at the end of the conversation, he stayed seated behind that desk and as we went out said in the same matter-of-fact manner, 'If I had my way I would shoot the bureaucrats one by one. Goodbye.'

Back in Hyderabad, we had to find our way to the offices of an NGO, which this time stood for Non-Governmental Organization. There was the normal urban Indian chaos on the roads which were enveloped in all-too-familiar clouds of black fumes, but we did get one unusual admonition from the police. Among the many signs they'd put up at road junctions urging drivers to obey the rules of the road there was one we'd never seen before. It asked us to remember that 'Only bulls charge on the red'.

The NGO was headed by a man who would once have been in the firing line, if Ramoji had his way, but who was now on his side. Dr Jayaprakash Narayan had been a highly successful member of the Indian Administrative Service but he jumped ship to head an NGO called Lok Satta, or People's Power. Among its aims is the promotion of 'the peaceful, democratic, transformation of the Indian governance process to enable India and all Indians to achieve their full potential through good governance'.

Dr Jayaprakash Narayan was an example of the opportunities to move up the ladder which do exist in India, so often portrayed as rigidly hierarchical with a caste and sub-caste system that sets everyone's position in stone. His father had been a railway guard and he'd been educated at a village school, but he'd gone on to become a doctor of medicine and then passed the stiff examination to get into the Indian Administrative Service. Looking as slim and young as he did when he joined the civil service back in the seventies, he was very keen to convince me that he was not one of those bureaucrats who turn against their profession because their careers had been blighted.

'I was one of the most successful officers in the state,' he told me. 'I learnt a great deal, and I had a wonderful time. I received love and affection. So I wasn't frustrated. I left with twenty years still to go because, although I was convinced that good could be done within the system, that would require heroic acts and I thought I could do more outside.'

Nevertheless, he took a poor view of his former colleagues, blaming them rather than the politicians for the failures of the system, and agreeing with Ramoji that a politician at least had to face the electorate and could be thrown out, while a civil servant had a job for life. He maintained that the administration oppressed the people it was intended to serve, and was particularly critical of the police, saying, 'Without the police being so dehumanized they couldn't maintain the Indian state in its present form.'

I had recently read of an Andhra Pradesh NGO which had described Chandrababu Naidu's Vision 2020 as the Vinasha Vision, and Vinasha means 'destruction'. So I suggested to Jayaprakash Narayan that NGOs were like the press – congenitally hostile to governments.

'I personally wouldn't want to write off all of Chandrababu Naidu's efforts like that,' he said, 'but I do feel that decentralization is essential, and Naidu is using IT to tighten, not loosen, his control over the administration.'

There was evidence to suggest that IT was putting too much power in the hands of the chief minister. Already it was being used by Chandrababu Naidu for regular video-conferences with district officials, undermining their autonomy and the autonomy of local elected bodies. At one video-conference Naidu had announced that he was stopping recruitment of staff to municipalities, a decision that should have been the responsibility of the town councils themselves. He had told me he wanted to hand power back to local bodies, but at the same time he had delayed the current local body elections until the Supreme Court had ordered him to hold them. Lok Satta had campaigned for parents' committees in schools, but the Chandrababu Naidu government had watered down the act. Admittedly, according to Jayaprakash Narayan, that wasn't because he wanted to control every school, but because he didn't want to antagonize 300,000 teachers who, like the non-gazetted officers, supervised elections.

But centralization can help. I told Jayaprakash Narayan of a software recently introduced that kept records of all Andhra Pradesh's roads, when they were last repaired and what state they were now in. One of the chief minister's most senior advisers told us these records had shown that in one area, four roads resurfaced only last year were already in a deplorable condition again. All four roads came under the same assistant engineer, clear evidence of corruption. Wasn't this a better way of allocating money for road maintenance and checking that money was properly spent than the old system whereby local politicians, officials, and contractors colluded on decisions and their implementation?

Jayaprakash agreed. 'It's very important not to condemn IT, or Chandrababu Naidu, out of hand. We must be selective, and give praise where praise is due.'

I felt it was important to go further than that, to err on the side of generosity in judging Chandrababu Naidu's reforms. 'After all,' I pointed out, 'Naidu is the most high-profile reforming politician in this country. If he's seen to fail then surely that will only give ammunition to the vested interests who don't want to see any reforms at all.'

Jayaprakash Narayan's answer was not particularly generous. After accepting that there was something to be said for my view, he went on, 'We can't exaggerate the impact of the reforms. For instance, Andhra Pradesh is not doing as well in investment as is being put about.'

Chandrababu Naidu was by no means unaware of the criticisms of his reforms, and of the need to ensure that they had an impact in villages, where, after all, most of the voters lived. He had started schemes to involve villagers in development projects, he'd formed irrigation-water users' committees as well as those parent committees. Millions of village women had joined his extraordinarily successful micro-savings and credit schemes, and efforts were being made to see that IT wasn't just used to deliver government services in cities like Hyderabad.

When we visited Mahbubnagar, headquarters of one of the poorest districts of Andhra Pradesh, we found a massive database being created, as computer operators loaded information from a survey of 735,000 households, spread over 1,555 villages, information which would be used to issue automatically documents like caste certificates, ration cards, deeds of property and land holdings. Well, not quite automatically. The bureaucracy had managed to retain a hold on the system by insisting that every document must be signed by the most senior official. The mandai revenue officer in Mahbubnagar justified this by saying, 'Only I will have the right to sign, otherwise the system will be misused by clerks. There is every chance of misuse, I can tell you.' But signature or no signature, the new system would undoubtedly reduce the opportunity for the clerks to harass, and demand money for doing what they were paid to do.

This was accepted by two of the more prosperous farmers in Gangapur, one of the villages in Mahbubnagar district. Standing at a crossroads in the centre of the village, G. Shekhar, who farmed twenty-seven acres of unirrigated land, a large holding by Indian standards, told us, 'Because of computers the working culture is faster than before. They used to harass us immensely. That has come down, not vanished, but come down.' His friend K. Narsa Reddy, who only had ten acres, was less certain: 'Computers have come to the mandais,' he agreed, 'but people have not used them, they are not yet able to exploit them.'

On the other side of the crossroads a group of women, dressed in what at first sight looked like patchwork quilts, were discussing at the top of their voices the difficulty of getting work as labourers. When I got closer I could see their skirts were made from brightly coloured patterned cloth and their blouses were embroidered with mirror-work. Rows of coins hung like medals over their breasts.

Only one older woman squatting on the ground had no coins – an indication that she was a widow. Their arms were covered with cream-coloured bangles, a few were ivory but most plastic. Some had rings made from one rupee coins and all had elaborate white metal ornaments hanging from their ears. These were Lambadas, one of the poorest castes. The women knew of Chandrababu Naidu's scheme to give villagers control over development schemes, but said that hadn't meant they'd been given any work, which was what mattered. They did have plots of land and a school, but when they went to complain about the teacher who didn't bother to teach, an official dismissed them saying, 'When you and your forefathers never studied, what do you want to have your children taught for?' They were enthusiastic members of Chandrababu Naidu's micro-credit schemes, but when it came to computers and e-government, they'd never heard of them.

A group of forlorn men sitting on the pieces of a broken statue of Nandi, the bull who always accompanies the god Shiva, were equally uninterested in computers. 'Computers are waste talk, rubbish,' one of the younger farmers said.

'They do nothing for us,' another lugubrious farmer agreed. 'They didn't stop five farmers committing suicide in this village last year because the rains failed and there was no crop, and they have failed again this year. If we go to our land we will just start crying, so we come here and have a bottle of liquor.' He then smiled sheepishly, appreciating the irony of the situation, and told us that he owned the liquor shop.

Apparently, in spite of the crop failure he still sold four hundred bottles of palm toddy every day at 3 rupees 50 a bottle. But then he claimed an average day's business should be two thousand bottles.

It was clearly by no means self-evident in the village of Gangapur that Chandrababu Naidu's campaign for good governance was making any difference. But then these were early days, and the chief minister himself admitted that there was much still to do. Would he be given the time to complete his programme, and if he wasn't, would his successor take up where he left off? Tata Consultancy Services obviously had a vested interest in the programme succeeding, but when we met one of their executive vice presidents I did not get answers to those questions prepared by the public relations department.

Dr M. Vidyasagar had until recently been a research scientist, 'on the border of maths and engineering' as he put it, who had established one of the defence ministry's research laboratories. The son of a brilliant mathematician who had migrated to North America, Vidyasagar himself had obtained a Ph.D. from Wisconsin University and taught in several North American universities. Then, at the age of forty, he decided that he wanted to bring up his daughter in his own country. He also wanted to show that Indians didn't need to go down the brain drain to succeed as scientists, that it was possible to do good research in India, and build good institutions too. When his godfather, who was the chief scientific adviser to the defence minister, retired and Vidyasagar found his successor unimaginative he resigned and was snapped up by Tata Consultancy Services. Within one year, he'd built up a team which had come up with marketable products.

Vidyasagar did not believe that IT was a panacea for all the evils of governance.

'You have to begin by recognizing the limitations of IT,' he warned me, 'it can't eliminate corruption, and we shouldn't give that impression because it will be discredited. IT won't, for instance, stop files being deliberately lost, but you will be able to tell who deleted the file and when. Also, if you want to reform and then monitor the system, it is a good tool. Look, for instance, at the way Naidu monitors the power supply situation. Andhra Pradesh power is much better than it was.'

'How successful do you think Naidu has been so far?' I asked.

'Well, I think he has put Andhra Pradesh ahead of other states in IT but what surprises me is that, when he started as chief minister and he was politically weak because everyone saw him as usurping NTR's throne, he was putting systems in place. In those days IAS officers were enthusiastic, and Naidu was approachable. But in 1999 he got a massive majority, and with that he could have done more but somehow he seems to have lost it.'

'Is this because there has been so much criticism of his continually harping on about IT? Is he reluctant to push it now?'

'I think our system is resistant to change because vested interests don't want it to be any less porous.'

Vidyasagar identified three elements who were opposed to reforms – politicians, bureaucrats, and intellectuals. Like almost everyone else we'd spoken to, he blamed the bureaucrats more than the politicians. While working for the defence ministry, he had come across cases where secret information was leaked, and had come to the opinion that bureaucrats were 'far more susceptible to the temptation to leak information than politicians'.

Vidyasagar was the first person I'd met to include intellectuals in his cast of villains. He dismissed them as 'full of self-loathing', and 'not proud of being Indian', saying this contributed to the low expectations people had from anything Indian, including the administration. But he thought things were changing, and that many of his peer group were proud of their 'Indian experience'. He was particularly opposed to those intellectuals who were fervent advocates of secularism, accusing them of 'doing nothing but heap scorn on Hinduism'.

Vidyasagar wore Western clothes, his beard and his hair were neatly trimmed, only the red dot on his forehead indicated that he was a believing Hindu. I discovered he was more than that, he was intensely proud of his Brahminical tradition, and that was the reason for his poor opinion of secularists.

'It's nonsense to claim that the Brahmin brain, and Brahmin practices, can't go with modernity,' he maintained. 'I want to spread Brahmin practices but I don't want to make them exclusive to any one caste.'

I had first met Vidyasagar at a lecture organized by the Andhra Pradesh government's IT adviser, Dr Hanuman Chowdary, who was a member of the RSS, and I had imagined Vidyasagar might also be a member of that sect. However, he told me, 'I have nothing to do with them, although I am not surprised you should ask that question because the secularists have created such an atmosphere that now if you say that you are a practising Hindu you are told you must be RSS. Many of the RSS's ideas are childish. To boost the Vedas they try to discover that the sages of old already knew what scientists today claim to be discovering for the first time. I don't believe in finding quantum physics in the Vedas. The Vedas are much more important than some discovery in physics.'

'So how can India recover its past and overcome the problems of its present?' I asked.

Without any hesitation, Vidyasagar replied, 'I can't speak for India, but personally now I would like to give eighty per cent of my energies to alternative forms of web-based education and access to information for villagers, and twenty per cent to government reforms.'

Vidyasagar 's house was only a hundred yards or so away from the headquarters of the new party fighting for a separate Telengana. As we came out we had to make our way through the crowds and the parked cars jamming the roads. Here was the obvious threat to Chandrababu Naidu's reforms – politicians who put personal ambition before principles and voters who voted for them. Less obvious, but acknowledged by almost everyone I had talked to, was the threat from the self-serving bureaucracy. Only Vidyasagar had pointed out the threat from intellectuals who had undermined India's pride in its past. Their contribution to the sense of inferiority which has led so many Indians to expect nothing better of their country than the present corrupt and moribund system of governance is considerable. If the reforms started in Andhra Pradesh should fail, it will reinforce the belief that it's inevitable India should be badly governed.

The Sufis and a Plain Faith

Our flat is on one side of the Delhi–Agra road in what is known as Nizamuddin East. On the other side of the road there is a bus stop. To the casual traveller there would appear to be nothing to mark it out from any other bus stop in Delhi. The traffic is jammed by buses pulling up in the middle of the road, passengers fighting to get on board, and cycle and scooter rickshaws vying for business. One person only stands out from the dull mediocrity of modern Delhi dress. Wearing a white turban with a tail stretching down the back of his long red coat, he is posted there to guide potential patrons of Karim's restaurant through the crowded alleys of the Nizamuddin *basti*, the settlement surrounding the tomb of Hazrat Nizamuddin Auliya, one of India's most revered Sufi saints. Karim's, down one of the narrowest alleys, is owned and managed by a family that once cooked for the Mughal emperors and claims to have invented Mughlai cuisine. Follow Karim's man into the basti and you enter a different world. Here Western shirts and pants have not ousted long white kurtas and loose-fitting pajama trousers, and every man seems to be wearing an Islamic cap. There are not many women to be seen and not much to see of those there are, covered as they will be from head to toe in black burqas. The shop signs are in Urdu written in the Arabic script. Butchers carve great hunks of buffalo meat, kebabs turn over charcoal grills, and live chickens await their fate. There is no sign of any of India's renowned vegetarian cuisines. Money exchangers openly offer to accept Pakistani rupees, although this is not officially approved of either side of the border.

If tourists are not in the hands of the man from Karim's, they will probably be threading their way through the lanes towards the *dargah*, or shrine, of Hazrat Nizamuddin. Muslims from abroad, as well as every corner of India, come here to consult the *pirs*, or holy men, whose families claim to be descended from the sister of the saint. Pilgrims come to say their prayers at Nizamuddin's tomb and to hear the *qawwali*, the ecstatic songs of devotees in love with God. But first tourists have to pass a modern, seven-storey concrete building, topped by the minarets of a small mosque. Built right up to the edge of the alley which runs through the middle of the basti, out of place beside the traditional buildings of the dargah, this is the Markaz, the headquarters and training centre of the Tablighi movement which was founded in the twentieth century, and now has missionaries working in all parts of the world teaching a puritanical Islam which abhors colourful Sufism.

In earlier centuries it was the Sufis who converted Indians to their Islam which, with its rituals, its music and its emphasis on love of God, is not too far distant from *bhakti*, or devotional Hinduism. But in modern India the Tablighis, with their Islam pared to the bone in the deserts of Arabia by the eighteenth-century Wahabite movement, have a wider influence among Muslims. The pirs of the Sufi shrine fear they are losing their traditional influence to the Tablighis.

Very little is written about the Tablighis who are usually dismissed as 'fundamentalists'. I have myself always been suspicious of that definition, thinking it maligns the entire Islamic world, when there are many Muslims who should never be described as fundamentalists in the pejorative sense. So we decided to look more closely at this movement and its relations with its Sufi neighbours it disapproves of so strongly.

Finding out about the Tablighis didn't prove to be so easy. A Tablighi businessman, who had made a fortune turning buffalo bone into junk jewellery in the back streets of Old Delhi, gave us the name of one Yusuf Saloni to contact in the Markaz. But he warned that Gilly should not go with me as women were not allowed inside the building. The first entrance to the Markaz was closed but, through the bars of the gate, I could see a long dingy passage with what looked like lockers on both sides. A group of Tablighis standing outside were distinctly unhelpful. Before they would pass on any information, they first wanted to know who I was. Explaining that I was writing about their movement did not create a good impression, and when I asked how I could find Yusuf Saloni a grim, middle-aged man with a charm bypass growled, 'He's gone for Haj' – the annual Muslim pilgrimage to Mecca. I wondered whether anyone else could help me but he said 'no', and turned his back on me.

Not confident that Yusuf Saloni would see me when he got back, we decided to seek advice from a Muslim scholar who was known to be close to the Tablighis. Maulana Wahiduddin Khan proved far more approachable. When we rang him he willingly agreed to see us both, and there was no question of Gilly not being welcome. The maulana is well known for his irenic views on Hindu–Muslim relations. He is a staunch opponent of the more aggressive Indian Muslim leaders. In an article in the *Times of India* carrying the headline 'Not By Grievances Alone', he had urged his fellow Muslims to stop whining, face up to reality, and get on with their lives. He warned them that they were being misled by leaders who kept harking back to the days when they were the rulers and dwelt on 'slights (imagined or otherwise) to the Islamic psyche'. He called on Muslims to become 'a creative minority'.

The maulana had opposed the Muslim leaders who took the dispute over the Ayodhya mosque on to the streets, and it required courage to do that in those emotionally charged days. He wanted Muslims to rely on the courts to save the mosque and used to say, 'demonstrations create more heat than light'. After the images of the Hindu god Rama with his consort Sita had been installed on the site of the destroyed mosque, Wahiduddin accepted that it would be very difficult to rebuild it. He asked Muslims to leave that to the Hindus' conscience, and travelled extensively putting forward his two-point formula – Muslims should forget Ayodhya and the Hindus should forget all the other mosques they claimed were built on sites of temples which had been destroyed.

The headquarters of Maulana Wahiduddin's Islamic Centre and his home are in the residential area of Nizamuddin West just down the road from the basti. Two security guards check your credentials before you are allowed into his house – there are plenty of Muslims who don't approve of his peaceful politics. He met us in his book-lined study on the first floor. Born in a village in eastern Uttar Pradesh in 1925, his father died when he was only five. 'I was orphaned like the Prophet,' he told us. 'The best training is being an orphan. You are in the best position to create self-esteem, confidence, sacrifice, and hard work. They say in English it's not facility but difficulty which makes men.'

Wahiduddin eventually went to a Muslim theological college in the nearby town of Azamgarh, but the impact of his earlier village education stayed with him. 'Other Muslim leaders,' he said, 'were born in cities so they got a political angle in their thinking because it was in the cities that there was political activity. In a village I spent my time with nature so I was able to preserve my nature. God saved me from those political activities.' He regards Islamic organizations which get involved in politics like the Taliban in Afghanistan, the Jamaat Islami in Pakistan or the Muslim Brotherhood in Egypt as 'deviations from Islam'.

The maulana explained that in spite of their missionary zeal, and the appearance of being fundamentalists, the Tablighis too were apolitical. They followed his school of theology, with the difference being just one of tactics or targets. The maulana uses his scholarship to target 'educated people'. With his loosely tied white turban, long white hair, untidy beard trimmed only across his lips, and thick black-rimmed spectacles, Wahiduddin looked every inch the Islamic scholar. He also firmly believed in the value of scholarship. 'I'm able to persuade educated people to be good Muslims by reason,' he maintained. 'The Tablighis go for the ordinary Muslim through their mosques.' How then do the maulana and the Tablighis relate to political Islam, with its demand for Nizam-e-Mustafa, the rule of the Prophet, and Shariat or Muslim law? The maulana holds there are two types of Muslim organizations, those who believe in what he calls 'external change', changing the political system, and those who believe in changing Muslims themselves. 'They believe that if you change the system everything will be all right,' he explained. 'We believe there is a heart. If the heart changes the whole body will be good. Therefore a change of system depends on a change of the internal heart. We are the only two organizations who think like that.'

The maulana spoke slowly, pausing often to make sure we were following him. He was keen to convince us that his theology was thoroughly orthodox, that he was teaching the Qur'an and Sunna, or the traditions of what the Prophet did during his lifetime. Gilly noticed a copy of the Bible in among the maulana's Arabic books, and this led to a discussion of the Islamic attitude to other religions. According to Wahiduddin there is nothing in the Qur'an or the Sunna which says you should not respect other religions, rather the other way round. He told us the story of the Prophet seeing a funeral procession passing through a street in Medina, and standing in respect for the dead person. One of his companions asked him, 'Oh, Prophet, that was the funeral of a Jew not a Muslim and yet you stood up in respect.' The Prophet answered, 'Was he not a human being?' The maulana had contributed a chapter to a book presented to the Pope during his last visit. In that chapter he'd pointed out that Jesus and Mary were mentioned ten times more than the Prophet in the Qur'an.

Wahiduddin did admit to having difficulties with idol worship, because in the Qur'an God said he would forgive anything except *shirq* or worship of something other than Him. But the maulana still insisted that religious freedom was one of the basic human rights, and conversion was not a duty of Muslims. He saw his duty as, 'Introducing Islam and presenting Islam in a correct manner so that millions no longer believe it is a religion of violence and hatred – that impression we must not give.'

The general impression of the Tablighis is of a militant missionary organization, but Wahiduddin insisted, 'They do not believe in evangelizing.' In a book he'd written on the Tablighi movement he'd quoted Maulana Mohammed Yousuf, son of the movement's founder and his successor, as saying, 'Unless one has firm conviction and has moulded one's way of life accordingly, one fails to become a good Muslim morally, and he who does not become a good Muslim himself is ill-equipped to spread the message among others.'

That quotation, according to Wahiddudin, demonstrated that the founder's prime purpose was to reform Muslims themselves, not to make converts from other religions.

Yet the Tablighis were charged with responsibility for a mass conversion which has gone down in history. On 19 February 1981 a few hundred Dalits, members of the former untouchable castes, were publicly converted to Islam in Meenakshipuram in the southern state of Tamil Nadu. This led to an outburst of Hindu activity. Some was of the *mea culpa* variety, with Hindu priests prostrating themselves before Dalits, members of a Hindu former royal family being anointed by a Dalit priest, and in one state high-caste Hindus sitting down to feast with Dalits in five thousand different temples. But other activities were to have long-term consequences. In particular, a vast Hindu rally proved to be the launching pad for a campaign to arouse Hindu fears of the power of Islamic petro-dollars, and 'the sinister designs of Islamic fundamentalists'. From this grew the revival of the demand to destroy the Ayodhya mosque and the riots which followed it.

The Tablighis denied, and still do deny, any responsibility for the Meenakshipuram conversions, but they can hardly be surprised that their secrecy arouses suspicion, especially in times when terms like Islamic fundamentalism, and militant Islam, are so loosely thrown around that many believe they apply to all Muslim organizations.

The Tablighi movement made an unpromising start. Its founder Maulana Ilyas was deeply shocked when he came to learn that the Mewatis, a Muslim community who lived not far outside Delhi, kept their Hindu names, celebrated Hindu festivals and even worshipped Hindu images. To remedy this and to teach what he believed was true Islam he decided to set up schools in the area. But one day Ilyas was introduced to a young man who had just completed his education in one of the new Islamic schools and was shocked to see no beard or any other sign that he was a pious Muslim. That led to a change of tactics. Ilyas decided that young Mewatis must be removed from an environment which seemed unredeemable and brought to the mosque in Nizamuddin basti where he was based. There they were educated in Islam, guided, and counselled by devout Muslims, and kept busy round the clock. This proved more effective, and was the beginning of a movement which was to spread throughout the Muslim world.

Ilyas himself was neither an impressive preacher, with his stutter and his complex style, nor was he an impressive person, physically so weak that he was thought too feeble to work in the family bookshop, and so thin that Mewatis used to describe him as a skeleton. Yet he was able to inspire young men to go out in groups from the mosque in Nizamuddin to teach Islam, rewarding them with nothing more than his blessing: 'I entrust you to God and pray for you. May God accept our humble services towards His path.'

A contemporary of Ilyas wrote, 'Anyone who saw the tabligh parties of Mewat, travelling on foot, with blankets thrown on their shoulders and Sparaas (sic) tucked under their arms and parched grain or bread tied in a corner of the mantle, their tongues engaged in *zikr*, eyes showing the signs of nightly vigil and the mark of *sajda* on the forehead would have been reminded of the martyred companions of the Bir-Moona who were killed while going on the mission of teaching the Qur'an and imparting the knowledge of the Shariat or the orders of the Holy Prophet.' The martyrs were a party of missionaries who were slaughtered by hostile tribesmen during the life of Muhammad. The tribesmen had enticed Muhammad's followers into their territory on the pretence of wanting to hear the message of Islam. To Christians, the Tablighi missionaries might bring back memories of the story of Jesus sending out his disciples.

According to Wahiduddin's book on the movement, Muslim men come to Tablighi centres for intensive training and then go out in groups. They make for mosques where after prayers they invite members of the congregation to join them for a discussion. Sometimes the elders of the congregation object and the Tablighis withdraw. They never force themselves on anyone, and this reasonable attitude often leads to a change of heart among congregations originally suspicious of them. Once the Tablighis have been accepted they invite members of the congregation to sit round them and then ask them to recite the prayers that they are commanded to say five times a day. Mistakes in their Arabic are corrected and Tablighis point out that even a mispronunciation can alter the whole meaning of a sentence. Often Muslims who are regular worshippers don't know all the prayers they should say and the Tablighis will fill that gap in their knowledge. They will tell them that there is a ritually correct way of washing your face before saying prayers, and show them how to stand and where to put their hands. They teach the recitation of the Qur'an, but according to Wahiduddin they don't give an exposition of the meaning of the verses – that is left to scholars like him. Great stress is laid on the significance of the simple Muslim creed, the Kalima-e-Tauhid – there is no god but Allah, and Muhammad is his Prophet. There is not much theology in the Tablighi message. The emphasis is on the benefits to be gained by saying one's prayers regularly, observing rituals, and setting time aside to spread the message.

Nizamuddin, from where Maulana Ilyas started, is now the centre of a powerful international movement. Inside the forbidding Markaz no quarter is given to modernity. According to Wahiduddin there is no television, no radio, and no newspapers. An international organization with tentacles which spread into remote villages in every continent is run without benefit of telephone, fax or of course e-mail. The humble postcard is the usual method of communication. Word of mouth is the way of spreading the message. Ilyas's son Maulana Mohammed Yousuf once wrote, 'In order to make this mission public, the advertising media, newspapers, advertisements, posters and so on should be avoided as far as possible, for the whole of our work is unconventional. The real way of working is to address people individually, to impart education by approaching people, and forming groups of people to work together.'

That seemed to explain the Tablighis' reluctance to meet me. Nevertheless I still asked Wahiduddin whether, in the traditional Indian style, he could 'use his good offices' to get me to meet someone from the movement. He agreed but a few days later rang me back to confess failure. 'These people are not living in this century,' he said. 'They don't know what the media is.'

Gilly though found a rather different explanation when she met an active Tablighi preacher at a wedding she went to in a small town nearly a thousand kilometres away from the organization's headquarters. 'You see,' he told her, 'everything we do is for the Prophet, and if we look for publicity, if things are published about us, it means that our motives are not one hundred per cent pure. Ambition, self-glorification, ego – these begin to creep in.'

The Tablighis are not alone among Muslims in their reluctance to have a dialogue with the media. The Pakistani scholar Akbar Ahmed, who has spent many years in Britain, had to face suspicious questioning from his fellow Muslims when he started to appear on British television and radio regularly. He was asked, 'Why are you talking to the enemy?' and some even suggested he might have 'sold out'. Islamic suspicions are not entirely unjustified. If religion masks God, the media does tend to mask religion. It's so convenient to divide the world into modernists who support liberalism and Islamic fundamentalists who support terrorism. But peaceful Islamic movements which do not explain their beliefs and practices will be misunderstood, they will be taken as supporters of violent revolution. That dims the light that they shed.

In India the Tablighis' isolation keeps them away from Muslim politics. They do not take up Muslim causes, but nor is their voice of moderation heard in the noisy and often violent debate between the advocates of a secularism which seems to respect no religion, and a nationalism which carries with it the danger of only respecting one. They play no role in the search for the middle road between those two unsatisfactory alternatives. The Muslim historian Mushirul Hasan has told the Tablighis that isolation need not and should not be the answer to living as a minority in India. He has written, 'Islam in India has survived without compromising on its essential tenets, not in isolation from other cultural, intellectual, and religious currents, but in close interaction with them. The spiritual guides of the Tablighi Jamaat [movement] are perhaps unwittingly engaged in reversing an ongoing and dynamic historical process.' But it's clear that the Tablighis cannot be classified as Muslim fundamentalists if we take the usual definition of that term, which includes the ambition to impose Islamic rule. What's more they do manage to live peacefully beside other Muslims with whom they profoundly disagree, and there are no quarrels more bitter, more prone to violence, than those within religious families.

Whatever else can be said against the dargah of Hazrat Nizamuddin Auliya, not much more than a stone's throw from the Tablighi Markaz, no one can accuse it of being isolationist. Some would say they are a little too anxious to cash in on Nizamuddin's reputation as a miracle worker six hundred years or more after his death.

Before the pilgrims reach the passage leading to the dargah, they have to run the gauntlet of young men representing the restaurants who feed those who can't afford to feed themselves. One restaurant is called Garib Nawaz, or Refuge of the Poor, which was the title of another great Indian Sufi saint, Sheikh Moinuddin Chishti. The salesmen pester pilgrims and tourists to buy meal tickets. Five rupees will get one of the expectant crowd squatting in front of the restaurants a few roti baked in a tandoor and some gravy.

With or without their hearts touched and their wallets lightened, visitors to the shrine then dive into a narrow passage, flanked on either side by stalls selling the accoutrements required to worship at the tomb of the saint – gaudy green, yellow, purple, or red cloths to cover the saint's tomb, fragrant dark red roses, sticks of incense, prayer beads, and packets of small white sweets which become sacred food when blessed by the saint. There are souvenirs too, cassettes and books. It is not unlike a downmarket version of those cramped commercialized passages which comprise Christianity's Via Dolorosa in Jerusalem.

The main business of the shrine is problem solving. As pilgrims proceed down the passage they come to a small office, not much more than a cubbyhole excavated out of the wall, but covered with expensive white marble. It's a spiritual surgery advertising 'Solution of all kinds of problems relating to business, health, marriage, arising from jadu (magic), tona (spells), etc.' But most pilgrims prefer to take their problems to Nizamuddin and so they hurry along the passage until they emerge from the darkness through an archway into bright sunshine and a courtyard paved with white marble. It's open to the sky but surrounded by buildings on all sides. One of them is the prayer hall of a red stone mosque built by the sultans of pre-Mughal Delhi. Majestic in its simplicity, it dominates the tombs around it. The first tomb the pilgrims encounter is that of the poet Amir Khusrau, Nizamuddin's most famous disciple. A little further on are the marble screens surrounding the tomb of Jahanara, the elder daughter of the emperor Shah Jahan. He built the most famous tomb in the world, the Taj Mahal, for her mother but his daughter's resting place is marked with the inscription, 'Let nothing cover my grave save green grass for grass well suffices as a covering for the grave of the lowly' Then comes the most elaborate tomb of all, the square shrine topped by a white dome ornamented with vertical stripes of black marble under which Nizamuddin himself is buried.

As they enter the dargah, pilgrims are greeted by a line of men in the garb of old-fashioned Muslim gentlemen, they may even see a plum-red fez with a black tassel, a rare sight today. These are the pirs of Nizamuddin.

According to orthodox Sufi tradition the status of pir is only granted to a spiritual master, but in Nizamuddin it has become a hereditary title, passed on from father to son. Most pirs, and there are hundreds of them in Nizamuddin, are no longer spiritual advisers but facilitators, middlemen between supplicants and the saint. A pir will guide a pilgrim through the rituals of worshipping in the shrine of Nizamuddin. They will demand a financial commitment, written in a ledger – a sum of money for the school, a sum of money to feed the poor, a sum of money for the shrine itself. The pirs also claim the power to ward off evil and foretell the future. They write out *tawiz* or amulets – perhaps one of the ninety-nine names of God, perhaps a phrase of the Qur'an. These amulets are worn around the neck, or upper arm, or waist for protection.

Although we had often been to the dargah, I'd never gone into the saint's tomb. Somehow it didn't seem right for a non-Muslim to do so. This was absurd because Indians of all religions pray there. Perhaps that was just an excuse for the fear I have never got over, the fear of doing the wrong thing. We deliberately chose the morning, a time when the dargah is usually quietest. As no woman is allowed inside the sanctum sanctorum, the chamber of the tomb, Gilly sat on the cool marble pavement outside. I felt in my pocket for a handkerchief to cover my head, and walked with the pir I had chosen as my guide through one of the arches of the verandah surrounding the chamber. The arches were decorated with delicate blue, maroon and green floral patterns, and crystal chandeliers. Women, their heads covered, their lips silently repeating prayers, sat on the floor of the verandah. A carved marble screen separating them from the chamber was covered with red threads and scraps of ribbon they and others before them had tied when they asked for favours from the saint. I bowed my head to pass under a low lintel and entered the darkened chamber. Nothing could be seen of the tomb itself because it was covered by layer after layer of brightly coloured cloths and rose petals. Devotees were adding more sheets to that pile and scattering rose petals on top of them. A prostrate devotee had poked his head under all those *chadars*, as the covers are known, and I wondered whether perhaps he was kissing the tomb. Above the tomb was a wooden canopy inlaid with mother-of-pearl. It was difficult to circumambulate the tomb, as ritual required, without disturbing devotees sitting cross-legged with their hands held up in prayer. The smell of incense took me back to Christian services of my childhood in the chapel of the Anglo-Catholic Oxford Mission to Calcutta, but there was nothing Christian about the sound of the lone *qawwal* and his harmonium in the courtyard outside.

It is easy to mock the piety of those who are drawn to Nizamuddin's tomb, and to condemn the worship of the saint because of some venal pirs. But the tomb reminded me of a Christian priest in Wells cathedral who spoke in awe of 'these prayer-soaked walls', not all the pirs are there for the money, and Sufism is one of the great schools of mysticism which is still flourishing today.

We wanted to understand Nizamuddin better, and so Gilly turned for advice to Ilmi Sahib, a man whose name actually means knowledgeable, and is one of the wisest of our friends, a scholar of Persian and Arabic and a poet. Although much more sympathetic himself to the Tablighi point of view, he immediately recommended we call on Khwaja Hasan Sani Nizami, a pir who edits a magazine which he described as 'literary and semi-religious'.

Hasan Sani Nizami's father was also a khwaja, a traditional title of respect. Although Hasan Sani Nizami was the fourth son in the family, his father knew even before he was born that he would succeed to the title of pir, that he would inherit the right to take *murids* or disciples, and initiate them into Sufism. That is why he was named after his father. Hasan Sani Nizami actually means Hasan Nizami the Second. Hasan the First was a considerable figure under the British. He was invited to meet Edward VIII on his ill-fated visit to India as Prince of Wales. He found an irritated prince complaining that he'd been able to see virtually nothing of India because of the limitations put on him by considerations of ceremony and security. Delighted by the prospect of having a talk with a 'real Indian' the prince gave so much time to the pir that his carefully prepared schedule was disrupted. When Edward ran into matrimonial difficulties, Hasan the First wrote him a letter saying that the people of India had a tradition of devotion to their *badshahs*, or emperors, and were most upset to think that he was not allowed to choose his own bride. This friendship with British royalty, though, never stood between Hasan the First and the leaders of the freedom movement who were fighting the Raj. Jawaharlal Nehru, even as prime minister, would always find time to call on him.

A gifted writer in Urdu, in fact inventing an informal, colloquial prose style entirely his own which won him a large following, Hasan the First was also a man before his time. Some of the pirs had attracted scandal by taking on women as murids. To satisfy women's need for spiritual advice, and for solutions to their problems, while at the same time avoiding gossip, he authorized his wife to practise as a pir. She was a practical woman who found a way of combining her spiritual gifts with sound common sense. Many of those who came to seek her help were mothers who couldn't breastfeed their children. Realizing that the problem was often dietary she would write a tawiz in saffron on a plate, then tell the mothers to wash the plate in half a pint of milk four times a day and drink the milk.

Hasan Sani has never married, believing he would not have been able to fulfil his responsibilities if he had. He sees people in a small sparsely furnished room leading off the courtyard round which the family house is built. It's behind the dargah. Old-fashioned and courteous, he offers all his visitors tea but he limits his own intake to three cups a day – one before sunrise, one at breakfast, and one in the evening. He wears the traditional Muslim loose-fitting white cotton clothes, topped by a cap. When we met him it was a bright yellow, pointed cap.

I bent down to take off my shoes before entering his room, but he laughed and said, 'There's no need for that. I know that's not an English custom, because when I was small my father employed an Anglo-Indian nanny for his sons.' That seemed rather surprising in such a traditional Muslim family until the pir explained. 'He wanted us to learn manners and a little English.' But his father found that the boys' English was improving at the expense of their Urdu, and that was the end of that experiment. We conducted our conversation in Urdu, a language in which Gilly is far more fluent than I am.

The Sufi tradition has been passed down the centuries by pirs to their murids. It's believed that the secret wisdom they impart was first given by the Prophet to his son-in-law Ali. The secret is an interpretation of the inner meaning of the Qur'anic sayings, a meaning which goes deeper than the teachings of the orthodox clergy. Scholars believe that Sufism draws on a much earlier source too, the ancient Egyptian Hermetic wisdom which dates back to the time of the Pyramids, thousands of years before Muhammad. It's an Egyptian, Dhul-Nun al-Misti, who is given credit for putting the varied strands of Sufi thinking into some sort of shape in the ninth century after Christ. The classical philosophy of Sufism was written by the Spaniard Ibn al-Arabi in the thirteenth century, and in that century Sufi poetry reached what many would argue is its highest point with the verses of Jalaluddin Rumi who lived in Turkey.

According to one of the great modern scholars of Sufism, Annemarie Schimmel, the practice of Sufism is based on meditation of death. To illustrate that she quoted these lines of Rumi written to console his friends when he was about to die,

> If death's a man – let him come close to me
> That I can clasp him tightly to my breast!
> I'll take from him a soul, pure, colourless;
> He'll take from me a coloured frock, no more!

The aim of the Sufi mystic is to come so close to God that there is no room for fear, to lose oneself in God. So great is this sense of closeness to God, that mystics sometimes seem to be saying they become God. This is of course blasphemy for orthodox Muslims. They insist that even the gap between the Prophet and God was absolute. To give the vaguest impression that the gap might be bridgeable is to diminish the unique glory of God. In the tenth century the mystic Al Hallaj did feel he had come so close to God that he was God. He was executed for blasphemy by the caliphal government in Baghdad. At his execution he thanked God for revealing 'the glories of Thy shining countenance'. Then he went on to pray for his enemies, 'You have made it lawful for me to behold the mysteries of Thy inner consciousness and made it unlawful for others. As for these others Thy servants, zealous of religion, desirous of Thy favour, who have gathered to kill me, forgive and have mercy on them, for if Thou hadst revealed what Thou hadst hid I should not suffer this.'

A modern Jesuit scholar who studied the Sufism of the Nizamuddin dargah found a murid whose pir had suggested that a man in search of God was like a deer who spent his whole life looking for the source of the scent of musk, and only at his death came to realize that the source was within him. The murid went on to say, 'In the same way Allah is in you, and in me, but we do not know this. It is the pir who will teach us this knowledge.'

Sufism has, therefore, very much the same goal as the mystic traditions of other religions – direct communion, many would say union, with God. But Sufism differs in the tradition of the pir and the murid. The approach to God has to be made through a pir, and the subjection to the pir has to be as complete as the subjection to God – so much so that another offence to orthodox Islam can creep in. The murid can come to regard his pir as his god. Rumi fell wholly under the influence of a wandering mystic known as Shams. He believed Shams was the dispenser of the divine grace which inspired his poetry. He even took on the pen name of Shams, and once confessed,

> Whether it be infidelity or Islam, listen:
> You (Shams) are either the light of God or God, *Khuda!*

While we were talking to Hasan Sani a man came in with a nervous, sickly boy aged about ten who had just been diagnosed as suffering from jaundice. Hasan Sani put his hands on the boy's head, repeated an Arabic prayer and then blew on the boy. After that he gave some practical advice recommending a diet and a doctor who practised the Muslim Yunani system of medicine.

When the boy left I asked Hasan about the belief that pirs can perform miracles. He said, 'I try to tell people that I can't perform miracles but people believe I can. Some people tell me the power was in your pir and his pir before him and that goes into you as their representative without you knowing it.' He told us about two miracles that had been credited to him but asked us not to relate them as he didn't want to give the appearance of claiming to be a miracle-worker.

'Was the father of that boy one of your murids?' Gilly asked.

'Yes,' the pir replied, 'I have thousands of murids. I have never counted them nor did my father.'

Many more want to become murids of Hasan Sani, so many that he can't always cope with the demand. When he travels sometimes the crowds are too large to allow him to take the hand of each murid and perform the initiation rites, so he asks them to form a line joined to each other by pieces of cloth. Then he takes the hand of the postulant in the front and the spiritual power travels down the line like electricity down a wire. He admits that many of those murids he never sees again. So how then does he establish such a close relationship with his disciples that they come to see him almost as God?

In Hasan Sani's case the centre of his life is his pir, his father. He has built a white shrine in traditional Indian Islamic style with an onion-shaped dome to house his tomb, and next to it is a hall where we attended the *urs* or annual commemoration of Hasan the First. The invitation card described him as a 'Sufi Saint and Littérateur', and most of the speeches concentrated on his literary achievements. From the speeches it became clear that history had not done him justice as he'd been overshadowed by the fashionable school of writers based at the Muslim University at Aligarh. Hasan Nizami had not only been a brilliant writer but a prolific one too. We were told he sometimes dictated to three transcribers at the same time, concentrating on subjects which had never before attracted literary attention – 'kerosene oil', 'matches' and 'owls' to name but three. To my horror, Hasan the Second announced that I would chair the function, and so I had to sit cross-legged on the floor behind the long low table which separated the VIPs from the rest of the audience. Gilly had the honour of being the only woman to sit with the VIPs. All the other women sat at the back of the hall. Fortunately my role was purely ceremonial. I was just a presence and the pir himself conducted the proceedings, introducing each of the long line of speakers.

At first, there were only the occasional low murmurs of approval when someone made a particularly telling point, but after Hasan Sani had announced that clapping was in order, every speaker, good, bad or indifferent got a round of applause. The loudest clapping was for a pir who had come from the only other shrine to rival Nizamuddin in popularity, the dargah at Ajmer in Rajasthan where Sheikh Moinuddin Chishti, one of the earliest saints to bring Sufism to India, is buried. He spoke not of Hasan the First's literary achievements, but of his life and spiritual message saying, 'Khwaja Hasan Nizami was a great Sufi because he understood and told his people that you must be outside the world and yet in it. You must be detached from the world but work hard. And that is what he did. All his writings, if you read them properly, had some point to them, they are instructive to those who understand.'

Many others have pointed out this difference between Sufism and other forms of mysticism which call for retreat from the world. The Sufi is not allowed to withdraw to a monastery or retire to a hermit's cave. In his introduction to *The Sufis* by the Sufi Master Idries Shah, Robert Graves wrote, 'Whereas Christian mystics regard ecstasy as a union with God, and therefore the height of religious attainment, Sufis admit its value only if the devotee can afterwards return to the world and live in a manner consonant with his experience ... Sufis have always insisted on the practicality of their experience. Metaphysics for them are useless without practical illustrations of prudent human behaviour, supplied both by popular legends and fables.' At the urs we were told a story to illustrate this point.

A man decided to renounce the world and become a wandering Sufi mendicant. He deserted his wife and children. Many years later he returned to his own home, begging for food. Despite his altered appearance and his unkempt beard, his wife recognized him. She gave him some wheat flour. But when the beggar took out a series of pots and pans from his bag to cook his dinner, she hit him as hard as she could with both hands on his head and screamed, 'So it was only me you were leaving! You said you were going to renounce the world but you're still carrying it around with you!' The moral of that story is the hypocrisy of false renunciation. Sufis are not expected to give up all to follow their spiritual master.

Nizamuddin himself had been a major public figure. During his ninety years he lived through the reigns of seven sultans several of whom regarded his independence and popularity as a challenge to their authority. When the two sides clashed, it was the sultans who came off worst. According to a brief biography of the saint on sale in Nizamuddin, one of the rulers, Qutubuddin Khilji, jealous of the huge crowds Nizamuddin drew, ordered him to leave the city. He was immediately struck down with severe and apparently incurable colic and so his mother rushed to Nizamuddin to beg for forgiveness. The saint told her to bring a letter from her son handing over the kingdom to him and a bottle of the ruler's urine. When she returned with them Nizamuddin dipped the abdication document into the urine saying, 'Such is the regard that saints have for earthly kingdoms.' A better-known example was made of Ghiasuddin Tughlaq who was openly hostile to the saint. This sultan also wanted him out of the city, and sent him a letter warning him to clear out before he and his army returned from Bengal. Nizamuddin read the message and remarked, 'Delhi is far away.' So far away, in fact, that the sultan never arrived. He was assassinated by his son on the banks of the Jamuna outside the city and buried in the tomb he'd built for himself at Tughlaqabad, his splendid new capital. Its outer fortification still stands, a forlorn reminder that the works of kings and emperors pass away, while the words and the deeds of saints live on.

Hasan Sani explained to us that Sufis believed Hazrat Nizamuddin was still alive, and that was why he was able to intercede for those who sought his help.

The speeches, or papers as they were called, had lasted for more than three hours, and there had only been one short break for prayers, so I was relieved when Hasan Sani announced that the seminar was running over time, and asked the remaining speakers to be brief. One overcame that difficulty by reading his speech at double speed, another by promising to speak for just ten minutes and then ignoring that commitment. Eventually Hasan Sani had to pull the last of the scheduled speakers away from the microphone by the sleeves of his kurta. But there were still the VIPs to come. They included a member of the Finance Commission, a vice-chancellor, professors and an emeritus professor too, indicating the respect Delhi's Muslim elite has for Hasan Sani and his father. Just as I thought it was all over Hasan Sani insisted that I came to the microphone. The limitations of my Urdu ensured that my speech was brief. It was nothing more than a gentle rebuke to Hasan Sani who had promised I could come to the urs as just another member of the audience. By then he was so anxious to close the seminar and take his guests to dinner that he almost forgot one VIP, the vice-chancellor of Delhi's Muslim university, Jamia Millia. He made the important announcement that Hasan Sani had agreed to hand his father's papers to the university library so that his words and deeds, which had been in danger of fading away with the generation of those who had known him, would now be kept alive.

While we VIPs were enjoying our dinner of chicken biryani, mutton korma and aubergine, all cooked in rich spices, in the courtyard of Hasan Sani's house, he retired to a small room to say his prayers again. Robert Graves said Sufis were a sect 'bound by no religious dogma however tenuous'. He considered it a mistake to think of them as a Muslim sect because they are at home in all religions. According to Idries Shah, 'Sufism is not a religion, it is religion.' He regards Sufism as the essence of all religions. But Hasan Sani holds that a Sufi must practise Islam, must be a good Muslim, a *panch namazi* who turns to Mecca to say his prayers five times a day. He maintains that Sufism cannot be separated from Islam but is 'real Islam'.

This argument is particularly important in Nizamuddin because Tablighi theology considers many Sufi practices unIslamic, and the Tablighis in their Markaz are told they must not go to Nizamuddin's shrine just round the corner. They look askance at the ritual of the dargah, regarding it as corrupted by Hindu practices like scattering flowers, burning incense, and tying coloured threads. The Tablighis see prostration before the tomb as idolatry. The belief that Nizamuddin is still alive is heresy. Pirs are charlatans because there can be no intermediary between a Muslim and God. At a higher theological level Wahiduddin Khan told us that the Sufi philosopher Ibn Arabi believed in the Hindu concept of Advaita, or what is known as monism, which states that all reality including God is one. Islam holds that God and his creation are absolutely separate. The scholar said to us, 'The early Sufis were good. Then came the Sufism from Iran, in this there is much that is alien to Islam, not part of Islam.'

Perhaps nothing causes more offence to the Tablighis than the music of the Nizamuddin shrine, and the belief that it can create mystic ecstasy. There is no verse in the Qur'an which prohibits listening to music, nor does a ban emerge from the stories told

about Muhammad, the Hadith. In fact two stories indicate that the
Prophet didn't entirely disapprove of music. One tells of the Prophet
returning home on the feast of 'Id to find his young wife A'isha and
some of her friends singing. His companion admonished them but
the Prophet said 'let them do what they are doing because it's their
'Id.' That story was told to us by Wahiduddin Khan, but at the same
time he said that Islam abjured all aids to worship, audio and visual –
no music, no pictures. He explained, 'There is a Hadith – "Worship
God as if you are seeing him". So the whole concentration has to be
on seeing him, not on seeing or hearing anything or anyone else. If
you can't manage that then you should worship God as if he is seeing
you.' As the orthodox liturgy and ritual are at the heart of their
teaching, Tablighis abhor music.

Whatever the theological rights or wrongs of the issue, the
connection between Sufism and music is ancient, and in Nizamuddin
it's sanctified by the tomb next to the saints – the tomb of his best-
known disciple the poet and musician Amir Khusrau.

Khusrau was what would now be called a fusion musician,
combining the Indian tradition with the Turkish and Persian
traditions he had been brought up in. He was the father of qawwali
– sacred poetry about loving God set to music which evoked such a
response that one saint, buried not many miles from Nizamuddin,
died in ecstasy induced by listening to it. This Sufi form has long
influenced modern secular music. Many superhit Bombay movies
have featured qawwalis whose lyrics refer to human rather than
divine love. The Pakistani qawwal, the late Nusrat Fateh Ali Khan,
who in his short life became almost as famous in world music as
the Indian Ravi Shankar, collaborated on American film scores and
Indian pop music videos and films.

One of our oldest acquaintances at Nizamuddin, Farid Nizami,
belongs to a family which traces its roots back to the qawwals of
Amir Khusrau's time. We had often heard him performing qawwali
in front of Nizamuddin's tomb on a Thursday evening and on the
saint's festival days. When we phoned him to ask for his help in
writing about the dargah, he invited us to his home. The family
lives in what were once the dargah kitchens. We bent down to enter

the windowless vault with its low, arched ceiling and greeted his father. Although he no longer sings he still presides over the joint family of seventeen living in the dargah. The 'party' had been out until seven in the morning and two of the younger members, boys still in their teens, were stretched out on the floor fast asleep. The head of the house sat cross-legged on a low *takht*. He was wheezing like a pair of punctured bellows but, that apart, was remarkably alert, if Farid is really right in claiming he is one hundred years old. The measurement of age is not an exact science in India. Farid maintains his grandfather lived until he was 123 years old with his eyes and his teeth in fine fettle until the end. I could see where Farid got his leonine head and firmly stated features from. Like a lion too he had a great mane of hair stretching down below his shoulders.

Farid is a respectful son, but there is a disagreement within the family on how the qawwal tradition can be kept alive. His father complained to us, 'Now my family performs for drinks' parties. When I was young we would never do that. We would only perform in dargahs or Sikh *gurudwaras*, or churches.'

'My father tells me off like this quite often,' Farid admitted, 'but what can I do? We are under pressure. I also, thanks be to God, know the classical style of qawwali, but if you have a crowd of one hundred and only two want to hear the old style what can you do? Qawwali has become very light, very popular.'

Farid and his party still perform classical qawwali in front of Nizamuddin's tomb. There they also sing Hindu hymns known as *bhajans*, in line with the tradition established by Hazrat Nizamuddin Auliya and Amir Khusrau. Nizamuddin is known to have been moved by bhajans in praise of Hindu gods, and Khusrau described himself as a Hindu Turk. Farid explained, 'Bhajans and the music of other religions are all linked to God and make you remember him.'

A few days later, Farid invited me to a gathering of Sikhs from California at which the party was performing. Farid was the lead singer and he and his brother both played harmoniums. There were two younger members of the family on dholak and tabla to provide the characteristic qawwali beat, and for percussion there was a tambourine and a novelty that Farid has introduced, two small pieces of plate glass which, skilfully handled, rattle and clatter like ponies trotting on a cobbled street.

This was the lighter qawwali, designed to entertain and flatter. Gesturing towards the Sikh baba, or teacher, lying back regally on a settee and clad in golden turban and cloak, Farid sang,

> 'The whole world comes to your court,
> a river of generosity flows there.'

The couplet was repeated, repeated, and repeated with great zest by the rest of the party. A contented smile lit up the baba's face. The young Sikh at his feet massaged him even more vigorously. A five hundred rupee note fluttered on to Farid's harmonium. Those who understood the words chorused, 'Wah, wah.' The white American Sikhs reminded me of something a critic had once said of the Western audiences who went to hear Nusrat Fateh Ali Khan, 'He might as well have been belting out the pages of the telephone book.' Yet he was a megastar, and on a lesser scale Farid entranced the Americans who couldn't understand a word he sang.

Although the Tablighis and Maulana Wahiduddin Khan disapprove of music, ever since the days of Amir Khusrau music has been a common bond between Muslims who subscribe to a less severe theology and Hindus. The renowned Indian historian Mohammad Mujeeb has written, 'By the end of the fourteenth century, the devotional character of Hindi songs and the appeal which the language made to the Sufis brought Hindus and Muslims closer together than any other influence.' It was music and Sufism's other affinities to the bhakti, or devotional tradition of Hinduism, which spread Islam in the countryside. Sufi pirs brought with them colourful ritual, inspiring music, the comfort of surrendering to a teacher, and the ambition of a mystical union with God. The bhakti gurus were teachers, their faith inspired music and poetry, the gods adored were often colourful manifestations of the Almighty, and their worship was the path to union with God. The two traditions grew so close that it is not always possible to disentangle them now.

For example, scholars still argue over the religious affiliation of the fifteenth-century poet Kabir who has a Muslim name. Some argue that he was a devotee of Vishnu, others that he was a Sufi, others that he worshipped a Hindu concept of a formless God. Some stories of his birth say he was born into a family of Muslim weavers, others that he was a Brahmin baby adopted by Muslims, and others that he was a Dalit – a saint of the people still known in those days as Untouchables. Scholars also debate whether certain mystical traditions thought to have deep roots in Hinduism are in fact flowerings of Sufi teachings.

It was these two traditions which maintained harmony between Hindus and Muslims in the countryside. One of the leading eighteenth-century Sufi mystics always attended the celebration of the Hindu festival of Diwali, watched performances of Krishna's life, and even had visions of Rama and his brother Lakshman. Today, in spite of all that politicians have done to destroy that harmony, visitors to the Nizamuddin dargah may well see Sikh turbans among the Muslim caps, and the reddened partings of Hindu wives tying threads to the walls of the tomb in the belief that the saint may deliver them a son.

Hasan Sani says that Nizamuddin dargah is losing out to the Tablighis, because Muslims feel the latter 'know religion'. The Tablighis certainly have a simple message and the missionary zeal to put it across. They go out to preach that message, while the pirs wait for followers to come to them. The Tablighis are in tune with the Wahabites and so attract those young men, with some education but seeing no chance of joining the elite, who seek self-respect in emphasizing their religious identity. They look for an Islam which puts up a fight against what they fear threatens that identity–Western materialism, atheism, moral anarchy, and cultural colonialism. This is a stereotype of the West, but then the Western view of Islam is a stereotype too. What matters is the truth as people see it not the truth itself, and that presents another difficulty for the dargah. We now live in what to many seems to be a rational world, a world it is possible to know and control, a world in which science has ousted the supernatural, in which magic and miracles are not possible because they offend against the order imposed by science. Weber described this process as 'the disenchantment of the world.' So what future can there be for a dargah which deals in enchantment, magic, and miracles?

Part of the answer lies in the return of enchantment. What is postmodernism but a revolt against overweaning rationalism? Scientific fundamentalists continue to claim they have dealt with God, but are they now any more intellectually respectable than religious fundamentalists? Spaces are opening up again in which there is room for the possibility of divine intervention. Many of course have always admitted, and still do, to an emptiness in their own lives which only the spirit can fill. Magic and miracles are only the crudest manifestations of a world where there is room for enchantment. Nizamuddin and the other Sufi dargahs of the subcontinent represent a profound religious tradition, the saints buried there were spiritual masters. All too often it has appeared that the spirituality they taught has been replaced by devotion to them. But, as with all other religions, the Sufi light has never been finally extinguished, there have been saints in every generation.

In the early part of the twentieth century, years before Ravi Shankar took the West by storm, the musician Inayat Khan was making his mark outside India. Debussy was so impressed by his music that he started to take an interest in ragas. The Russian composer A. Skriabin came to believe that Eastern music had much to give to the Western tradition. But Inayat Khan gave up his music to bring his religion, Sufism, to the West, saying, 'To serve God one must sacrifice the dearest thing, and I sacrificed my music, the dearest thing to me ... Now if I do anything it is to tune souls instead of instruments, to harmonize people instead of notes.' He used a metaphor often found in the poet Rumi to describe himself, 'I have become the divine musician's flute, and when he chooses he plays his music' Inayat Khan went on to found the World Sufi Movement, which had a profound impact in the West. As a Sufi he taught the need to take faith into the life of the world, not to withdraw from it, saying, 'I can conceive of no loftier mission than this: to teach philosophy to the West and learn its science, to impart purity of life to Europe and attain to her loftier political ideal, to inculcate spirituality to the American mind and acquire the business ways of her merchants.' But in the end Inayat Khan's body was laid to rest in Nizamuddin, where for him it had all started with the Sufism of his native country, India. Today, behind the ancient dargah of Nizamuddin you will find a modern mausoleum dedicated to the twentieth-century saint, and if you are there on a Friday evening you will probably find some members of Farid's family performing qawwali.

Farmer's Reward

On the night of 4 February 2001 Ningappa Basappa Hiregannavar, a thirty-five-year-old farmer, told his wife that he was going out to discuss the family's financial plight with one of the elders of the village of Javur in the southern state of Karnataka. His wife, who was sitting on the earthen floor of the shack they lived in, said nothing, just continuing to breastfeed their third child. Golden maize, still unhusked, lay piled up in one corner, a continuous reminder to the husband and the wife of the crisis they were facing.

Ningappa came from one of the more prosperous families in the village. His father had owned thirty-two acres but, after his death, the family had split up, and the land had been divided between his three sons. Ningappa had moved out of the family house and for the last seven years had been living in this shack. Wooden beams supported a slightly sloping tiled roof, the walls consisted of corrugated iron sheeting and, when Ningappa had run out of that, he had made do with maize straw. He had inherited part of the family debt when the brothers separated, and since then low prices or poor crops had driven him further into the hands of moneylenders. Now he was desperate because he couldn't even sell his maize. There was no demand in the market and he didn't believe the government would bother to buy from a farmer as small as he was.

The village elder's shop was just opposite the home where Ningappa had lived until the family broke up, very much a pukka house, built of bricks with a thick coating of mud for insulation. Although it was nine o'clock, the village elder, Mahabaleshwar Mallappa Desai, was still doing good business, and so the farmer wandered around the lanes of the village. Returning at ten o'clock, he found there were still customers and so he continued his meandering until the shop emptied and he could sit down and confide in Mahabaleshwar.

'We are all in debt, farmers are everywhere,' the elder comforted him. 'I have bigger debts than you do.'

'But my debts just keep growing,' Ningappa sobbed, 'and what hope do I have now of ever providing my family with somewhere to live? I feel disgraced, I have nowhere to show my face, living as I do. I come from a respectable family and my wife and children are reduced to living in a hut.'

Mahabaleshwar tried to calm him. 'It's a matter of patience. These things come round in circles. I am older than you are, I've seen it all before – two or three bad years and then a good one or two, but we never get out of debt, nor do the moneylenders want us to. We survive and so do they.' Leaning forward he patted Ningappa on the face and said, 'Come on, you must be a man. Crying won't help you.'

But Ningappa wasn't going to be consoled. In a voice still choked he replied, 'There's no point in my surviving. My family would be better off if I killed myself, at least the government would have to pay compensation and they would have some money.'

Mahabaleshwar didn't take this threat very seriously and, seeing that there was no way of helping the farmer in his present mood, made no attempt to restrain him when he got up and walked out into the darkness. Shortly afterwards he heard a young man running through the village shouting, 'Come quickly! There's someone trying to drown himself in the tank.'

The whole village rushed to the tank but in the dark no one could see any sign of the farmer. Some men mounted guard on the tank, others fanned out into the fields to search for him, but it wasn't until after dawn that a village boy found Ningappa hanging from a tree. His noose was a cotton lungi.

Ningappa's suicide was only one of several such stories we were told about in Karnataka, one of India's more prosperous and better administered states. In the village of Sutagatti for instance, not far from Hubli, the second largest town in the state, a young and heavily indebted farmer called Irayya Basayya Mukhashivayyanavar had killed himself. We were directed to the house of his uncle.

We found the women of the family sitting on a platform under the porch of their house shaking wheat grains in winnowing baskets. Tamarind pods were spread out to dry at their feet. I broke one open and sucked the tart pulp inside which is one of the main ingredients in south Indian cooking and reputed to have many medicinal qualities. Two stick figures, not unreminiscent of Lowry, painted on the wall, held up a white lingam of Shiva on an ochre background. The lingam was flanked by serpents, symbols of fertility and ancestor worship. This kind of folk painting has been described by one art historian as timeless. A long discussion between the artist, one of the women winnowing wheat, and our interpreter never quite clarified which festival she had painted it for.

News of our arrival was not long in reaching the head of the household, Basayya, who came hurrying up the lane wearing a long white kurta and dhoti. His forehead bore the three white lines of a worshipper of Shiva, his hair was uncombed, his grey beard might have been stubble or might have been intentional, and his walrus moustache lacked any precision. He could have been taken for a deliberately dishevelled holy man, but he was a working farmer.

Basayya took us across the road to the house of his nephew Irayya, the farmer who had committed suicide, and introduced us to his family. A younger brother sat glumly against some sacks of grain saying nothing. His mother and sister were no more communicative. So it was left to the uncle to tell us what had happened.

This was another case of a joint family splitting up, leaving thirty-two-year-old Irayya, the youngest of the brothers, with just two and a half acres. He had sown potatoes, cotton and maize but a small river flooded his land in heavy rains and his crop was destroyed. He tried again with *jowar*, or sorghum, but once more the rain went against him and the yield was only two sacks of grain. 'There was a weed problem too,' the older farmer said, 'and then there was the well too. That turned into bad luck because other farmers went in for borings and so the level of the water under the ground sank and his well dried up.'

'Did he give any warning that he might commit suicide?' I asked.

'No. He was discussing his wedding and his brother's, both were planned, so it looked as though he had the intention to live a normal life, and then one day we found him hanging in the shed he'd built near his land.'

In the dead farmer's pocket was a list of all his debts. They included money the village accountant, a minor official, was demanding before he would register the transfer of Irayya's share of the family land.

'The village accountant has been suspended,' said Basayya, 'but what good does that do now? It won't bring our boy back. Compensation has been paid too, but that won't bring him back either.'

The government had given a hundred thousand rupees, a local minister ten thousand, and Karnataka's only former prime minister, Deve Gowda, who at the time was trying to make a political comeback, another ten.

As we rose to leave, I asked our interpreter to explain how distressed we were by this story, and to offer our deepest sympathy. The family of the dead farmer just folded their hands and didn't even say 'namaste'. No attempt was made to detain us for the traditional hospitality shown to guests. But Basayya insisted that we should go back to his house where we were given *poha*, savoury pounded yellow rice, and sweet tea.

Our interpreter, Hemant Kumar Panchal, wore a green khadi shawl wherever he went, the emblem of the farmers' movement which had rocked Karnataka in the eighties, but he was not a farmer by birth. He was one of the many Indians who are still prepared to sacrifice the prospect of 'the good life' for what they see as the cause of their country. I have found them in many different places, struggling for all sorts of causes. Hemant I had first met when he came to Delhi to discuss restarting the farmers' movement, but on an all-India basis this time.

Hemant's father, Dr Y. C. Panchal, was a distinguished professor of crop physiology who had spent most of his life teaching and researching in the agricultural university of the town of Dharwar, not many miles away from the villages we were visiting. His was a very strict upbringing. 'My mother was a great disciplinarian,' he told me as we drove away from Sutagatti, 'a dictator in the house.

We had servants but she made me wash my own clothes and clean my utensils myself.'

The strictness paid off and Hemant passed the highly competitive entrance exam for the prestigious Indian Institute of Technology in Chennai, which was Madras at that time. A German professor, on a temporary teaching assignment there, once told me he wished his students back home were half as good as the students in Chennai.

Engineering is considered one of the most promising careers in India, but Hemant wasn't tempted by stories of large salaries and opportunities abroad. He gave up university because he wanted 'to work for farmers'.

This, he told me, had not been well received at home. 'There was a hue and cry in the house. It was very difficult to cope with my parents at that time but somehow I passed through it.'

Where did this philanthropic urge come from? While at school Hemant had met boys who were connected with left-wing underground movements. They wanted him to join, and he admitted he had been 'slightly attracted to the ultras'. But he came to the conclusion that the underground movements, Marxists for the most part, 'lacked social roots and total strength'. He felt they didn't belong to the countryside, and were propagating an alien ideology unsuitable for India. He smiled. 'All my friends laughed at me. They said revolution wasn't brought by the people but by activists. But I still couldn't draw out from them what they wanted to do apart from be anti-government, and somehow I felt if I wanted to achieve anything I would have to get close to the people.'

Hemant's views were strengthened by reading Gandhi. It was from him that he learnt how 'to face villagers and get on with them'.

Reading is one thing and putting it into practice is another. When Hemant, just eighteen years old, did buy ten acres of land in a remote part of northern Karnataka and go off to 'become part of a village', all his friends thought village life would be too tough for him and expected him back in Bangalore within two months, but he is still farming that land himself.

Once he was accepted in the village and felt at home there, he joined the farmers' movement and soon became accepted as a leader. He was now taking us to a village, Morab, where he said the farmers were particularly active. He had called a meeting so that we could get a first-hand account of the problems they were facing.

Morab was obviously a village which commanded clout because, although its population was only ten thousand, it had a branch of the Vijaya Bank in the main square whose signboard proclaimed that it was wholly owned by the government of India. Opposite was the Panchayat Bhavan, the concrete box which housed the offices of the village council. Inside about forty farmers were waiting to meet us, among them were at least two Muslims. We were taken to the top of the table where the most important people were seated. On my right was the secretary of the council, an official of the government who was the only member of the village elite not wearing traditional clothes. Next to him was the elected head of the panchayat. On my left there was a member of the district council, a farmer who owned fifty acres. There were boards on the wall bearing the names of the members of the panchayat committees, some of whom, including the vice-president of the panchayat, were women. When we asked why none of the women had come to the meeting we were told they were busy at home, indicating that perhaps they were just there to fulfil the quotas required by the law and that real power still lay with their menfolk. A blackboard listed details of the work in progress under the supervision of the council – pukka instead of mud flooring for the houses of twenty-two Dalit families, a drain for the road which runs alongside the temple, improvements to the school, and a veterinary hospital.

Hemant stood to open the proceedings. Stroking his wispy black beard and adjusting his green shawl, he thought for a moment or two before starting to explain our mission. Although by no means substantial in size, he commanded the farmers' attention. After embarrassing me by exaggerating my influence and importance, he told the farmers, 'No politicians pay attention to our problems, and the bureaucrats are entirely against us so it's very important to get the help of the press. We must put our problems to them.'

There was no embarrassed silence when he opened the meeting

to the farmers, inviting them to tell us about their problems. Voices from all round the table told us that prices were below production costs, the market had collapsed, and the government was doing nothing. A farmer standing at the far end of the hall shouted, 'We harvested the maize in October and we still can't find a market for it six months later.'

When I asked about the government's decision to enter the market, buy in a big way, and so, hopefully, raise the price of maize, there was a chorus of protests.

'They haven't procured a tenth of the crop.'

'You mean a twentieth.'

'The government does unscientific purchasing, they haven't succeeded in raising the price in the market.'

'There's no profit for us in the government price, and the market means a definite loss.'

'The big farmers in the village will see that their produce gets taken up by the government, but if you only have forty quintals what hope is there for you?'

Hemant managed to restore some order, and the meeting turned into a veiled attack on Mr Hanchinal, the prosperous farmer sitting at the top of the table with me. There were complaints that big farmers were able to rig the markets and ensure that the government procured their produce first.

'They are not really farmers,' said a young man whose crumpled kurta contrasted with the sleek appearance of Mr Hanchinal. 'They are farmers-cum-merchants.'

'Merchants-cum-farmers, you mean,' interjected his neighbour, looking hard at Mr Hanchinal, who smiled wearily, acknowledging that he was a target, but said nothing.

An elderly man, sharp-featured and with wily eyes who had been anxious to speak for some time held up his hand again, and Hemant invited him to have his say. He proceeded to give a lengthy lecture, replete with convoluted phraseology, on scientific pricing. I was not surprised to learn that he was a lawyer-cum-farmer. It eventually transpired that scientific pricing meant farmers should get costs plus twenty-five per cent.

Mr Hanchinal intervened for the first time. 'Although a guaranteed price is what we need, we will never get it. But what we can demand is a bigger market, and that means exports. The government doesn't even announce its import–export policy until after the crops are handed to the merchants. There should be no restrictions on exports, but of course there should be restrictions on imports. I have been told that the World Bank has been very critical of the government's ban on exports and the way they annouce their export policies so late.'

No one told him that the World Bank would certainly not approve of a ban on imports either and the debate returned to the government's grain procurement policy. The lawyer re-entered the fray, complaining that his maize had been stuck for twenty days at the procurement centre. Every day he had to go there, and to look after his grain he had to employ a watchman round the clock.

'The delay in lifting from the farmers is because they are waiting for a bribe,' he explained.

Another farmer added, 'Yes, and if you bribe you will get your cheque quicker too.'

Hemant then raised the question of credit. Few Indian farmers have cash flows adequate to provide for the purchase of their seeds, fertilizers, and other inputs. They have to borrow each sowing season. When Indira Gandhi nationalized the banks more than thirty years ago, one of the reasons she gave was to provide rural credit so that farmers did not fall into the hands of loan sharks. The local branch of the Vijaya Bank should have been doing just that. But the farmers were united in their condemnation of the banking system. All complained that the procedures for raising a loan were so cumbersome and time-consuming that the money arrived well after it was needed. So, in spite of Indira Gandhi, farmers still went to private moneylenders even though they charged four per cent interest a month plus a one per cent surcharge. One farmer said there were twenty private financiers flourishing in Morab village alone. Another whispered into Hemant's ear, 'There's one over there, sitting next to your guest.'

Mr Hanchinal did not rise in defence of private finance.

Hemant then spoke for some time on the need for farmers to unite if they were to press their demands effectively. He spoke quietly, his hands folded in front of him. There was no rhetoric, no gesturing, none of the tricks of the orator's trade, but he held their attention as he reminded them of the heyday of the farmers' movement when the government had really been shaken, and of the defeat they had inflicted on a chief minister in the election to the state assembly. But after the speech was over one of the farmers said, 'The movement depended on emotions aroused by the police firing on us when we were demonstrating. That sort of emotional reaction cannot last for long.'

For some reason this brought another farmer to the subject of drink. 'Liquor complicates matters,' he said. 'Poor farmers turn to liquor. They earn forty rupees a day and then spend it on liquor so they are weakened. Small farmers are addicted to this because of tension.'

On cue, a drunken farmer who had been ejected from the hall twice, staggered in for the third time. The meeting broke up with Mr Hanchinal trying to restrain his colleagues who had grabbed the drunk and were frogmarching him out of the hall, cuffing him around the head to help him on his way.

The village seemed to be drowning in maize, pile after pile of golden grain waiting to be bagged, the tissue-paper-thin dried sheaths of the corn cobs littering every lane. As we left Morab, we passed a mechanical thresher producing yet more grain. The rattle of the machine turned to a roar each time a basket of corn cobs was poured into its mouth. A chain of girls passing the baskets from one to the other kept its hunger at bay. The farmer, who was not taking an active role in all this, was a surly, silent man who rebuffed our efforts to discuss prices and discover why his threshing was so long delayed.

We drove down what is known as a village road, in reality not much more than a potholed cart track, past some of the varied crops of northern Karnataka. Hemant commented on the cost of bad roads to farmers, increasing transport expenses and damaging vehicles even as uncomplicated as bullock carts. A white-eyed buzzard swooped dramatically over the fields of tall jowar whose leaves were turning brown as the harvest approached. A few black leaves still hung from the dismal stalks of sunflowers already harvested. We stopped to pick – steal would I suppose be a more appropriate word – some green *channa*, or chickpeas, and to look at a field of golden safflower, a crop I couldn't remember seeing before. Hemant explained it could only be harvested at dawn when the dew had softened the prickly plants. That might have been one reason why it hadn't caught on in the way he thought it should have done, because it was sturdy, resistant to drought and pests, and produced an excellent edible oil.

Before we reached a tarmacked road, we came upon a farmer who was willing to discuss the maize crop. He, his son, and his wife were working in the middle of a field, without any protection from the sun, shovelling grain into sacks. We took them to the shade of a tamarind tree to discuss the economics of their harvest.

Hemant had invited Dr Rajendra Poddar, a young agricultural economist to travel with us. Dapper in his light-blue shirt with button-down collar and dark-blue trousers, he looked out of place beside the farmer in his sweat-stained, frayed white shirt and dhoti. The farmer's son was only wearing a lungi tucked up above his knees and a vest. But the economist was not an armchair or air-conditioned academic. He had come up the hard way. His father was a farmer who could barely read and write, but had the enterprise to be the first person in his district to irrigate his land, thereby transforming the culture of the surrounding villages, which had previously depended on rain-fed agriculture.

After detailed questioning in which Dr Poddar used the skill of an economist and the knowledge of a farmer, he drew up a balance sheet of the maize crop which showed that the expenditure, including interest at five per cent a month on the crop loan, was 6150 rupees per acre, and income from the sale of the grain was 3960 rupees. So the net loss per acre was 2190 rupees. As the farmer had sown eight acres of maize, his total loss was 17,520 rupees. His income would have been higher if he had gone to the government procurement centre, instead of selling to a private trader at a hundred rupees a sack less than the official price, but the farmer, rubbing his head covered with thick grey hair, explained, 'Nobody cares if you go to the government. At least with the private trader I get my money at once and it's much easier. I don't have to take my grain anywhere either. He comes and collects it.'

His son added, 'It's probably more profitable too, what with all the interest we would have to pay while we waited for our money from the government.'

'That would be less if you'd borrowed from the bank,' Dr Poddar pointed out.

But the farmer had an answer to that too. 'We couldn't. We already had a debt of 23,000 rupees with the State Bank of India, which meant no other bank would have lent to us.'

So what was the point of farming if you were going to make a loss? For the farmer it wasn't just money that counted. 'Owning land is a matter of prestige and it would be a disgrace if you didn't farm it. When our joint family broke, I only actually owned 2.3 acres of land, but to keep up my standing as a farmer I have leased nearly 6 acres. Now I find my son and I have to work elsewhere to have money for household needs.'

'Do you mean labouring?' asked Dr Poddar.

'Yes, sometimes on bigger farmers' land, sometimes whatever we can get.'

'How can you go on like this? You are losing money.'

'I have hopes. The last two years have been very bad, maybe the prices will improve next year.'

'What about your debts?'

'I will use the money from this crop to pay the moneylender and the bank can wait. Everyone owes money to the banks here, and there's no disgrace in that. If they want to take my land, we'll see what happens. It's not that easy for them.'

Much to the disgust of Hemant and Dr Poddar, our first night in northern Karnataka had been spent in one of those modern Indian hotels whose management hoped that fancy sanitary ware would disguise faulty plumbing. Hemant had booked us into the guest house of the Dharwar Agricultural University where his father had taught and Dr Poddar had studied, but we had lost our room to the state agricultural commissioner and his entourage. Hemant and Dr Poddar were determined that this evening we would arrive there in time to secure our accommodation. However their determination conflicted with Hemant's insistence that we fulfil a schedule which all our lengthy discussions had delayed beyond any hope of completion. In the end we compromised by postponing a visit to Hemant's own village, but we still arrived at the university well after dark.

The next morning we went to see the much-criticized procurement arrangements for ourselves at the Amargol branch of the Karnataka State Warehousing Corporation.

Queues of trucks and tractors, waiting to pass over the one and only weighbridge, stretched the entire length of the warehouses and disappeared behind them. There were more queues on the main road outside. On the verandah of the warehouse office farmers jostled each other to get their documents recorded by just one bald-headed, bad-tempered clerk. They also had to register their vehicles with the police for some reason the sub-inspector on duty was unable to explain.

A crowd, anxious to express their frustration, gathered around us. Some had been waiting for twenty-four hours to complete the complicated process which involved queuing first to get their loaded vehicles weighed, then queuing to get them unloaded, and finally joining a third queue to have their empty vehicles weighed, and all this was only the end of the story. All the farmers complained of long waits, one as long as two months, at local procurement centres before they were allowed to bring their maize to these warehouses.

A young farmer, who was also a transporter, was particularly vocal. 'They should have started procurement here months ago,' he insisted. 'They have only just started buying, and the rate they are going most of the grain will start losing quality. If it's not properly stored it loses quality after six months.'

'Why do you think they have only started buying recently?' I asked.

Back without any hesitation came the reply: 'Those suicide reports. Only when they face a crisis do politicians get worried.'

Gilly focused her camera on him but he put his hand across his face. She said there was no danger of the photograph being seen on television, but he was not reassured.

All this maize was an embarrassment to the central government. It already had a massive stock of grain. One economist had recently calculated that if all the sacks stored by the government's Food Corporation of India were lined up they would stretch for a million miles. Yet millions of children in India are still chronically undernourished, and the government itself admits that thirty-six per cent of the wheat it allots to those who need subsidized food doesn't reach them. It gets eaten by insects and rats, or falls into the hands of private traders.

The Amargol warehouses were already stacked to capacity, and so the grain was now being unloaded down the road in what had once been a factory for manufacturing gears. The business must have failed because there was no sign of any machinery, and the factory had become a gigantic barn fast filling up with sacks of maize. An official who was meant to be grading grain was fast asleep at his desk. One group of coolies was sitting on the floor eating lunch. Another group was slowly unloading a lorry. Three men, bare-chested with their backs protected by cotton cloth knotted over their heads, laboured to lift a sack weighing ninety-six kilogrammes on to the back of a fourth coolie. He tottered precariously across the uneven terrain of the grain mountain and threw the sack down, yanking it into place with a grappling hook, reminiscent of the longshoremen in *On the Waterfront*. The hook tore the sack and grain dribbled out. It was obvious that, contrary to the principles of good inventory management, the first grain to be stored, the bottom of the mountain, would be the last to go out of the warehouse. But the Food Corporation doesn't have to bother with those sort of considerations because its costs are subsidized by the government, and it faces no competition.

The banking system, we were to discover, was no less antiquated and inefficient – the farmers' complaints about credit were as justified as their criticism of the procurement system we saw at Amargol. Hemant and Dr Poddar took us to meet the manager of the Malaprabha Grameen (or rural) Bank in Navalgund, a town where police opened fire for the first time at the height of the farmers' movement in which Hemant had played a prominent role.

The branch was a narrow room on the ground floor of a small house. Into it were crowded the clerks, the counter, and the benches where farmers waited for clerical complexities to be unravelled. The manager had no office of his own but sat at the entrance. Behind him were the safes. The wooden notice on his desk identified the manager as 'K. G. Ballarwad, Bachelor of Science, Bachelor of Law'. A small man, greyed by twenty-two years drudgery in the bank, I felt certain that he would be bound by rules which prohibited him from talking to the press. But not at all – he was most polite and very communicative.

He agreed that the process for getting a loan was somewhat complicated and could put off potential borrowers, especially if they were not very well educated. He counted the obstacles a borrower had to negotiate on his fingers.

'Before he can even ask for a loan he has to produce, one – land records, two – records of rights, three – no dues from the government, four – records of all land revenue paid, five – no dues certificates from other banks, six – land valuation certificates, seven – no dues from agricultural societies, and if he is a minor, permission from the court.'

'How does he show he doesn't owe money to any bank?' I asked.

'He goes to each bank to get a certificate.'

'How many is that?'

'Seven commercial banks and two cooperative banks.'

'Nine altogether,' I said in amazement. 'He has to go to nine different banks.'

'Yes, I suppose nine, and even after all these safeguards our recovery rate is only fifty-five per cent.'

'Fifty-five per cent, you mean nearly half the loans go down the drain?'

'If you put it like that, yes. It can be worse than that. We had to move this branch to Navalgund from the village where it was established because non-payment was eighty-five to ninety-five per cent.'

A clerk pushed a heavy, bound ledger in front of the manager – The Register of Cheques, Bills, and Drafts Deposited for Collection. He signed the entry in the ledger, opened an ink pad and stamped the cheque that went with it, explaining that he had to sign every transaction, which meant a thousand signatures a day.

'But don't you have any other supervisory staff?' I asked.

'Yes,' he replied, 'I have two who are classified supervisory staff, but under the bank rules they are not allowed to supervise.'

Mr Ballarwad was neither a faceless nor a heartless bureaucrat. He realized that the complexities of the banking system drove farmers into the hands of the moneylenders. 'In our area we are trying to stop private lending,' he said, 'but farmers are in the habit of taking private loans. When the bank loan is overdue they will go to the private financier to get money to repay it.'

Dr Poddar quoted an unnamed British author who had written: 'The Indian farmer is born in debt, lives in debt and dies in debt.'

'Is reborn in debt too,' added Hemant.

We had asked Hemant to introduce us to one or two of the teachers at the agricultural university but I was horrified when, on our way back to Dharwar, he told me the vice-chancellor was going to round up all his professors to meet us. There was no getting out of it, so the next morning we walked down the wooded hill from the guest house, with the neatly set out fields of experimental crops below us, to the administrative building which dominated the campus. Indo-Palladian in style and crowned with a dome, it gave the impression of some seat of classical learning rather than the headquarters of a comparatively new agricultural university. We walked up the stairs to a large room where some sixty academics sat round a U-shaped table waiting to hear me speak. I protested that as a mere Bachelor of Arts with no research behind me in any subject, I had no right to address an assembly of scholars. I wanted to learn from them, not speak to them. But I did describe briefly the complaints we had heard from farmers and asked what their views were on the agricultural problems of Karnataka.

There seemed to be universal agreement that agricultural research had focused on production and ignored 'post-harvest' problems. One plant physiologist led the breast-beating, 'We forgot the market. Now the stark reality is staring us in the face. Farmers come to us and say, "We did everything you told us to produce crops – now tell us where to sell them." This bitter lesson has only just been learnt.'

But according to an agricultural marketing specialist, it was the farmers' fault for ignoring an obvious fact. 'Every market has an absorption level,' he said. 'They have ignored the consumer base. I have the seeds available and so I sow, have the resources so I grow, a farmer says, but without market there should be no growth at all.'

Several academics then pointed out that there would be a bigger market if there had been more investment in food storage facilities and food processing industries, some of them blaming the government for this. Others criticized the government for a lack of crop forecasting. But the marketing expert interjected to say that farmers and academics alike were too dependent on the government and ought to do more for themselves. He was shot down by a colleague who said, 'No, the government should come in in a big way to help agriculture.'

When Hemant suggested what was needed was 'a model neither capitalist nor socialist', I said, 'That's the holy grail we are all searching for.'

In the end, the vice-chancellor, while not ruling out the role of private capital and initiatives, put much of the blame on the government saying, 'They are on the side of the consumers entirely. All they want is cheap food. Every IAS officer should be made to stay in a village and work with farmers for one year, then the problems will be solved. Only if an IAS officer shows he can run a marginal farm should he be allowed to occupy a secretary to government chair.'

Seniority is still respected in India, and the word 'sir' is frequently to be heard but, comparatively young though he was and junior in the academic hierarchy too, Dr Poddar was not overawed by the vice-chancellor.

'What we have is a problem of localized over-production,' he said, as if pronouncing the final verdict. 'Since the sixties our main emphasis has been on production, but by the eighties we had the problem of supply management and we should have concentrated on that.'

After the meeting in the university we left to fulfil our commitment to Hemant's village. On the way I asked Dr Poddar how there could be a surplus in a country where the government itself admitted that almost one third of the population didn't get enough to eat. The infrastructure, he believed, was part of the problem – not enough effective investment in road construction and maintenance, electricity supply, and storage. Produce wasn't able to move from markets where there was a surplus to those where there was a shortage. The government had made matters worse by restricting movement between states. The history of procurement hadn't been a happy one either. It had failed to guarantee fair prices in surplus situations, much of the food was destroyed in storage, and what did get into the public distribution system didn't reach those who needed it most because of the two inevitable flaws in anything the government did – corruption and inefficiency. But Dr Poddar didn't want to paint 'a totally negative picture'.

'It's not all bad news,' he assured us. 'Indian agricultural scientists have made tremendous contributions. DCH32 cotton, for instance, is a great revolution. Farmers have shown great willingness to try new varieties of seed and new methods too. That is why we face these difficulties now. But the government should have seen this production problem earlier. They have a plan for industry but no plan for agriculture which, although so many people depend on it for their livelihood, has been starved of capital. Even now, with all these World Bank and IMF economic reforms, the emphasis is on industry and commerce, not on agriculture.'

Although Karnataka is thought of as one of India's modernizing states, primitive methods of agriculture still survive. We passed one farmer driving two bullocks round and round in circles pulling a stone roller to thresh wheat. But it was the farmers who were getting the traffic to do the threshing for them that particularly upset Dr Poddar. Their harvested channa was liberally spread over the road so that vehicles would drive over it and separate the chickpeas from their pods.

'Apart from being lazy farming, it's very dangerous to do this on a highway,' he complained. 'Just look at those people squatting in the road and sweeping up the seeds, one of them could easily be run over.' Our driver was not amused either as time and again he was forced to brake by a thick carpet of channa straw.

There was some tarmac on the road leading to Belvatagi, the village where Hemant had bought his land and learned to be a farmer. On the outskirts of the village, Hemant pointed to a comparatively recent plantation of coconut palms and fruit trees, a rare sight in this area with its long tradition of arable farming.

'That's what we should be doing now if traditional crops are failing,' said Hemant. 'Let the farmer be in the field for a challenge rather than waiting for protection.'

But Hemant himself was still very much an arable farmer. Standing in the middle of the six acres of jowar he had planted, he plucked a head which had turned white, and chewed one of the seeds. 'Not quite ripe,' he exclaimed. 'If it was I would have to crunch it, you would hear the crack.' Last year his jowar had fetched 650 rupees a quintal, this year the market rate was only 400.

He pointed to a shami tree explaining, 'That was the tree I ran round when the villagers tested me. They said, if you are a farmer, lift a sack of grain and dump it on a tractor trailer. I lifted the sack, ran away from the tractor round the tree and then back to dump it just to show that I was more than fit to be a farmer. After that I was accepted in the village.'

Hemant had also conducted an experiment in self-sufficiency. He had stayed in a hut on his land and grown what he needed. 'I didn't break down,' he told us, 'and I found I only needed one hundred rupees a month for cash purchases.'

When we reached the village we stopped at a bilious-green, concrete building which doubled as a village hall and temple. The corrugated iron roof of the porch was supported by wooden pillars and a red postbox attached to one of them added to its utility. At the back of the hall, across the entire width of the building, was a gallery of colourful and carefully framed calendar art. Most of the major deities and local saints were represented, including Akka Mahadevi, the revolutionary woman poet and saint of medieval times who threw away even her clothes in a gesture of social defiance. She was depicted, as she generally was, covered only by her long tresses and standing in front of her beloved Lord Shiva's faithful servant, Nandi the bull. Arranged beside her were the heroes of the independence movement. Below, at the very back of the hall, were a black stone image of Veerbhadra, the heavily mustachioed son of Shiva, and five lingams of Shiva himself.

Once again the villagers had been summoned to meet us. Fortunately two of them had worked outside Karnataka and spoke Hindi, and so the interpretation problem wasn't so acute. Vilas Kulkarni, whose dyed black hair didn't match the white stubble on his chin, had worked in a factory in Mumbai but had come back to the village because there was no one to farm his family's sixty-four acres. He backed the vice-chancellor's criticism of commerce. 'With the bad seeds we get now, the yield of cotton has gone down from twenty-four quintals a hectare to less than one,' he complained. 'As for the pesticides we buy, they have no strength in them.'

'If you dunked a pest in them neat, it wouldn't die,' chipped in another farmer.

There was universal dissatisfaction with the irrigation department too.

'We are tail-enders, so the water never reaches us until all the villages further up the canal have taken theirs, and then it's too late,' one farmer protested.

Another bemoaned the leakages in the canal and the lack of maintenance.

A third said, 'If we complain to the irrigation department about the state of the canal they tell us to go away, and do nothing themselves.'

I asked the farmers about the plantation we had seen and Hemant's suggestion that the future might lie in that direction. That was scorned by the second Hindi speaker, Maharudrappa Virappa Kuruvinashetti, who replied, 'When that plantation farmer balances his books at the end of each year, he has to sell four acres of land. If we copy him we will all have to join the One Up There in two years – we will have to commit suicide too.'

Maharudrappa had worked in the central government's commission promoting the manufacture and marketing of hand-woven cloth and other traditional village products, but he'd got fed up with being transferred from region to region and so had come back to his village. His loose-fitting white shirt and striped pajama trousers didn't give him the appearance of a man of means, but at least, with his savings from his government job, he'd been able to set up a tea shop to supplement his income from farming. Inevitably he insisted that we repaired there.

In the darkness of the café the kettle itself seemed to be on fire, so high were the flames from the kerosene stove. As we drank sweet tea and ate fresh, hot samosas, we discussed the fate of wrestling as a sport. The village had two traditional *akharas*, or wrestling pits, with mud floors and Indian clubs as gym equipment, but the young men now preferred to play cricket. We were introduced to a soldier back on leave from Kashmir where he drove supply lorries. He maintained that it now took a fifty thousand rupee bribe to get recruited into the army. We tried to discuss Hemant's role in the farmers' movement as well, but he wouldn't have that, saying, 'Most of the time I was away, and affairs here were looked after by an elderly colleague who died recently. She was my main support, and dealt with the police and the officials when they came here, and she prevented them auctioning debtors' lands.'

Nevertheless the farmers insisted that Hemant had made 'great sacrifices'.

In north Karnataka we had discerned the plight of arable farmers, but as we set off on the long drive down the national highway to Bangalore, Hemant promised to show us villages where vegetable farmers were facing equally severe difficulties. We passed the granite hills of Chitradurga, ringed by the snaking walls of a seventeenth-century fortress and reached Tumkur, where the crowds of cars at the Perfect Iddly House, testified to the quality of their steamed snacks, served on banana leaves. As most other people on the highway seemed to be doing so, we decided to take an *iddly* and coffee break before turning on to a lesser road which led us to much lusher and greener countryside than that around Dharwar. Finally we left this road too, and turned down a track past a village tank choked with purple water hyacinth, past a low but ancient stone temple, and tall peepul trees, until we reached the heart of Surd-henapura village. We stopped in front of a modest, single-storey house, which had been the home of Ashwathnarayana Achari, a vegetable farmer who had ended his life by committing suicide.

He had gone to his fields and drunk pesticide after selling the last of his cauliflowers and tomatoes at a price so low that he couldn't pay off any of his debts. It had been a long and painful death, twelve hours after he drank the poison. His neighbours showed us a report of the death in a local paper but, in spite of this, the local member of the state assembly had not bothered to come to the village, although it was barely ten kilometres away from his home.

Ashwathnarayana had left a widow and two sons aged eighteen and fifteen whose hair was sprouting again after being shaved as part of the ritual mourning. They showed us a framed photograph of their father as a young man – earnest, unsure, eyes fixed on the camera. On the glass of the frame the family had pasted the three white lines of a *shaivite* across the farmer's forehead and a scarlet dot between his eyebrows. The elder son had started working with his father but, when I asked whether he felt he would be able to take over the farm and run the household too, he was very uncertain.

'If my father couldn't manage how can I say I can?' he mumbled.

The day before he'd taken twenty kilogrammes of tomatoes to a market and sold them for just fourteen rupees. Transport there and back had cost ten rupees.

The boys were not very talkative. Stunned by their father's death and overawed by all the attention they were receiving, they left the talking to Pushpavati, a niece of the farmer who lived almost next door.

'My uncle had just received his electricity bill, was in debt for fertilizers and pesticides, for labourers' wages, seeds and household rations. He took loans from traders and from friends and relatives. He had sold his bullocks and cow but still couldn't repay his debts. Things wouldn't have been so bad if at least the market worked fairly for us, but the commission agents we sell our vegetables to rig the prices, and then they deduct a fee from us which is illegal. It's banned by the government.'

As usual other villagers had gathered around us and an elderly man interrupted Pushpavati: 'He was a self-respecting man and he didn't want to go back on his word.'

Adjusting her blue sari, impatiently she agreed, 'Yes, he may have done it out of self-respect, but if we all kill ourselves what will happen to our children?'

The villager ignored this and went on, 'He was hard working but, despite good crops, he couldn't make ends meet. He waited for two years for the situation to improve, for prices to go up. But no one thought he would do this. He was a pious man with knowledge of herbal medicines and was so close to all the village that he used to give free medicines at his own expense.'

Pushpavati, although one of the younger wives of the village, did not hesitate to challenge the elderly villager:

'That's quite right, he did value the respect of the village, but he needn't have gone so far. He used to talk about his debts a lot but his family and friends all assured him saying it's not that much of a problem because every one of us is in debt.'

Pushpavati then darted inside her house and emerged with a sheaf of papers.

'Look at these ... My father-in-law's mortgaged two acres of land with the Cooperative Bank. Here's an electricity bill, but unlike my uncle I am not worried about it because I won't pay it and nothing will happen. And then there's our jewellery. Look at this.'

It was a receipt from a pawnbroker in Bangalore who had lent 600 rupees against a gold ring. The interest was twenty-one per cent and the ring had to be redeemed within one year or otherwise it would be sold. There was another receipt for gold earrings and a gold chain, they had fetched 6,800 rupees from a different pawnbroker but on the same terms.

To have pawned the family jewels seemed to be almost a badge of honour. The men standing around us fell over themselves in their anxiety to show us receipts kept in their shirt pockets. The whole village seemed to be in hock, and this was only some twenty miles from Bangalore, India's fifth largest city, and particularly prosperous as a centre of India's current success story, the IT industry.

When we left to drive to Bangalore we saw that the city's prosperity had spread almost to the doorstep of Pushpavati's house. Just down the road there were two 'out of town developments'. They were apartment blocks set in gardens which clearly never lacked water. One was called California, the other Monte Carlo, and they might have been situated there too, so remote they seemed from the village of Surdhenapura.

As we were entering Bangalore itself, Hemant pointed out a lake saying, 'The city has three hundred lakes, but half of them are extinct now. They are being converted for housing, and they call that development.'

When I first visited Bangalore in the sixties it was a garden city. With its parks, one a forest in the centre of the city, its lakes, its avenues covered with a green canopy of rain trees, its altitude of three thousand feet above sea-level and the temperate climate that goes with the height, it became a victim of its own natural assets. Mumbai (then known as Bombay) and Chennai (formerly Madras) had far exceeded Bangalore in importance during the British Raj, but after independence many businessmen and industrialists moved from those crowded, chaotic cities to green, cool Bangalore. At the beginning of the twentieth century the Indian Institute of Science was founded there and just before independence came the Raman Research Institute. They gave Bangalore a reputation for excellence in science which attracted nationalized hi-tech industries like Hindustan Aeronautics as well as the private sector. Then followed the IT wallahs. To add to all those pressures post-independence,

Bangalore also became the capital of one of India's largest and most progressive states. The result has been described by Maya Jayapal in a history of her city which is a delight to read, 'Bangaloreans who once boasted of their garden city now do not use that term for obvious reasons. Their hopes for the future, fuelled by the city's readiness to move on to the national, even international, platform have been belied at least for the moment by their innumerable travails like environmental pollution, haphazard expansion and piece-meal planning.'

To the casual visitor there is certainly very little evidence of any planning. The wife of a nineteenth-century commissioner of Bangalore complained that the palanquin she used to get about the town stopped every hundred yards to allow for a change of bearers. The average speed of the traffic which now enveloped us was probably not much faster than Lady Bowring's palanquin, and we stopped for much longer periods than would have been necessary to change bearers. At one traffic jam I noticed the board outside a branch of the nationalized Bank of India. It advertised 'computerized tele-banking' – a far cry I thought from Mr Ballarwad and his thousand signatures a day in the small up-country town of Navalgund.

In other respects too Bangalore does have a modernity, a veneer which is not to be seen in rural Karnataka. Mahatma Gandhi, in his loincloth, would be horrified by the shops on the road named after him, full as they are of the latest branded fashion wear from the West. He would be even more shocked by the pubs. Bangalore was the first Indian city to develop what it calls 'a pub culture'. In the 'Underground', which has the London Underground's logo as its inn sign, a music channel vied with a news channel on television sets at opposite ends of the bar. The noise made conversation difficult, if not impossible, and the lighting, or lack of it, allowed for all sorts of amorous activities the Mahatma would have deplored. It was too dark to see whether any such activities were taking place in the far recesses of the bar without being inquisitive, but the names of the cocktails would have made it difficult for the management to discourage them. Among the specialities on the Underground's list of drinks were 'Sex on the Beach', 'Silk Panties', and 'Ants in the Pants'. Less special were 'Blow Job', 'Slippery Nipple', and 'Virgin's Kiss'.

In the Raj, Bangalore, dominated as it was by its military cantonment, was a peculiarly British town and perhaps it's significant that now, very much a city and India's most Westernized city too, it has not tried to obliterate its British past and remove all evidence of the colonial rulers. King George V has been dethroned from the India Gate in Delhi, and as far as I know there isn't a single statue of a British ruler, officer, or administrator in any prominent place there. In Bangalore, Sir Mark Cubbon, the first commissioner, still sits astride his horse, and the central park still bears his name. On the edge of that park, Victoria has not been dethroned, nor has her son Edward VII. Although Victoria's son was not renowned for his piety, it's said that the sculptor so positioned his statue that its nose pointed directly at the cross on the altar of Holy Trinity Church. Despite Winston Churchill describing Indians in derogatory terms, and opposing their independence to the end, Bangaloreans are proud that he served in their city as a subaltern and will tell you with delight that he still owes his club thirteen rupees. Eighteen citizens of Bangalore started the legal action which saved the British red stone High Court building from being pulled down in the name of progress, and when a few years later the judges needed more space, the annexe to the courts was built in the same Graeco-Roman style.

But this being India where counter-action follows action as day follows night, it is perhaps not surprising that Bangalore was also the first city to see a revolt against modern Western culture with an attack on a Kentucky Fried Chicken outlet. And for all that Bangaloreans saved the British High Court, opposite it stands one of the very few grand public buildings to have been constructed in India since Independence. Karnataka's Vidhana Soudha, or State Assembly, is a vast grey stone building, with architecture incorporating four different Indian styles. The central portico supports a dome surmounted by the national emblem, the Ashokan lion. The portico is flanked by two long wings with lines of arches fronting verandahs piled one on top of the other. There are smaller domes at both ends. Over the portico are the words 'Government's work is God's work'. One might be tempted to add, 'If that's so, God help God', but perhaps that would be a little unfair because governance in Karnataka is better than in most states.

It was in the Vidhana Soudha that Habib Beary, who had been BBC correspondent in Bangalore when I was bureau chief, and was still the corporation's man there, took us to meet the agriculture minister. Inside the impressive façade were numberless offices built around a courtyard. But Habib knew his way and, what's more, was sufficiently well known for us to avoid the security procedures which are the bane of modern India.

The minister T. B. Jayachandra was taken by surprise. 'Don't they have cameras?' he asked Habib in Kannada.

'No, they are writing a book, and you don't need cameras for that.'

The minister recovered from his disappointment and, when we'd explained the purpose of our visit said, 'Suicides are becoming inevitable. There is unprecedented production, it's the same in the whole of India and so the prices have fallen and farmers are facing a lot of problems.'

The minister of course put the blame for the crisis on the central government because Sonia Gandhi's Congress Party was in power in Karnataka and the Hindu nationalist BJP was governing in Delhi. 'They must give permission to export,' he maintained. 'Onions went up in price, the BJP lost the election for Delhi's state assembly because of that, and so now they've banned all agricultural exports. They don't have a policy. Now, in maize they are acting under pressure from north Indian cattle and poultry feed manufacturers who want to keep prices low.'

He was not optimistic about procurement solving the farmers' problems, because he didn't think the government would be able to buy more than ten per cent of the maize crop, and its efforts so far had made 'no dent' on the market. He was not optimistic about the food processing industry providing a market either, even though it was a Congress Prime Minister, Rajiv Gandhi, who more than ten years previously had set up a food processing ministry to develop that industry. He dismissed the ministry's efforts saying, 'The entrepreneurs are not interested. They say it's seasonal work, but we have ten agro-climatic zones and can grow any crop in the world around the year.'

The minister may have been in his early middle age, it was difficult to tell, so sleek was his grooming, so immaculately black his hair and moustache. He had a restrained smile, as if a full-blown grin might give something away, but spoke quite freely and had a good mastery of his brief, which is not always true of ministers. A farmer himself, he was particularly concerned about the terms of the WTO which obliged India to accept imports of agricultural products. He owned a plantation of areca palms which produced betel-nut for paan, and even the price of that essentially Indian commodity had collapsed. The farmers we had talked to blamed the slump in areca-nut on the recent earthquake in Gujarat. Apparently Gujarat was a big market for paan. But the minister blamed the WTO, claiming that areca was being imported from Indonesia and the Philippines disguised as dried fruit. He accused the central government of 'falling prey to the dictated terms of the developed countries'.

I pointed out that the WTO agreement was signed when the Government of India was in the hands of his party, but he had an answer to that. 'We are not raising the tariffs as allowed under the WTO. The government is more concerned with the consumer, so it uses imports to bring down prices. We need to assess and then import, now they import without assessing the demand. As the state government we only monitor production. The Government of India controls prices by giving licences to import and export.'

As usual in politics everywhere in the world, suicides weren't the minister's fault. There was someone else to blame.

On our last morning in Bangalore, we drove with Hemant through the mercifully light traffic at six o'clock in the morning to see what was happening to prices in the vegetable market. Dispirited farmers sat by their produce, waiting with little or no hope for a commission agent to auction them. There were peas, green peppers, fat red chillies, tomatoes, carrots, cucumbers, and ladies' fingers which seemed longer and thinner than the northern variety. Most of the vegetables were in the open because the covered area couldn't even begin to cope with the demand for space. There were no stalls and very limited storage arrangements. Tractor trailers and lorries stacked high with vegetables were unloaded by coolies. They trotted with sacks on their backs or baskets on their heads, threading their way through the piles of vegetables and the crowds of buyers and sellers, somehow not slipping on carpets of cauliflower leaves, or tripping over pavements and potholes concealed by those carpets. Small time retailers sat cross-legged on the ground in front of their stock. Among their customers were two intrepid young nuns buying vegetables for their convent. But the main business was done by the auctioneers who stood on sacks of the vegetables they were selling to wholesalers. All round the market could be heard the familiar patter – 'ten rupees, ten rupees, ten rupees, eleven, eleven, twelve, twelve, twelve, twelve, sold for twelve'. Clerks stood by the auctioneers to note down the details of the seller and the buyer. I was reminded of racecourse bookmakers.

Although farmers had no faith in these commission agents, they still tended to go back to the same one time and again. The auctioneer from B. M. Raman and Sons had a Rexine bag hanging over the front of his gaudy shirt to hold his takings. He told me that tomatoes were selling at fifteen rupees per sack for the smallest, twenty rupees for the next size up, and twenty-five for the large ones. The day before it was even worse. The best price had been twenty rupees because so much produce came into the market.

I couldn't understand the point of the auctions as the produce seemed to go for the same price throughout the market, but the commission agent assured me that the price was established by supply and demand, and auctioning was the best way to work out that equation. He laughed when I told him what the villagers thought of commission agents, 'Oh, they always say we rig the price, but they keep on coming back. If we are so bad why don't they go to the government-run markets?'

'Because they don't have the capacity,' Hemant intervened, 'and there is red-tape there, but they do often get a better price, and the produce is at least weighed. Here no one knows how much there is in a bag or a sack, they can only guess.'

'What about the so-called illegal commission charged to farmers?' I asked.

'They are a tradition and if the government says they should stop, let the government stop them,' replied the auctioneer, impatient by now to get on with the morning's business.

The market was quintessentially Indian. Unmanaged, unmodernized, it functioned only because everyone knew their role, played it without prompting, and allowed others to play theirs. But the Indian system does not achieve a very high level of efficiency and Bangalore's market certainly didn't seem ready to launch Karnataka's vegetables on to the global market.

In spite of the farmers' anger at the prices they were paid for their produce, there was no sign yet of an organized protest in Karnataka. But this was the state which had been at the centre of the farmers' movement in the eighties, a movement in which more than one hundred farmers had been shot by the police, a movement which had brought down one Karnataka government, a movement that had paralysed the administration. So the last time we sat down with Hemant to drink that special form of coffee, the south Indian decoction, I asked why the farmers seemed to be taking their troubles lying down this time.

Hemant thought for some time, twiddling his coffee cup before replying. 'I think the difference is that there were very specific grievances then. In 1979 the government started to demand that we pay water tax, a levy on irrigated land, and then charges for using the water. The farmers couldn't pay even if they wanted to, the demands per acre were more than the farmer would make from that acre.'

'But aren't today's prices a specific grievance too?'

'Yes, but no one seems to believe that even if they protest the government is capable of doing anything about prices. Although it broke up in the end, the farmers' movement was a total success – we never paid those taxes.'

Soft-spoken Hemant was the most mild-mannered of men.

During our travels I had sometimes been impatient with his inability to keep to our schedule. There always seemed to be just one more person he had to meet, one more household we had to call on, before we could move to our next destination. Whenever I put my clumsy foot down and insisted on moving, he smiled, ignored my obvious irritation, and usually we did move on. Even when we didn't, it was just not possible to be angry with Hemant for long, because of that smile – not a superior or a long-suffering smile, just a smile.

I wondered how he had survived in the turmoil of an Indian agitation where everyone is permanently enraged, no one speaks, they only shout, and violence is the first not the last resort.

'We were no pushover, I can tell you,' Hemant assured me. 'During the early eighties I saw how the officials and police treated people and how they extracted corruption. People would come to us with their complaints and we would literally drag the officers before the people. Court-martial them and get them to give the money back. They called us goondas, but even the police were afraid of us.'

'I have only known you for a week but I just can't see you doing that sort of thing.'

'Well, I had one secret. I did hate the police and bureaucracy but I never lost my temper, except on one occasion and that was something different. Late one night I'd heard a woman in my village screaming because she was about to give birth. Her men were away drinking. There was no one else to help and so I carried that lady nearly a kilometre to the road and then hitched a lift in a truck to Navalgund and had her admitted to the civil hospital. The next day I went back and found her lying in the dust in the porch of the hospital, with sweepers sweeping all around her. She had delivered her child and had been thrown out. I went to the doctor and asked, "What is the reason for this?" He was rude and said, "If you are so concerned, start a hospital of your own." I lost my temper, caught him by his collar and took him to the lady. Then I beat him, kicked him, and asked whether he would do the same to his own wife.'

Even telling this story Hemant didn't raise his voice. 'All the staff were telling me to kick him more,' he went on calmly. 'The doctor started crying, then other doctors came, including a lady doctor, and they said, "Don't worry, we will take care of her."'

For all his gentleness, Hemant had been arrested twenty-three times and spent a total of two years in jail during the movement. In a country which has still not turned its back on the ethics and ethos of its colonial rulers, the police used the summary powers of arrest provided under an act the British passed after the First World War to curb the nascent independence movement.

'Repealing that act was one of our demands,' Hemant said, 'but that didn't happen for another ten years. It has gone now, so I suppose that is another success for us.'

I still wanted to know why a once-effective farmers' movement was now so paralysed that it wasn't protesting against their present plight. So I pressed him again.

'You arrested even policemen and dragged them before people's courts, brought about the downfall of Indira Gandhi's chosen chief minister, you defied the administration and never paid those taxes and charges, but what has been the long-term impact of all that; has there been any?'

'Not much, I have to admit. As the movement grew in Karnataka and spread to other states, its hold on the farmers was recognized by politicians, but this is where the trouble came. The politicians wanted to take over the movement and they did this by co-opting our leaders. Many of them made their careers on the backs of the farmers.'

'So it was politics and politicians which broke the movement,' I suggested.

'Well, yes, but the fact is that the farmers respected those of us who did not go into politics. Our mistake was to protect and give our support to political leaders who didn't have direct contact with the people.'

At last a certain urgency entered Hemant's voice. 'Look at India – the tribals rose in protest, the fishermen, the farmers, the weavers, the Dalits, the workers. All over India the mindset is there to protest, but what is the response in the long run? It's appalling.'

'Why is there so little response?'

'Political impotency. We have to address that. For all the protests and risings, local bodies are dens of vested interests, state assemblies are swayed by vested interests, and parliament manipulated by them. The problem is that there is no dialogue between the activists. Every one is fighting on their own line. It's high time for young, cosmopolitan activists to take the lead and begin a process of democratic reforms. I want to start networking with different groups – rural, social, environmental, farmers' organizations, even individuals, and to build them into a team, and my journey has started.'

We both wished him well on his journey, but I have to say if there's one failing Indians do admit to, it's weakness in teamwork.

A Tale of Two Brothers

Delhi has more embassies and high commissions than almost any other capital in the world, all competing with each other for guests to adorn their cocktail and dinner parties. For a journalist seeking to widen his circle of sources, diplomatic functions serve little purpose because guest lists are recycled from one party to the next. During the heyday of Indira Gandhi, the years after her victory over Pakistan and the liberation of Bangladesh, diplomatic drawing rooms and lawns were particularly barren because she was known to frown on the gossip that circulated there. One of her closest confidants – Dinesh Singh, a small but handsome politician of princely origin – was thrown out of the prime minister's charmed circle, known as her 'kitchen cabinet', when she heard that he had been boasting of his proximity to her on the cocktail circuit. Dinesh always insisted that he had never claimed to have had a relationship with Indira Gandhi, and I find it hard to believe that a politician as canny as he was would ever have been so indiscreet, but his banishment served notice to all members of the ruling Congress Party to treat diplomatic invitations with the utmost caution. So it was with some surprise that at the Queen's birthday party on the lawns of the colonial bungalow, which is the official residence of the British High Commissioner, I was introduced to Sant Bux Singh, a Congress member of parliament who had made a name for himself as a speaker on foreign affairs.

On hearing my name, the MP burst into laughter and said, 'Oh, you are the BBC man who is not very popular with our beloved leader.'

I was disconcerted by this direct approach and puzzled that a Congress MP could speak of his leader with even mild sarcasm. Before I could recover, this strange politician said, 'Good company is in short supply in this city. We must get to know each other.'

At that moment Sant Bux's attention was distracted by one of the political operators who haunt such functions, seeking contacts to fix for and contacts to fix through. 'Sant Buxji, we haven't met for many days,' the unctuous apparatchik whined. 'We have so much to talk about. We must meet. There are such essential matters to discuss.'

'No, there are not,' said Sant Bux, dismissing the toady in mid-flow; and saying to me, 'We can't talk here, we'll spend all our time being interrupted by twerps like this, but phone me and come and have a drink one evening.' Giving me a playful smile he moved on to another clump of guests, with his creased, wide pajama trousers, cut in the style of his home city of Allahabad, flapping about his ankles. Defying the dress instructions which decreed formal wear, Sant Bux hadn't bothered to get his kurta pressed either, and his distinctly home-spun Nehru jacket was reddish brown flecked with gold instead of the regulation black.

I rang the next day and was invited that evening to the government flat Sant Bux had been allocated as an MP. Although not a bungalow set in its own garden, the top-of-the-range official accommodation, the ground-floor flat was more spacious than the rooms Sant Bux was to find himself in as his political fortunes declined. A scruffy servant showed me into the room where Sant Bux was sitting, a spittoon by his side and a bottle of Henke's whisky, one of the cheaper and more sugary brands of Indian-made foreign liquor, on a table in front of him. Although Sant Bux took no care about his clothes – he was wearing a stained, creased kurta – he considered himself attractive to women, and maintained that experience had borne this out. His lived-in face was unusual; nothing seemed quite in proportion, not ugly but certainly not conventionally attractive. Heavy-framed spectacles hid his bright brown eyes, which sparkled with humour. Gilly always said it was his personality not his appearance which attracted women to Sant Bux.

He waved me to a chair, emptied his mouth by spitting a red stream of paan into the spittoon and said, 'You must be wondering why I wanted to see you.'

'Well, yes, I suppose I am,' I replied.

'You see, I know all about you, and what I've learnt makes me think you would be someone entertaining to talk to,' he giggled as though we were conspirators. 'I know why Indiraji is angry with you too, and anyone who can make a joke out of the Maruti project must have a sense of humour which is in short supply round here, especially an English sense of humour.'

'Not a very good joke, I'm afraid.'

Sant Bux ignored that and went on, 'I was at Oxford and that's why I want an Englishman to laugh with me. There's nothing more exciting or sinister about my inviting you here. There are no secrets I have to give you, although I might be able to give you a nudge occasionally.'

The Maruti project to manufacture a people's car was causing problems for Indira Gandhi. It was the first challenge to the supremacy of the Hindustan Ambassador, the British Morris Oxford of the late forties which is still manufactured in Calcutta. Under India's particularly virulent form of socialism and central planning, known as the licence-permit raj, no one was allowed to invest in the automobile or any other industry without the government's permission. This led to crony capitalism, with some industrialists managing to bribe their way to a licence and others paying to have potential competitors frustrated. Inevitably, therefore, eyebrows were raised when Indira's younger son, Sanjay, was given a much-sought-after licence to manufacture a people's car, named after the son of the wind god Maruti. But fortunately for the Ambassador, and unfortunately for the people of India, Maruti, far from going like the wind, was at this time still going nowhere. Sanjay's limited experience, an unfinished apprenticeship at Rolls-Royce in Crewe, was insufficient for the task he'd set himself. This was embarrassing his mother and so I wasn't surprised when her spokesman protested about my reporting that the opposition were saying the people's car should be called 'ma roti' which means 'the mother is crying' rather than Maruti.

Sant Bux agreed it wasn't a very good joke. 'I think I might have done better if you'd come to me,' he said. 'But it is typical of the sycophancy surrounding Indira that you should have been hauled in for something so slight as that. We Congressmen are meant to believe that Indira is a goddess who can do no wrong, so I suppose your joke was blasphemy.'

I was to discover that Sant Bux was rarely bitter, just mildly sarcastic. When I asked him how he put up with this stifling atmosphere in the Congress Party he replied with one of his wry smiles.

'As a Congressman I am expected to believe that Indira gets her mandate from God, the divine right of Nehrus. Well, I believe in God but I don't believe in Indira, so where does that leave me as a Hindu? Socialism is my party's creed and so I am supposed to believe that my government's mandate comes from the people, but seeing my fellow MPs, I can't believe in the people, so where does that leave me as a politician? But there is nowhere else to go, all the other parties are even more half-baked, and who knows, I might be able to do some good here.'

By this time, the glow of Indira Gandhi's victory in 1971, the surrender of the Pakistan Army and the creation of Bangladesh, was fading fast. Maruti was not the only questionable deal to corrode the Iron Lady's image. The economy was in trouble too, with the world oil price rise and the constraints of the licence-permit raj, the burden of unproductive nationalized industries, and a disastrous attempt to take over the trade in food grains at a time when India was already suffering from drought and a shortage of food.

Many of Indira's problems arose from her socialism, and so I asked Sant Bux, 'Doesn't the present mess undermine your faith in socialism?'

'You might think so, but Indira doesn't understand the difference between socialism and populism. For her what matters is that she gives the poor the impression that she is on their side, that she is serious about her election slogan, *garibi hatao*, eradicate poverty, even though her policies may actually be increasing poverty.'

'So is it all a fraud?'

'No, I wouldn't exactly say that. You only have to watch Indira at an election meeting and you can see she has a remarkable rapport with the poor, especially poor women, and there must be something

genuine about that. I think part of her problem is that she doesn't
see any alternative to this populist socialism, and her advisers don't
have the balls to tell her she is wrong. They always say she is the only
man in the Congress Party.'

I already felt sufficiently confident about our friendship to ask,
'Where does that leave you, neutered too?'

That provoked a high-pitched laugh and a splutter before he
replied, 'Not a *hijra* but on the sidelines.'

Sant Bux and I found we had much in common. He loved to
talk of his days at Oxford where he became a friend of Zulfikar Ali
Bhutto, the Prime Minister of Pakistan who was eventually executed.
He used to say, 'Zulfi was always too clever by half.' Oxford, and later
Lincoln's Inn, left their mark on Sant Bux's humour, and his attitude
towards authority accorded with the attitude I had never grown out
of since my days as a rebellious schoolboy and undergraduate in
England. We shared too a deep interest in politics, and loved the
gossip which went with it. Then there was religion, and it was Sant
Bux who first opened my mind to the richness of Indian philosophy.
We looked at God through the bottom of many glasses of Indian
whisky.

The crisis facing Indira Gandhi deepened. She attempted to revive
her image as the Iron Lady, the indisputable leader of the nation,
by crushing a national railway strike ruthlessly, and ordering India's
first nuclear test, but she was unable to stem the tide of opinion
and events running against her. India's economic plight forced her
into a humiliating surrender to the World Bank and IMF, which
insisted that she backtrack on some of her socialist policies before
they would bail her out of a balance of payments crisis. The veteran
socialist Jayaprakash Narayan, known simply as JP, who was seen by
many as Mahatma Gandhi's successor, was gathering more and more
support for his campaign against corruption. He was accusing Indira
Gandhi of 'raping democracy', and calling for 'total revolution'.
The march on parliament he led was described by Inder Malhotra,
a journalist Indira Gandhi herself respected, as 'one of the biggest
demonstrations the capital has ever seen'.

All this was heady stuff for journalists. We are not immune to personal feelings and I have to admit I was not sorry that Indira Gandhi was being taught that she couldn't take the Indian people for granted. But Sant Bux, who was no great admirer of Indira Gandhi, saw the dangers to democracy in all this excitement. During one of many evenings we spent together he said, 'The JP movement has got out of hand. It amounts to bringing the people out on the streets to pull the government down, and that should be done through the ballot box. This is going to have grave consequences whichever way it ends.'

'But JP says he doesn't want to drive her from power, that he's willing and indeed anxious to face her in an election.'

'At the same time he is calling for "total revolution". What does that mean? You tell me, and don't all revolutions end in making things worse? You are a student of theology. You know about the unclean spirit going out of a man only to be replaced by seven others and the last state of that man is worse than the first.'

I had to agree with Sant Bux. I have always believed in evolution rather than revolution and JP had certainly not spelt out what he would do with India once he'd swept Indira away.

The crisis came to a head in 1975. Violent demonstrations against corruption had forced her to dissolve the assembly in the state of Gujarat even though her party had not lost its majority in the assembly. She imposed President's Rule, that is rule from Delhi, and resisted the demand to hold an election for fear of a defeat which would undermine her invincible reputation. But then her archenemy Morarji Desai, a veteran colleague of her father she had dismissed as finance minister during the crisis which had split the Congress Party six years earlier, went on hunger strike demanding elections in Gujarat. Morarji was a Gujarati, as stern a self-disciplinarian as his guru and fellow Gujarati, Mahatma Gandhi. Some argued that he was principled, others that he was stubborn. Whoever was right, Indira knew the octogenarian was capable of carrying his fast to the end and so, rather than risk bearing the blame for that, she accepted defeat and called the election. The day the results from Gujarat came in, showing that the Indira magic did not always work, a judge of the Allahabad High Court found her guilty of minor breaches of the electoral law. The judge declared the prime minister's own election null and void and debarred her from any elected office for six years. An approach to the Supreme Court resulted in a temporary compromise which allowed Indira to stay in power until the appeal against the Allahabad judgment was heard but banned her from voting in parliament. JP and Morarji still demanded vociferously that she resign and Indira decided enough was enough. She arrested both of them along with many other prominent politicians, including some from her own party, and declared a State of Emergency.

Even more frenzied sycophancy became the order of the day in the Congress Party. To question the Emergency even in private was gross disobedience and there were spies everywhere to report back to the prime minister's coterie, now overtly dominated by her younger son, the would-be car maker Sanjay. But when I phoned Sant Bux to ask whether we could still meet he said, 'Of course. It'll be even more fun. I'll have plenty to tell you.'

When I next went to Sant Bux's flat, I found the tea cosy over the telephone. 'Must be careful about bugging,' he said. I wasn't quite sure whether to take him seriously or not.

Pouring out a glass of whisky for me, he went on, 'Do you know you were nearly given a good bottom spanking, when the Emergency was declared?'

I didn't know, and so Sant Bux went on to tell me how one of Indira Gandhi's most trusted advisors had summoned the information minister and ordered him to 'Send for Mark Tully, pull down his trousers, give him a few lashes, and send him to jail. He has reported that a senior cabinet minister has resigned in protest against the Emergency.' The information minister was the mild-mannered Inder Gujral who, many years later, became prime minister for a short time. Fortunately for me, he first checked All India Radio's monitoring reports and found no evidence of that report and so went to Indira Gandhi who told him to ignore the order. But Gujral paid a price. He was considered too soft to handle the press the way the Emergency demanded and was dismissed.

Gujral was replaced by Vidya Charan Shukla, the tall, imposing

son of one of the stalwart chief ministers of the Nehru days. Sant
Bux knew him well. 'Vidya is a bit of an ass,' he said. 'He does
not have the political skills of his father, they've got lost somewhere
on the way. But he is dreadfully ambitious and will do anything to
push his career. I can't imagine he'll do Indira's reputation any good.
What she needs is tactful, skilful handling of the press. Old Vidya is
already behaving like a *thanedar* in charge of a police station.'

Vidya Charan did soon become known as Indira Gandhi's
Goebbels. He enforced strict censorship and from the start was
determined to show that he could control the foreign as well as the
Indian press. With the BBC's vast listenership to its Hindi and other
Indian language services, I became a prime target. It was Sant Bux
who told me the information minister was telling Sanjay I was a spy.

'Do you know why?' he asked.

'No.'

'Because you have tried to learn Hindi,' he replied, coughing and
spluttering with laughter.

When he'd recovered himself he went on, 'What an idiot. You
a spy! I suppose I'd be one of your agents, perhaps Vidya thinks I
am. A fine pair we'd make, neither of us would be able to keep our
mouths shut. Anyhow your Hindi would need a lot of improvement
for you to be a spy.'

Sant Bux also greatly enjoyed the time when I was summoned
early one morning by Vidya Charan to explain how only the BBC
had come to know that a bomb had exploded in the compound
of one of All India Radio's stations. The minister was somewhat
crestfallen when I told him, 'We haven't come to know, but now
that you have told me about it I will broadcast the news.'

'There you are,' Sant Bux said. 'Vidya has been caught in a mess of
his own making. Because people can't get reliable news they believe
every rumour that's doing the rounds. The rumours get recycled by
the intelligence people, so the government comes to believe them
too. Some intelligence idiot must have told Vidya you'd broadcast
news of that bomb.'

Sant Bux was right. What made matters even more complicated
for Vidya Charan and me was that one common way of giving

rumours some authenticity was to claim they'd been heard on the BBC.

After a month or so Vidya Charan ran out of patience and ordered the expulsion of all those foreign correspondents who refused to sign an agreement to abide by the censorship, which was so strict that you couldn't even report what the opposition said in parliament. The BBC rightly refused to allow me to sign and so I was given twenty-four hours to get out of the country. Sant Bux came to the impromptu party I held on the night that I left. In the eighteen months I was back in London, I often remembered the assurance he gave me as I was leaving for the airport, 'Don't worry. This lunacy can't last. You will be back.'

What depressed Sant Bux most in the early days of the Emergency was the sycophancy which it was assumed, whether rightly or wrongly, that Indira and Sanjay demanded. He was appalled when the Congress Party president said, 'India is Indira and Indira is India.' The president, Dev Kanta Barooah, was also well-read and highly intelligent, and Sant Bux had always thought of him as one of the more congenial members of his party. 'I can't understand how Dev Kanta can bring himself to say that,' Sant Bux had said to me. 'He read history and he must know that he'll go down in history as a prize ass.'

Barooah's words have indeed gone down in history.

Sant Bux had pride and self-respect, and was never going to fit into what came to be known as 'Congress culture', which was shorthand for dishonest flattery of the Nehru family representative who happened to be leading the party at the time. He was born into the family of a minor raja who ruled over a landed estate in northern India and, for all his socialism, Sant Bux never entirely threw off his feudal upbringing.

One of the people who understood him best was Maurice Zinkin, his boss when he joined the Indian subsidiary of Unilever after returning from Oxford and Lincoln's Inn. Zinkin had been one of the last recruits to the elite Indian Civil Service, or ICS, before Independence and with his knowledge and experience of India, had not surprisingly been sent back when he joined Unilever. He described Sant Bux as 'a combination of regal outlook and leftist beliefs, a sort of Stafford Cripps'. Like me, he also remembered Sant Bux as a conversationalist. Zinkin once said to me, 'Of all the sales managers, he was very much the one my wife and I enjoyed talking to on equal terms.' He insisted that Sant Bux had never been sycophantic. Zinkin had admired him for his 'detached intelligence' and believed he would have become a director of Hindustan Lever if he had not been lured away by politics.

When Indira Gandhi had first come to power she had used Sant Bux's detached intelligence to make effective speeches on foreign policy for her in parliament. During her battle with Morarji and the old guard for control of the Congress Party, she listened to Sant Bux's honest advice but, by the time the Emergency was declared, she demanded attached intelligence, and would not listen to independent counsel.

Still, Sant Bux could never bring himself to acknowledge that there was no hope for independent-minded politicians in Indira's government. For all his detachment, all his disapproval of sycophancy, his insistence on honesty, and his refusal to flatter, he did hanker after office. He sent Devendranath Dwivedi, a close friend, to see Kamlapati Tripathi, one of the few Congress veterans Indira still trusted. Dwivedi later told us that when he asked the veteran to suggest Sant Bux's name to Indira for a post in her government, Kamlapati had asked, 'Does Sant Bux need your recommendation? Doesn't he know me well enough to come directly?'

Dwivedi had replied, 'He insisted that I should approach you. He's not very good at doing this sort of thing.'

Indira was looking for a replacement for Dinesh Singh, the raja who had unwisely allowed rumours to circulate about his relationship with her. Kamlapati thought Sant Bux would be an ideal candidate because he came from the same feudal caste and background and the same state. When he raised the matter with the prime minister, she said, 'Yes, but doesn't he have a younger brother?'

Kamlapati was shocked. 'But,' he protested, 'there is no comparison between Sant Bux and Vishwanath Pratap. Sant Bux is a good speaker, English-educated, competent, experienced. His brother is a novice.'

Indira replied, 'I need a novice.'

According to Dwivedi, Kamlapati's protest only strengthened Indira's resolve. Insecurity was an important part of her personality. She thought Sant Bux was too smart for her to handle. So she wanted a man less independent-minded and Vishwanath fitted the bill.

One of Indira Gandhi's biographers described her when a young woman as 'an odd figure of loneliness and self-reliance'. Hers was the loneliness born of a childhood and youth separated from her father by his long periods in jail, unhappy about his apparent lack of concern for her mother, witnessing her mother's pain as tuberculosis slowly claimed her, never having the chance to establish herself at any one school or university and form the lifelong friendships which are made in those days. To that loneliness was later added the experience of her days when her father was prime minister. She ran his household and became involved in his politics too, which led her to believe you could trust no one. When she herself was chosen to lead the Congress Party she knew she'd only been given the job because the old leaders thought she would be like putty in their hands. But at the same time she knew her position was unique and felt that she had a right to rule. When she was facing her first general election after splitting the Congress Party and driving out many powerful leaders, she told a journalist, 'The issue is me.' And Indira Gandhi saw to it that she remained the issue until she died.

It wasn't therefore surprising that Indira Gandhi preferred the novice she assumed would be malleable, to the politician she knew from experience was too honest to hold his tongue when he felt she was going wrong, who was too intelligent to subscribe to her one-issue politics. But in the end it was Vishwanath's honesty that would bring Indira Gandhi's family down.

Sant Bux had brought his brother into politics. He once told the author of an unflattering biography of Vishwanath, 'I just took him along with me to Mrs Gandhi and told her this is Vishwanath, my younger brother, and he wants a ticket for the Uttar Pradesh assembly, and she said all right.'

During the Emergency, while Sant Bux sat at home, with that tea cosy firmly clamped on his telephone so that the heresies he uttered didn't reach the ears of Indira's spies. Vishwanath on the other hand remained deputy commerce minister and was even promoted to minister of state just before the end of the Emergency. Inevitably his enemies accused him of surviving by joining in the sycophantic chorus singing the praises of Indira and Sanjay. Vishwanath, however, has always strongly denied this, pointing out that he was a member of a group of Congressmen who had the courage to tell Indira Gandhi it was unconstitutional and politically unwise to extend the life of parliament during the Emergency. He was never a member of the inner circle surrounding Sanjay. In a small spartan office in an outbuilding of the VIP bungalow in what remains of Lutyens's New Delhi, where he is entitled to live as a former prime minister, he said to us, 'Singing praises of the leader is part of Congress culture and it is one thing to play that game. Politically also I was loyal to her; that I had promised to myself because she had brought me into politics. But when it came to one's conscience and wrong administrative actions I wouldn't do it.'

I first met Vishwanath with Sant Bux just after Indira Gandhi had called a general election and I had been allowed to return to Delhi. He had come to ask for advice about the seat he should ask for. Sant Bux, with foresight, said, 'I shouldn't bother too much. We are all going to get trounced after what Sanjay has done with his family planning campaign in the Emergency.' Vishwanath in those days was very much the younger brother. His was certainly not a lived-in face, there was something unformed about him, unsure. He looked as though he was in constant fear of something dreadful happening, and his sharp intake of breath indicated that he felt something dreadful had indeed happened when his brother criticized Sanjay in front of a journalist.

Unlike Sant Bux, Vishwanath was not sociable, nor was he confident in company. He was born to the raja's second wife and had a lonely childhood, being adopted by the rajah of a neighbouring estate who had no son of his own. Sant Bux often said, 'Vishwanath is no one's. He has no loyalties because of his adoption.'

Sant Bux's skill lay in dealing with people. Vishwanath's political capital was a justifiable reputation for honesty in financial matters, which was eventually to carry him to that victory over the Nehru family and then on to the prime ministership. He was young when he started to build his reputation for honesty by distributing all the lands he had inherited from his adopted father to the landless. There is room for some scepticism about this move. Much of the land was barren, the estate was mortgaged up to the hilt, and new legislation abolishing large estates would have meant adopting complicated and questionable legal tactics to hold on to many of the acres he had inherited. But at the same time it has to be said that Vishwanath was never someone to bother unduly about property or living standards. An admirer of his showed me the government bungalow in Delhi he moved out of when he became prime minister. With his influence he could have persuaded the public works department to do something about the leaking taps, the exposed wires, the damp patches and the dilapidated decoration, but he hadn't bothered.

Although Vishwanath never saw himself as a *darbari*, or courtier, of Indira Gandhi he did become one of her favourites. He told us, 'She pampered me.' He continued to nurture his reputation for honesty, always refusing any donation to election funds which could possibly be described as 'tainted'. Lying in Delhi's most prestigious private hospital strapped to a dialysis machine, he admitted it had all been a bit of a farce. 'I would not take money myself, but I would say, "If you want, give to the party." Politicians started from hypocrisy by making false declarations to the election commissioner about their expenses. After all, it's not much to say you don't take money yourself. You can't stand on a high pedestal as long as elections are funded by non-accounted money. Perhaps you don't use that money yourself, but you know it is being used.'

When Indira Gandhi chose him to be the chief minister of her home state, Uttar Pradesh, one of the most prestigious positions in Indian politics, he had to get elected to the state assembly. He told us with a wry smile how, during that election campaign, he'd banned his workers travelling in jeeps, telling them to use motorcycles or bicycles. He himself travelled by bus. He then went on to admit, 'I didn't risk losing by these economies. I had the biggest attraction going for me because everyone wanted to have the chief minister as their MLA, thinking that he would do a lot for the constituency. No political party put up a candidate against me and I won ninety-eight per cent of the vote. So that election can't be counted in expense terms.'

In a later and much more hard-fought election for the parliamentary seat of Allahabad, Vishwanath very publicly stated that all the expenditure was being met by the people. He even set up a stall at his house so that workers had to pay for their own tea. The only concession he made was to serve free tea late at night.

As chief minister, Vishwanath promised to eliminate criminal gangs plaguing the countryside by a certain date. The police had some considerable successes, but when the date had passed there were two attacks by gangs in which sixteen people were killed. Six of the dead were Dalits, the former Untouchables. Vishwanath sent his resignation to the governor and immediately informed the press, without telling Indira Gandhi first. He thus gained the reputation of being one politician who admitted to his failure and did not cling to his 'chair' until he was pushed off it, a politician who put honour before office. Political gossips maintained that he only got up from his chair because he was going to be pushed, that Indira Gandhi was about to sack him. She had been embarrassed by the many allegations about the police killing innocent people in what they called encounters with dacoits. Vishwanath, however, told us he didn't inform Indira Gandhi he was quitting because she would have said 'no'. Although denying that he resigned to boost his reputation, he did tell us, 'I had a massive response from the people after I stepped down.'

I remember Sant Bux's words at the time: 'My brother is growing up. From the boy who wouldn't say boo to a goose, let alone Indira, he's gone to the man who has challenged her authority, he's committed lese-majesty by resigning without asking her permission.'

Indira was reported to be livid that Vishwanath had put his principles before loyalty to her, but his gamble paid off. She still needed him to balance the caste equations of her cabinet and so appointed him commerce minister. There was a problem about that. The commerce minister, with his dealings with businessmen and industrialists was expected to be one of the party's main fundraisers. However, as Vishwanath explained to us, an exception was made in his case.

'When Rajiv called me to say that Indira wanted to induct me into the cabinet, I asked which ministry. He replied, "Commerce." I just looked at him. He understood and said, "You don't have to raise funds", and Indira left it like that.'

Unlike most Indian politicians Vishwanath didn't allow the interests of his family to interfere with his politics. It was one of his relatives, a close associate of Sanjay, who recommended him for the job of Uttar Pradesh chief minister, but Vishwanath refused to take that relative into his cabinet for fear of being branded a nepotist. When the Congress Party didn't give Sant Bux a ticket in the 1980 election which brought Indira Gandhi back to power less than three years after her stunning post-Emergency defeat, Vishwanath didn't come to his rescue for the same reason. It has been suggested, although never by Sant Bux, that Vishwanath actively lobbied against Sant Bux. Vishwanath himself denied this, saying that Sant Bux had already burnt his boats by not displaying the loyalty Indira Gandhi expected when she was out of power. He said the Congress president who had declared 'India is Indira and Indira is India' sidelined his brother. Sant Bux's friend Dwivedi said, 'If VP did play a role in his not getting a ticket, it was a low key role.'

At the time we suspected that Vishwanath might not have wanted Sant Bux's career to revive because he feared he would be outshone. Looking back on his life from that hospital bed, Vishwanath did admit, 'In our family we received intelligence in the same order as we were born. He had a very good sense of humour, and a talent for human relations. There was an element of envy, I have to admit, as so often happens between brothers. It's the younger brother who envies.' Vishwanath insisted, 'I would never overtly or covertly have done anything to harm Sant Bux but neither of us was perfect. Perhaps when questions of open support came, after the Emergency something crept in.'

But Vishwanath maintained that Sant Bux himself was largely to blame for the failure of his career. 'In Indian politics you have to do a lot of footwork,' he explained. 'Someone once told me, earlier the kingdom was in the crown, now it's in the sole of the shoe. The more you wear it down the more you will go forward. You have to do a lot of running around among the people, leaders, decision makers and darbaris – what you would call now networking. I used to ask him, why do you sit at home? Either write – you write beautifully – or you must run about, have a mass base, go to the people. Any leader you can impress if you have a mass base, otherwise you are entirely dependent on their mercy.'

At that time Sant Bux's home was Western Court, whose apartments were reserved for members of parliament. From the outside, Western Court still had all the appearances of a splendid colonial classical-style building, which sat well in the heart of the capital city the British built just in time to house the viceroy and his entourage before they wound up the imperial enterprise. But when you got inside Western Court, it was dingy, dirty, and down at heel. Sant Bux's small apartment was probably more shambolic than most because he didn't care about his surroundings or indeed, as mentioned earlier, his appearance. His wardrobe consisted almost entirely of crumpled white shirts and pajama trousers. When he took out his winter Nehru jackets they were full of holes. He would sit there of an evening with his bottle of Indian whisky on one side of the chair and his spittoon on the other. Even when I was away Gilly would often go to spend an evening with Sant Bux who delighted in speculating about the rumours that regular visits by a young, blonde woman might generate.

During our evenings together we would often talk about Vishwanath. Gilly and I both used to tell him that he would never get back into parliament as long as Vishwanath had influence in the Congress Party. I remember once saying, 'Vishwanath would dance naked in the street if it was required to prove his honesty and so he's not going to do anything to help a brother and risk being accused of nepotism. Rather the reverse, he will do what he can to keep you out.'

Sant Bux could never bring himself to accept that Vishwanath might block the revival of his political career, but he was too proud to test his brother by asking for help.

When Indira was assassinated and Rajiv succeeded, Vishwanath's career went up another notch. He was promoted to the finance ministry. There his campaign to clean up the Indian business world led eventually to a break with Rajiv Gandhi. As the minister in charge of the income tax department he started investigating the accounts of some of the most prominent family-run industrial houses. The industrialist Lalit Thapar was arrested, which did not amuse Rajiv Gandhi as he was the chairman of the board of governors of the Doon School – the Eton of India where Indira Gandhi had sent both her sons. There was outrage when the eighty-four-year-old S. L. Kirloskar, one of India's most respected industrialists, was interrogated from six o'clock in the evening until four o'clock the next morning. He complained, 'I have been publicly crucified even before being brought to stand trial.' But what finally induced Rajiv to step in was a report that Vishwanath had started investigating the business affairs of Amitabh Bachchan. He was 'the biggest ever' star of the Bombay film industry, and a longstanding friend of Rajiv who had just brought him into politics. Vishwanath told us he had not started investigating Amitabh Bach-chan. The report, he said, was put about by those who were aggrieved by Vishwanath and wanted to discredit him with Rajiv. Rajiv was in a jam. He couldn't sack Vishwanath without being accused of covering up for his friend and risking his own clean reputation, and so he transferred him to the defence ministry – not a very sensible move as it gave Vishwanath the opportunity to look into the murky world of arms deals.

Within a few months of crossing over from the finance ministry in the north block of the grandiose pink sandstone secretariat, to the defence ministry in the south block, Vishwanath learnt from the Indian ambassador in Germany that an Indian agent had been paid seven per cent in commission on a submarine deal. He announced an inquiry without consulting Rajiv. The prime minister first tried to get the home minister, Umashankar Dixit, to rein in his overzealous defence minister. Vishwanath described that meeting.

'Dixitji was far senior to me in the party, but he came from my state and was always fond of me. That day, however, he was very angry. "You don't understand what you are doing," he told me. "You are doing wrong." Waving his walking stick at me he went on, "You know I can't walk without a stick and you want to take away that stick. You are not so innocent not to know that the whole political system doesn't run without money." I couldn't make much of a reply except to stick to my point, which was that Rajiv himself had said there should be no middlemen, no agents, in defence deals.'

When the elder statesman Dixit failed to move Vishwanath, the prime minister summoned him. He remembered that meeting vividly. 'Rajiv was so enraged that he was red in the face. He asked how I knew the telex from the ambassador was correct. I said, how do I know it's wrong? It came through the correct channels in code, if it's not correct then it will come out in the inquiry.'

Rajiv then wanted to know what the result of the inquiry would be. Vishwanath's rather unsatisfactory reply was, 'If there is a dead body there has to be an inquiry.' Rajiv then changed tack and suggested Vishwanath should consider the international implications of the inquiry, saying that the manufacturing company had paid many heads of state and might go bust if it started revealing names, to which Vishwanath replied, 'My charge is not to run this company but to see that government orders are implemented.'

Vishwanath had always turned to Sant Bux for advice when he reached a crossroads in his career. I kept in close touch with Sant Bux during this crisis, and learned that he'd told Vishwanath, 'You can't go back on the inquiry without ruining the reputation you have for being a crusader against corruption, so you only have two alternatives. Either you stay on and allow yourself to be thrown out, or you search your heart, and if you think you have it in you to become prime minister, resign in good time.' Vishwanath did resign and did become prime minister, ending the reign of the dynasty he'd once served with such loyalty.

Vishwanath's departure from the cabinet couldn't have been better timed. Only four days after his resignation, Swedish Radio broadcast a story alleging that the armaments manufacturer Bofors had bribed politicians, army officers and bureaucrats, to secure a deal for what was known as 'shoot and scoot' artillery. That was the beginning of the Bofors scandal, which was to dog Rajiv until his death. Nothing was proved against him but the opposition was able to mount an effective campaign alleging that a family friend of Rajiv and his wife had been paid a commission in the Bofors deal and that Rajiv himself was covering this up. Vishwanath remained within the Congress Party, protesting his loyalty to the prime minister, denying that he thought Rajiv was involved in the Bofors deal, but at the same time addressing meetings around the country at which he demanded enquiries into the Bofors affair and information on Swiss bank accounts. He did nothing to stop his supporters at these meetings shouting, 'Desh ka neta kaisa ho, V. P. Singh jaisa ho!' – 'What kind of national leader do we need? One like V. P. Singh!' Once again Sant Bux advised him that he would have to resign, this time from the Congress, or make a humiliating retreat that would end his career for good. But Vishwanath waited to be pushed out, and Rajiv eventually obliged him by doing so. This gave him a martyr's crown.

Vishwanath's reputation for honesty, his apparent lack of ambition as evidenced by his resignations from office, together with a wave of sympathy because he had been expelled from the Congress Party, now paid dividends. To the dismay of the politicians who had been with the opposition all along, Vishwanath, the latecomer, overtook their popularity and rapidly emerged as the public's choice as the alternative prime minister.

Realizing that Vishwanath's only asset was his reputation for honesty, the Congress Party did all it could to make mud stick to his Teflon kurta. One morning, his brother summoned Gilly and me. We found him sitting in the smallest room of the latest MP's flat he had managed to borrow, the sunshine highlighting the dust on the table which was littered with the books he had taken out from the parliament library. He greeted us with a hoot of laughter strangled by his trying to keep his mouth shut so that we were not splattered with paan.

After getting rid of the paan, he leant back in his chair and asked us with a self-satisfied smile, 'Well, don't you want to know why I have asked you to come round at this time of the day?' We both nodded intently.

'Last night the telephone rang and when I picked it up a voice the other end said' – and he imitated a deep voice – '"Have you recognized me? I have recognized you. I need to see you right away." It was the voice of a senior cabinet minister.'

Remembering that he had drunk two whiskies and knowing the minister's hypocrisy, he asked whether he needed to come straight away, wouldn't tomorrow morning do? But the minister insisted. So, chewing another paan to disguise the smell of alcohol, he set off for the minister's office. There he was told he would be rewarded with a seat in the upper house of parliament if he signed the document the minister had produced. It was a statement acknowledging that he, Sant Bux Singh, knew his brother had undeclared accounts in foreign banks. At that moment another man entered the room and Sant Bux recognized him as a 'moneybag'. He got up from his chair, told the minister, 'If you want to fight Vishwanath, you must fight him politically,' folded his hands in a *namaskar* and left the room.

After that crude attempt to corrupt him, Sant Bux felt free of any obligation to the Congress, but he had still not joined Vishwanath's party. Sant Bux was thinking, 'How can I join my brother's Janata Dal?' and Vishwanath was thinking, 'Why hasn't he joined me when I am fighting the battle of my life?' To break this deadlock between two brothers too proud to ask each other for anything which might smack of a favour, I, for the only time in my BBC career, deserted the role of observer to become a participant briefly in Indian politics. I felt there was nothing wrong in trying to help a friend who I knew would never be in a position to do me a favour, nor would he do one if he could. So I suggested to him that I should

speak to Devi Lal, the powerful leader of a farmer's party from the
state of Haryana just outside Delhi, a party which he had merged
with the Janata Dal. Sant Bux was too proud to approach Devi Lal
himself but he was happy for me to do so.

Devi Lal was often known as Chaudhuri Sahib, the title given to
a village headman. He was a politician who made no pretensions
to sophistication, and was proud of his rustic background. As a
result most political correspondents wrote him off as a country
bumpkin. But I found Devi Lal's straightforwardness refreshing
and I admired the way he had maintained his links with the
villagers of Haryana even when he was chief minister of the state.
Whenever I've asked about Devi Lal in a Haryana village I've been
told, 'He is the only politician who doesn't come to beg for our
votes at election time, and then we don't see him until the next
election. Chaudhuri Sahib comes to the villages often and sits on a
charpoy and talks to us.'

Devi Lal had played a key role in bringing the quarrelsome
opposition to Rajiv Gandhi together to form the Janata Dal. He'd
had plenty of experience in dealing with politicians who were loyal
to no one except themselves. Politicians in Haryana were known as
'aaya Ram, gaya Ram', here today gone tomorrow. They formed and
broke parties without any thought for policy or principle. Fulfilling
personal ambitions and taking revenge on enemies were what
mattered. Devi Lal himself was sometimes described as a shunting
engine because he was a renowned breaker and maker of parties
but once he had shunted politicians into a new political formation
someone else usually pushed him aside and pulled the train out of
the station. Nevertheless he hadjust routed the Congress in elections
to the state assembly and ensured that this time he became chief
minister of Haryana.

We had first come to know Devi Lal well when he was robbed of
the chief ministership on a previous occasion, and had called a rally
to protest. Driving to the rally we were overtaken by a very small Fiat
filled with a large Chaudhuri Sahib bulging out of the back window,
arms flailing to flag us down.

We stopped and walked over to Devi Lal who growled, 'Come

with me. I want you to report what the government has done to prevent my people getting to Chandigarh to attend the rally.'

Without waiting for our reply, Devi Lal ordered his driver, 'Go!' The Fiat's engine roared, bald tyres spun, and Devi Lal hurtled away in a cloud of dust. We followed along the mercifully straight and reasonably well-maintained tree-lined highways of Haryana until Devi Lal's Fiat pulled up abruptly at a line of trailers attached to tractors the police had immobilized by pouring sand and broken glass into their petrol tanks.

Our next stop was a small fort on a hilltop, which was now a police station. Outside, tractors with their lights smashed and their tyres deflated stood in disarray. As we walked through the archway into the courtyard a shout went up: 'Chaudhuri Devi Lal zindabad!' and Devi Lal found himself surrounded by supporters who had been arrested on their way to the rally. The officer in charge of the police station came out and seeing Devi Lal, rushed towards him, head bowed hands folded. 'Chaudhuri Sahib, please forgive me. I was under orders,' he pleaded.

Devi Lal, a formidable figure more than six foot tall with the rugged features of a north Indian farmer, towered over the diminutive police officer. 'Idiot! You think I will never be chief minister again?' he bellowed. 'Just you wait. I will show you!'

'Please sir, one request,' entreated the representative of the law, by now sweating profusely.

'What do you mean, request? Shut up, and let these people go immediately, right now, at once.'

'But, sir, one request, it was an order, not my responsibility.'

'Shut up, I told you, and let these people go. You wait, I will remember your name.'

'Sir, sir, pardon me, not my fault. I was given ...'

But Devi Lal wasn't having any of it. He cut the terrified police officer short with yet another 'Shut up!' turned on his heels and marched out of the police station followed by his supporters.

When Sant Bux agreed that I could approach the formidable farmers' leader, Devi Lal was 'camping' in Delhi, an expression which goes back to the days when British officials in the districts were under orders to spend a certain percentage of their time travelling and that involved camping. Devi Lal had set up his 'tent' in Haryana Bhavan, the state guest house. From there he was playing a crucial role in planning the election strategy of the Janata Dal, and, importantly from Sant Bux's point of view, in the selection of candidates. When I went to see him he had just returned from a meeting to discuss the party's manifesto, which had not entertained him greatly.

'I am not good at this table work,' he told me. 'Do you know, I've lost count of all the many elections I have fought, but I can assure you of one thing. I have never read a single manifesto.'

We both roared with laughter and then I went on, diffidently, to approach the matter of a ticket for Sant Bux. Devi Lal put me at ease. 'Don't feel shy in making such a request. There is nothing wrong in trying to help a friend. I have heard that he is a good man, and his brother should look after him. But if he won't, why shouldn't I?'

A few days later I was woken about six o'clock in the morning by the telephone. I picked it up to hear the gravelly voice of Devi Lal say, 'Mark Tully Sahib, your work is done. Come down here right away.'

So I went to have a breakfast of curd, parathas, and vegetable curry with Chaudhuri Sahib and be told that Sant Bux had been given his old seat of Fatehpur, between Allahabad and Kanpur. I drove straight to Sant Bux who was now staying in another MP's apartment, and hammered on the door. A half-asleep servant appeared and pleaded nervously with me not to insist that he wake up Sant Bux so early, but I did insist. When Sant Bux eventually appeared, I simply repeated Chaudhuri Sahib's words, 'Your work is done.'

At first, all seemed to be going well. I heard from other sources that Fatehpur had indeed been allocated to Sant Bux. There was talk of the money he was to be given by party headquarters and he himself made an appearance on the platform of an election rally in Delhi. But then once again I was summoned to Haryana Bhavan early in the morning. A grumpy Chaudhuri Sahib asked me, 'What sort of a man is that Vishwanath Pratap Singh, who would cut his own brother's ticket?'

'Meaning what?' I asked.

'Meaning that Vishwanath Pratap Singh has not only cut Sant Bux Singh's name, he has taken Fatehpur for himself. At first when Sant Bux's name came up in the discussion he said, "Let's think about it, think about it," but eventually it became clear that he was not going to have his brother's name on the list.'

'To save his own reputation I suppose.'

'What sort of reputation does a man deserve who doesn't help his own brother? That is a question of honour.'

Chaudhuri Sahib also spoke to Sant Bux and told him he would continue to make efforts on his behalf, but it was all to no avail.

Sant Bux never rang Vishwanath to complain, to argue or fight with him. If he had done he would have learnt that Vishwanath had made it clear to his colleagues from the beginning that he wanted to fight from Fatehpur because it would be safe for him. He was from the feudal Thakur caste which dominated the constituency and was almost a local boy. Vishwanath's own election had to be guaranteed so that he would be free to campaign in the rest of the country. Once again a misunderstanding was created between the two brothers by their refusal to ask favours of each other. Sant Bux was deeply hurt by this but he felt there was only one course open to him. 'I am going to Fatehpur,' he told us, 'to campaign.' Then he paused before continuing, 'I am going to campaign for Vishwanath. I am going to shame him.'

Sant Bux did campaign, but there was little or no evidence that he shamed his brother.

Rajiv Gandhi failed to win a majority, and refused to attempt to break the opposition, which might well not have been too difficult as future events were to show. The president asked the Janata Dal to try to form a government. For Vishwanath it had been a one-issue campaign. He presented himself as a crusader against corruption and everywhere he went his supporters would shout the slogan, 'Not a raja but a faqir, the nation's destiny is in his care!' Throughout the campaign he had protested his innocence of any ambition, but his

profile had risen so high that voters and the press assumed he would
be the Janata Dal's candidate for the prime ministership.

When it came to electing the leader of the parliamentary party,
who would also become the prime minister, there was considerable
opposition to him within the Janata Dal. Devi Lal himself used
to describe Vishwanath as 'a parachutist' because he had not been
part of the historic opposition to Congress but had parachuted into
the movement as it was reaching a climax. Eventually, however, a
compromise was hammered out whereby the party would choose
Devi Lal as their leader, and he would then stand down in favour
of Vishwanath. To save Chaudhuri Sahib's honour, he would be
appointed deputy prime minister.

When this charade was over, Devi Lal phoned the BBC office.
He spoke to me first and asked me whether I thought he had done
the right thing. I congratulated him on his statesmanship, and he
seemed gratified, but then asked to speak to my Indian colleague
Satish Jacob. To him he said, 'I have made a fool of myself.'

Devi Lal realized that yet again he had been relegated to the
shunting yard.

Vishwanath's triumph was short-lived. The contradictions within
the Janata Dal, the conflicting ambitions, brought his government
down within a year. His reputation as a selfless politician was
besmirched by the ambition he had revealed. Vishwanath told us
that he had not sought to be prime minister, but that Devi Lal had
insisted saying, 'You be prime minister, people have voted for you.
They will chase us away if you are not appointed.' But Vishwanath
also admitted, 'I paid a heavy price. People have to find an ulterior
motive and they did in my case.'

Devi Lal was among the conspirators who brought down
Vishwanath, but once again the train was pulled away by another
engine, ironically a friend of Sant Bux from the days when they were
both in the Congress, the wily Chandra Shekhar. That was the end of
a career built on a reputation for honesty, a reputation Vishwanath
himself admitted was based on a false assumption.

Throughout his crusade against corruption he knew that others
were spending tainted money on behalf of himself and his party but

he insisted that there was never any 'quid pro quo', that money was never accepted for doing favours.

As for Sant Bux, he never recovered from what he saw as his brother's disloyalty. He left Delhi, where his only ambition lay, and returned to his house in Allahabad. There he seemed to lose all interest in life. We didn't know at the time, but his wife told us later that he had collected all his personal papers together in a bundle, given them to a friend and asked him to throw them into the Sangam, the sacred place in Allahabad where the Ganges meets the River Jamuna. He became ill but when we suggested he should come back to Delhi to consult with the best-known doctors, he showed no interest. The last time Gilly saw him before he died, he greeted her with the words, 'Why have you bothered to come and see me?' Tears filled her eyes and she replied, 'If I don't come to see you, who will I come to see?'

Sant Bux had started out with bright prospects but his career failed because he was too honest to flatter, or to ask for favours, even from his brother.

The Water Harvesters

At the beginning of the hot weather in 2000, the Indian media discovered 'the worst drought of the century' – there were even warnings of 'the worst famine of the century'. The drought was 'spreading like an epidemic', and agriculture was 'being pushed over the precipice'. Wells dug as deep as 1500 feet had dried up and so, for the first time, had a reservoir constructed 340 years ago by the Maharaja of Udaipur. 'Cattle-bone dealers have a field day', was one of the more macabre headlines. Women were filmed standing in long queues with brass pots on their heads waiting for water, and disconsolate farmers were interviewed standing on soil baked and cracked like crazy paving. State governments, anxious to squeeze as much money as possible for relief from the central government were jacking up the story too. The international press was not far behind, and it began to look as though the world was facing another calamity.

Within a month, though, most of the media, Indian and international, had lost interest in the drought. Perhaps this was because diligent searches by journalists had only revealed two cases of people who might have died of starvation. Perhaps, to be less cynical, it was because state governments were coping with the immediate consequences of what was certainly a severe water shortage by providing drinking water in tankers and fodder for cattle.

The disappearance of this story prompted me to pick up a remarkable book called *Everybody Likes a Good Drought* which had lain in my to-be-read pile far too long. Written by P. Sainath, an Indian journalist, it is among other things a harsh indictment of the reporting on those who live below the poverty line and the disasters that afflict them. After two years of investigation he came to the conclusion that journalists were only interested in what happened during disasters and in their immediate aftermath, they were not concerned about the causes of the disasters and the possible remedies. Sainath found one report that talked of 'perpetual drought and scarcity conditions' in an area with a more than adequate rainfall. The journalist did not explain how this anomaly had come about. Sainath did – destruction of the traditional irrigation systems, development schemes which did more harm than good, moneylenders, and the failure of land reforms. Sainath blamed a government development policy which had shirked the big issues, like ownership of land, and a development policy which did not involve those it was meant to help – it didn't even seek their consent. This was not widely understood, he maintained, because the mass media were becoming further and further removed from what he called 'mass reality'. But Sainath discerned a new mood among the poor. He wrote, 'In different parts of the country people are asserting themselves against great odds in different ways. In some cases these may not be the healthiest of ways. But all of them represent this reality, the ruled are no longer willing to be ruled in the old way.'

Gujarat in western India was one of the drought-stricken states, it was also the scene of a battle raging over the construction of a dam on the Narmada, the only major Indian river whose waters had not been harnessed. Opponents of the dam saw it as typical of the development policies that Sainath complained about. Without being consulted, thousands and thousands of villagers had lost their land to make way for the reservoir. The enormous cost of the project had left little or no money for reviving traditional methods of irrigation and preserving water. What's more there was a people's movement to stop the dam. Under the leadership of a charismatic woman named Medha Patkar they had succeeded in getting the World Bank to withdraw its support for the dam, and the Japanese government to withdraw a loan, although that decision was reversed. The movement had also forced the courts to take notice of their complaints. At the time of the drought, the judges were about to decide whether the dam could be completed or not.

Gujarat had been the home state of Mahatma Gandhi, the advocate of development by villagers for villagers, and if his influence lives on anywhere, it lives on there. So Gujarat seemed the obvious place to go to test Sainath's theories.

Local journalists are the unsung heroes of most foreign correspondents' stories, and so when I arrived in Rajkot, the capital of the Saurashtra region of Gujarat, I made straight for the office of a Saurashtrian paper. The paper was called *Fulchab*, or basket of flowers, a high-minded name for a high-minded paper, a name with a touch of the poetic for a paper whose first editor, Zaverchand Meghani, was described by Mahatma Gandhi as India's national poet. Dinesh Raja, the present editor, keeps large pictures of Zaverchand Meghani and the philanthropic businessman who founded the paper behind his desk. He does not have to bow to any commercial pressures because the paper is still owned by the trust set up by that businessman.

I was not the first person to drop in on Dinesh Raja. I found him presiding, like a benign Buddha, over an assembly of local worthies and some journalists from Ahmedabad, the chief city of Gujarat. All were very anxious to ensure I was correctly briefed on the drought. The most insistent was a man Dinesh Raja introduced as a 'veteran journalist'. Everyone in India has to have a status, a rank in a hierarchy, and in journalism when you graduate from senior to veteran it usually means you have retired. Hemant Pandya with his close-cropped, grey hair, his lean, lined face, his cheeks collapsed because of a lack of teeth, was clearly beyond retirement age, but that hadn't dimmed his energy or his enthusiasm. Determined to have his say first he rose from his chair, turned towards me and, with all the authority of his superior years, began a lecture.

'To understand this drought you have to understand Saurashtra, which is not like other parts of India. Here we say, "A man who doesn't respect the brave and the saints, is not a man at all."'

Seeing that I was not quite getting the connection between sanctity and drought, Dinesh Raja intervened explaining, 'The saints here, instead of advising their followers to retire from the world and live in ashrams as they do elsewhere, or asking for money to build temples, spread the message of social service. The effects of this drought are being mitigated by the tradition of social service the saints left us.'

This prompted the veteran to declaim, 'Service of the people is service of God; all the poor are God.'

I pointed out that this was also the tradition of Mother Teresa of Calcutta, but that was ignored and the lecture continued ... 'Here the saints were not just upper caste, they came from the backward castes, and the Dalits too who were despised elsewhere. We were more forward a hundred years back.'

Everyone burst into laughter and the old man sat down, satisfied at least for the moment. This gave the editor the chance to tell me about the support the saints of today had given to 'a people's movement' to mitigate Saurashtra's chronic water shortage by reviving traditional methods of 'harvesting water'. Apparently one of the leading saints – a term freely applied to Hindu holy men – had called a meeting of all his fellow religious leaders and told them to teach their followers in the villages that they had been misled by the government, with its emphasis on big new schemes which never 'delivered the goods'. As a result of this 'false propaganda', villagers had come to believe that traditional methods were out of date, too small-scale. The editor went on to say, 'Because of this drought and the people's movement, the villagers are now turning their backs on the government propaganda, and not only that, they're building the check dams and digging the ponds for themselves, not relying on corrupt officials and the contractors who loot the public. What Gandhi had dreamt of, villagers becoming self-sufficient and looking after their own needs, is coming true at last.'

Fulchab had played a role in the people's movement by running a campaign to promote water harvesting. The veteran journalist was determined that I should be aware of this. Leaning forward and jabbing his finger in my direction he proclaimed, 'The awakening of the people has been done here. This paper is the pioneer. It's a mission, a mission.'

The stout, homely Dinesh Raja sitting comfortably behind his desk, looking anything but a fanatic missionary, was content to allow others to take up the story of *Fulchab*'s good works. His former circulation manager, who was now a social worker, explained how *Fulchab* had organized a scheme to deliver water by tanker free of charge to the citizens of Rajkot. Gujaratis are great settlers. Some say as many as forty per cent of the people of Indian origin settled in Britain and forty-five per cent of those in America are from Gujarat. The Gujarati diaspora also spread throughout eastern and southern Africa and the Gulf countries. These prosperous business communities had contributed generously to *Fulchab*'s fund. While I was sitting in his office Dinesh Raja got news that a Gujarati settled in Bahrain had sent a cheque for the equivalent of two thousand pounds.

This prompted yet another outburst from Hemant Pandya. 'I told you. The press you are visiting is a mission. It's a mission which fought for the freedom of the people and now it's fighting for their freedom from the misrule of the rulers.'

Sitting in the offices of *Fulchab*, a paper I am sure Sainath would find less to complain about than most papers, I had been presented with the opportunity to investigate the 'worst drought of the century', to study the remedies and witness the people's rejection of their rulers. The editor of *Fulchab* also provided me with the place to start, the village of Rajsamdhiyala where, he told me, there had been a people's revolution. It had been led by the sarpanch or chairman of the village council.

Dinesh Raja rang the mobile number of the sarpanch, and learnt that he was in Rajkot. Within a matter of minutes he had joined us in the editor's office, and after a brief introduction he said brusquely, 'If you want to see why there is no need for a drought in Gujarat, come with me.'

Two grim, grey, stone towers still guard the gateway of the high school in Rajkot through which Gandhi used to run home as soon as classes were over. He wrote in his autobiography, 'I couldn't bear to talk to anybody, I was even afraid lest anyone should poke fun at me.' A strange beginning for a man who was to become the most prominent and outspoken critic of the politics and economics of his time. Gandhi believed, 'Independence must begin at the bottom. Thus every village will be a republic, or panchayat, having full powers.' So I assumed that the sarpanch who had done just what Gandhi wanted, had turned his village into a republic, would be a follower of his teaching. I was wrong.

Hardevsinh Jadeja wore a bushshirt, trousers, and a smart pair of shoes, not a stitch of *khadi*, the cloth woven by villagers which is the uniform of the Mahatma's followers. Gandhi always travelled by public transport and would never have owned a car. When I suggested we should drive to the village in my car, the sarpanch was somewhat offended that I didn't seem to realize he had a car of his own. A villager with a car and a mobile phone was odd enough in my experience, but worse was to follow from the Gandhian point of view. As he drove with dangerous determination through the traffic of Rajkot, which like all Indian towns didn't seem to have any rules of the road, instead of advocating Gandhi's simplicity of life and austerity, the sarpanch boasted of his own prosperity.

'They are talking of a drought,' he said scornfully. 'I've got a crop of bhindi, and it needs plenty of water. I expect it to fetch me at least eighty thousand rupees, and in these days when other farmers don't have water it might be a lot more – you never can tell with markets, can you?'

Hardevsinh had an M.A. in English from a college in Rajkot, but he didn't have much use for it. Cutting in front of a three-wheeler rickshaw to avoid a lopsided bus, so overcrowded it seemed in imminent danger of toppling over, he said, 'What matters to me is what I've learnt as a farmer. I'm of course a farmer by birth and I just increased my knowledge. My father used to earn one and a half lakhs from his vegetables. Now I earn more than ten, so you can see how much I've learnt.'

Eventually we extricated ourselves from the traffic of Rajkot and emerged on to the Bhavnagar highway where the going was smoother. Bhavnagar is a city to the south-east of Rajkot, on the Gulf of Khambhat. After some twenty kilometres we turned off the highway on to a track which was perfectly motorable but not tarmacked, and drove under a concrete arch inscribed with the words 'Rajsamdhiyala Gram Panchayat'. This was the border between India and the *gram*, or village, whose panchayat, under the leadership of Hardevsinh Jadeja, had declared unilateral independence.

Hardevsinh parked the car under the branches of a lone banyan tree on the edge of the village square. The panchayat must have once met in the shade of that tree, but Hardevsinh pointed to a new two-storeyed concrete building which was the parliament and secretariat of Rajsamdhiyala. 'It's where I rule from,' he said without a trace of modesty. A lean man, of only average height, with a narrow foxy face and, in spite of being past fifty, a mop of black hair which almost covered his forehead, Hardevsinh would not have stood out in a crowd. But when you talked to him, he had the manner and impatience of someone used to commanding obedience. As chairman he had a large office on the ground floor of the panchayat office building with photographs of his successful water-harvesting on the wall – small dams holding water in previously dried-up rivulets, and ponds which collected the rain and allowed it to percolate through the soil to raise the groundwater level. The Indian bureaucracy classifies these as 'minor irrigation works', as against the major dams and canals of which they are so fond.

Two farmers from a neighbouring village were waiting for Hardevsinh in his office. They had come to seek his help to buy cattle fodder on concessional terms from an agricultural cooperative of which he was a director. Unlike the sarpanch they wore traditional Gujarati clothes, white smocks outside white cotton trousers cut like jodhpurs, the more tight round the calves the more fashionable. Hardevsinh rang the cooperative office in Rajkot to warn them he would be there later in the day with the two farmers, ordered cups of tea for us, and asked me, 'Where would you like to begin?'

'I suppose we'd better start with water, hadn't we?' I replied rather diffidently.

'Well, the most important thing is to know where the water is. The government has built check dams all over the place and most of them are absolutely useless. What's even more stupid is that they have all the information to know where they should be built.'

He opened the drawer of his desk and took out satellite images of the underground water ducts and dykes of the area. 'Look at these,' he instructed me. 'They have helped us to harvest water so successfully. They show where it is to be found, where it is stored underground, and where there are fractures so that it can percolate from the surface.' Pointing to thick black lines looking something like railway lines on a map he went on, 'These are the dykes, and you can see how important they are to decide where to build the dams.' I couldn't. The dykes seemed to start from nowhere and end nowhere, and I was unable to see any significance in them. So to avoid showing my ignorance I changed the subject and asked how the water was shared in the village. He explained that the panchayat ran a scheme which supplied every house with tap water and maintained public wells in addition to those owned by farmers. In return every villager paid a water tax to the panchayat.

Water isn't the only thing that is taxed in Rajsamdhiyala. The village's government is financed by a house tax, a tax for cleaning the village, and a tax on vehicles including bicycles. And raising taxes isn't the only power that the panchayat has usurped from the government. It also acts as the court and the police. Statutory fines are prescribed. Among them are fifty-one rupees for dropping litter, one hundred and fifty-one rupees for drinking alcohol, and two hundred and fifty-one rupees for gambling. Anyone found guilty of 'eve-teasing', or making a nuisance of himself with a woman, has his head shaved and is paraded through the village. If there is a theft, the panchayat immediately pays compensation to the victim and takes on the responsibility of solving the crime. No villager is allowed to approach the police; that incurs a fine of five hundred rupees.

I was a little doubtful about keeping the police away. In India they guard their turf jealously – investigating crimes and dealing with complaints is a profitable occupation. But Hardevsinh insisted, 'The police don't come here because there is no work for them to do. There are plenty of other places for them to perform their duties. There are in every place, always, some ten per cent of people who are not willing to be law-abiding but in this village we can deal with them ourselves. We have a government of our own and we are free.'

The sarpanch took considerable pleasure in telling me the fate of a gang who had robbed a farmer and a Dalit of Rajsamdhiyala six years ago. 'We managed to locate two of them, members of a nomadic caste, and we thrashed them until they told us where the others where. We broke the legs of two, and eventually we caught twenty-five altogether and dealt with them. Since then no one has dared to enter my village,' he added with a satisfied smile. Rajsamdhiyala doesn't have a written code of law. Hardevsinh despises such refinements. 'Anyone who works according to a copybook will achieve nothing. There's no appeal, no court drama here, everything is decided on the spot, the same day, and is final.'

Although the sun was by now at its height, Hardevsinh insisted on showing me round his model village. He strode, swaggered would be a slight exaggeration, along the lanes which were remarkably wide and lacking in potholes. All the houses were built of brick and plastered with concrete, only the cattle-sheds were constructed of mud.

Hardevsinh was justifiably proud of Rajsamdhiyala.

'You don't see any flies because there is no dirt and litter,' he pointed out.

'There don't seem to be any pi-dogs either,' I added.

'No,' he replied. 'We don't have any love for them.'

'You are a mini-Lee Kuan Yew,' I suggested, 'a sort of benevolent dictator with a passion for cleanliness.'

The sarpanch agreed that everything in the village was 'compulsory', but preferred to describe himself as 'a mixture of Hitler and Gandhi'.

We came across three old men, their heads shielded from the sun by white turbans, sitting on the steps of a shop. The shop was a mini-department store selling virtually anything the villagers could require. The shopkeeper had been a landless labourer but the sarpanch had organized a loan for him to start up in business.

I asked the old men whether they thought this drought really was the worst of the century.

One replied, 'We were used to hardship and living without water. Some years it was bad, some years not so bad. Some years the crops were good, some years bad, and some years there was nothing to harvest. Not so long ago, I can't remember exactly when but I think it was in the time of Rajiv Gandhi, we had three bad years together. But usually one was able to find some drinking water in the wells. This year we are told there is none.'

'Told, what do you mean?'

'We are told there is none in other villages, and there are many complaints about what the government is doing, but here we have plenty of water because of Sarpanch Sahib.'

The other old men muttered in agreement.

I asked to see the area of the village where the Dalits lived. It is usually the poorest and most neglected part of a village, but here again the houses were brick built and had little gardens. A pair of bullocks with magnificent curved horns and humps behind the yoke were harrowing a field. I was surprised, because in a prosperous north Indian village that job would be done by a tractor. But Saurashtrians are notoriously canny and Hardevsinh explained how bullocks can still be more economical than a tractor because the capital cost is very low, they require no maintenance, their fodder is cheaper than diesel, and they can reach places inaccessible to tractors.

During our discussion on the village's government, Hardevsinh had told me of a case he had dealt with only that morning. A farmer protecting his land from nilgai, members of the antelope family also known as blue bulls, had erected a fence which crossed the irrigation channel of his neighbour. A complaint had been lodged at eight o'clock and by nine o'clock Hardevsinh had persuaded the farmers to accept a compromise whereby the fence was moved and in exchange the aggrieved party surrendered some less strategic land. We went to see what the decision meant on the ground and found a labourer already digging fresh holes for the fence. The two farmers from a neighbouring village who were still patiently tagging along behind us were amazed. One said, 'In our village this dispute would have ended up in court, costing both parties a lot of money.'

'And there would have been no end to the matter, no decision,' the other added.

'That's the advantage of not having courts,' said Hardevsinh with a satisfied smile.

So far I'd seen no water, no rivulets, no streams, no ponds, and when I asked Hardevsinh about this he replied, 'You won't, the water is all underground.' He took me to see a series of concrete dams in a river bed. Each dam was about three feet high. There was no water in the river bed but peering into a nearby well I could see some water deep down in the darkness at the bottom of the shaft. There didn't appear to be much water but Hardevsinh said, 'The owner is lucky to have any water. If it wasn't for these dams what little rain we did get last year would have run away. Because it was stopped, it seeped down to the underground storage. All we need now is a single flood and in two hours the wells will be recharged and the farmer can have irrigation from this well.'

As we re-entered the main square after my tour of the village, I was somewhat distressed to see a white van parked under the banyan tree. It seemed to be done up in the livery of the Gujarat police force. Had my story collapsed, was the hero if not a liar, given to exaggeration which made his testimony unreliable? When we got nearer it became clear that the van did indeed belong to the police, but this did nothing to deflate the sarpanch's confidence. He strode into his office and greeted the two burly police officers sitting in front of the desk.

'We were just talking about the police and here you are.'

One thing did seem clear – the two policemen had waited to get permission from the sarpanch before entering the village, what was more they seemed to know him well and be on good terms. When I asked how this could be, the older of the two, a heavy jowled, pot-bellied sub-inspector from the Special Branch in Rajkot, growled, 'The panchayat here is very helpful to us. Sometimes we come here to have *chae-pani*, tea and water. But we don't have any trouble with this village.' There appeared to be a sort of Interpol relationship between the republic of Rajsamdhiyala and the Indian police. The two would exchange information and cooperate when necessary. This time the police had come to ask permission to interview a villager who had once been friendly with an absconder who had escaped from custody after being charged with adulterating petrol. Permission was granted and the police went on their way.

The poor farmers from the neighbouring village were getting a little anxious about their appointment in Rajkot, but there was still one more thing I had asked to see. Because I wasn't going to get a typical picture of the impact of the drought in Rajsamdhiyala I'd asked the sarpanch to take me to a village which had not been affected by his enthusiasm for water harvesting. So we set off in his car for the village of Padashan.

On the way, we passed yet another unusual feature of Rajsamdhiyala, the village cricket ground with a practice match in progress. It was no lush English village green. There wasn't a blade of grass to be seen on the black sun-baked earth. We drove right up to the wicket – no player dared to object. I was relieved to see the game was being played with a tennis ball. A cricket ball would have been lethal on that hard pitch. Next to it two other pitches had been dug up and Hardevsinh assured me they would be covered with green grass by the time the season started in October. I found that difficult to believe. It was not a surprise, however, to learn that the sarpanch was captain of the village team, opening bat, and right arm leg-spin bowler.

On the way to Padashan we dropped off the two farmers from the neighbouring village, who were no nearer getting their fodder. They walked away uncomplaining after being dismissed without an apology and told to come back the next day.

As soon as we entered Padashan itself, I realized I was back in lethargic village India, its will sapped by dependence on the government, its hopes dashed by the unfulfilled promises of officials and politicians. We had difficulty in getting the car through the narrow, potholed lanes, and avoiding the mangy dogs so unloved in Rajsamdhiyala. Everywhere, it seemed, was littered with blue plastic bags. Flies buzzed around the open drains. Plaster was peeling off the wall of the temple in the centre of the village. There was no shortage of men young and old with nothing better to do than stare at us.

They gathered round us as soon as we got out of the car. Chairs were brought out and in no time at all we were in the middle of a discussion on the drought. A young man was sent to inform their sarpanch so that the diplomatic niceties could be observed. Hardevsinh was well known and highly regarded by the villagers, and no one wanted there to be any question of disrespect to him. A pot of tea appeared, but in Saurashtra it's drunk from the saucer, which to the unpractised is easier said than done. My hands trembled so much that I spilt most of the saucer's contents down my shirt.

While we were waiting for the sarpanch, I enquired about the impact of the drought. Apparently there was no water in the wells and villagers were entirely dependent on government tankers. Eight were meant to come every day, but there were the inevitable complaints about irregular supplies. Thinking of that headline about the cattle bone dealers, I asked an old farmer how many cattle had died in the village. 'I am not sure any have died,' he replied, 'but the cattle feed the government supplies is inedible so we have to pay a high price for fodder. In the big drought from '85 to '87 the government provided a cattle camp in every village.'

The *pujari*, or priest of the temple, said he could never remember a time when all the wells had been dry before. He didn't know of any cases of people becoming ill because of the water shortage, or of any migration from the village, but the village was suffering 'great hardship'. The farmers complained that although they had insured their crops with the cooperative, they hadn't been paid for last year's failure and they didn't have the money to buy seed even if the rains did come this year. I asked them why they hadn't followed the example of Rajsamdhiyala and built check dams to harvest water. The pujari replied, 'The government never did it for us.' I pointed out, 'Rajsamdhiyala has not had any help from the government.' An old farmer sitting in front of us, his hands clasped on top of his lathi, leant forward and said, 'The hand of God is not on us to have good leaders.'

At that moment the sarpanch arrived. He was a fine-looking man with neatly cut white hair and an immaculately brushed moustache, smartly turned out in trousers and a bushshirt which looked as if they had come straight off the ironing board. He had all the appearance of a man who could command authority, but when I asked him why he had not been able to organize the construction of check dams he replied, 'People here are not interested. Everyone in this village says why should we do it, the government should do it for us. The people are not helping.'

The villagers had all heard of the new scheme of the government to encourage water harvesting under which it guaranteed to fund sixty per cent of the cost of constructing dams if the village would find the remaining forty. But the old farmer clutching his stick was not impressed. 'The scheme was for ninety–ten, now it's for sixty–forty. How can we succeed?'

'He's suffering from pessimism,' Hardevsinh muttered to me, 'how can anyone do anything with that attitude.'

I asked the demoralized sarpanch what would happen if this drought lasted three years like the one in the eighties. He pointed to the heavens and said, 'The one up there knows,' and at that very moment there was a thunderous crack. But it wasn't the one up there replying, only a drummer opening the evening supplication to him in the temple by the village square. That was too much for Hardevsinh. Shrugging his shoulders in disgust he said scornfully, 'If you think doing puja to God or *sifarish* to the government is going to help you, you're mistaken. God hasn't done anything for us, nor has the government. We've done it all ourselves.'

After writing off the village, and the villagers from the sarpanch downwards, he strode off and I followed somewhat less confidently. I wasn't quite sure I wanted to be associated with the sarpanch's harsh words.

As we drove back to Rajsamdhiyala, the sun was setting behind a distant range of low hills rising abruptly from the flatlands of Saurashtra like unsightly slag-heaps. Hardevsinh noticed the banks of black clouds tinged rose pink and blood red by the last light of the sun. 'There could be rain tonight if there is a wind,' he said, and then added scornfully, 'it won't do that useless lot any good, the water will just run off their land.'

There were showers in some places that night and the next day I did see some water which had been harvested. But before that I was taken to meet one of the saints who had contributed to the water-harvesting movement. I was introduced to him by a comparatively lowly employee of the government's irrigation department who had taken leave from his job and had become the leader of a people's movement.

It was the editor of *Fulchab* who suggested I should also meet Mansukhbhai Suvagia who was credited with inspiring one hundred villages to build their own check dams in a region to the west of Rajkot. The water revolution, as Mansukhbhai called it, took off from a meeting in a village where three small dams had been built. News of this reached the chief minister of Gujarat and he agreed to attend a great assembly in the village. People came from all over Saurashtra and at the end of the proceedings they all raised their hands and took an oath to start harvesting water. Realizing that politicians' credibility was not of the highest, Mansukhbhai had also invited some fifteen saints to the meeting to add their influence to his campaign. He showed me a photograph of one elderly, and obviously much revered holy man, arriving enthroned on a tractor and accompanied by a procession of devotees. The tractor was got up like a traditional chariot with a richly embroidered parasol over the saint's head as a symbol of his dignity. Another photograph showed three saints handing over money to build dams. That, according to Mansukhbhai, who didn't share the *Fulchab* editor's high opinion of saints, was a rare sight indeed. 'This is the first time saints have given money,' he told me, 'they usually ask for money to build temples, now they are giving money for development.'

I was interested in meeting one of the water-harvesting saints, so Mansukhbhai agreed to take me to Karsan Das Bapu. We drove to the saint's headquarters and our car pulled up beside a large sandstone temple. There was no sign of any builders but bamboo scaffolding still clung precariously to the structure, and the hall, standing on a plinth, approached by some twenty steps, was as yet unoccupied by the gods. Next to the temple was a modern *dharamsala*, or rest house, for pilgrims and other visitors. On the opposite side of the spacious compound, lined with palm trees, was a long, low shed with a red corrugated iron roof. This turned out to be the dining hall. Sitting on the ground (the dining hall had no floor), we were served watery vegetable curry and even more watery daal, the standard fare in Indian religious establishments. Then we retired to bedrooms in the rest house and waited for the saint to receive us. As the time passed I became worried because I didn't want to miss a public meeting Mansukhbhai had scheduled for five o'clock, but Mansukhbhai didn't share my concern.

At last, we were shown into the saint's chamber, and seated below his throne, which was a bed rather than a chair. I was expecting a regal figure, someone demanding and accustomed to reverence, but eventually a slight, wizened man, clad inevitably in saffron robes, with thinning, oiled hair plastered over his skull, slipped into the room, went straight up to Mansukhbhai, embraced him, pinched his cheek and asked, 'How are you my friend?'

Karsan Das Bapu may have been a holy man but that didn't stop him having a sense of humour. When I asked him about the temple he was building he laughed, 'I suppose this young man has been telling you I am a beggar who takes money to build temples when what we need is dams.'

'Well, not exactly,' I replied. 'He did say saints used to do that but he also showed me a picture of some saints giving him money for dams.'

'Was I one of them?'

I didn't think so, but I didn't want to embarrass Mansukhbhai. Fortunately he spotted the trap before I could put my foot in it, and intervened, 'I knew you wouldn't expect any reward or any acknowledgement for your generosity. After all it says in the *Gita* that you should do your duty with no thought for the consequences.'

'Of course you are right,' chuckled the saint, leaning forward to pinch Mansukhbhai's cheek again. 'When we first met I told you that you were doing what we saints do, social service, but without wearing our robes. Now it seems you want to take over my job of teaching dharma too. Have you also told this man what I taught you – that God is everywhere including in water. Water is H_2O and God is the hydrogen in water?'

After Mansukhbhai assured him that he had not been teaching

me the theology of water, the saint went on to explain that if God was the hydrogen in water obviously we should not waste it, so it was our dharmic duty to harvest it.

The saint admitted he had needed convincing before he was converted to water harvesting. 'Local officials,' he said, 'told me it was all a waste of time and all that was needed was to complete the dam on the River Narmada, which they said would bring water to Saurashtra. But then I agreed to meet Mansukhbhai and I could see he was a good boy. So I went to see his work and realized that it was just jealousy speaking against him, so I gave him money.'

'What do you mean by jealousy, who was jealous?' I asked.

'In India no one likes to see anyone going ahead. They will always try to pull him down, especially if they are politicians who know they are unpopular and so fear popular leaders like Mansukhbhai.'

When we stood up to leave, the saint pinched my cheek and gave me an unusual blessing, 'Now you are my friend too. Of course, I don't know whether you are a good boy also, but I'm sure you will be now with Mansukhbhai to guide you.'

Now at last we were to see water. We drove past mile after mile of flat fields, their rich black soil prepared for the groundnut and cotton seeds which would only be sown if and when the monsoon came. There was no grass. The only vegetation was stunted, scrawny trees, scrub, and cactus. Last night's monsoon showers had bequeathed a few puddles which had not yet been dried out by the fierce summer sun. At last we came to a small village where we were greeted enthusiastically by the local doctor. Accompanied by half the village, he took us to what had been a dry river bed and there we saw black crows gulping water greedily and cows drinking contentedly from a pond which had built up behind one of Mansukhbhai's check dams. The doctor admitted, 'We were all doubtful about this scheme because we had forgotten the tradition of harvesting rain. Now we can see with our own eyes that it works. This water will take a long time to evaporate and all the time it's seeping underground too.'

By now we were more than two hours late for the meeting Mansukhbhai was due to address at the village of Bhalgam. When we did eventually arrive, a worried social worker, Madhibhai Vekaria, was waiting for us on the outskirts but he didn't receive an apology for the anxiety and inconvenience we had caused him. That didn't seem to worry him; he was just relieved that we had turned up in the end. As we drove through the village he leant out of the car window shouting, 'Mansukhbhai has come, the meeting will start now. The BBC man has come, the meeting will start now.' I didn't want to undermine his efforts to drum up a crowd by pointing out that I was longer a BBC man.

Villagers rose from the tea shop and from other stalls, from doorsteps and from the shade of trees, from all the places where they had gathered in small knots for the evening review of events local and national. They made their way to the barren land outside the village, the meeting ground. We went ahead of them to find that some people were already waiting patiently for us.

There was a wind that evening and so the social worker's introduction was interrupted by the microphone squawking and screeching. Various attempts to solve that problem by tying handkerchiefs round the microphone were eventually successful and by the time Mansukhbhai came to speak he could be heard loud and clear as he declaimed, 'For the last two hundred years you have bowed down under all your difficulties thinking whatever they are God will solve them. You have forgotten your own responsibilities and become lazy. I want this laziness to end and I want you to solve your own problems.'

Mansukhbhai spoke ad lib, never pausing to search for a word. Young, not particularly tall, and dressed in a long-sleeved white shirt tucked into his trousers with the obligatory ballpoint pen in the top pocket he looked like any other junior government clerk. Yet the village elders sitting in front of him, and their sons behind them, took this criticism without a murmur.

'I believe in God,' Mansukhbhai went on, 'but I don't want to unload all my troubles on to Him. I don't have faith in the government, so it's useless to unload your troubles on them. I have seen the power of the people. If you take that power into your hands you will see what you can achieve.'

It was difficult to tell from the phlegmatic faces of the villagers whether the message had hit home. But after the meeting, at a gathering of village notables in a house which surprised me with its opulence, I was assured it had.

No story in India is complete without allegations of corruption and water harvesting was no exception. According to Mansukhbhai it was because the chief minister of Gujarat was so moved by the meeting he'd attended that he had promised the government would finance sixty per cent of any water harvesting scheme if the villagers themselves put up the remaining forty per cent. He'd done this in spite of the fact that Gujarati politicians of all parties were totally committed to the theory that the Narmada dam was the one and only answer to Saurashtra's water problems. Not everyone agrees with Mansukhbhai's version of the origins of the chief minister's scheme, but nobody, not even officials, denied it had spawned corruption, especially in the district of Junagadh. There, according to press reports, the government had stopped handing out money because there was so much corruption.

Junagadh is about one hundred kilometres from Rajkot. On the way there I passed a small group of Jain nuns, recognizable by their thin white cotton robes. One nun, enthroned in a cumbersome wooden wheelchair, was being pushed by a lay woman. The rest were walking barefoot on a murderous Indian main road which made no concessions to pedestrians. I hesitated to stop and talk to the nuns for fear they would consider that an intrusion, but in the end I couldn't resist the temptation to satisfy my curiosity. I told the driver to turn the car round and go back to them. To my surprise the first nun I approached was quite willing to talk to me. She spoke softly and her speech was muffled by a white cloth tied across her mouth to prevent her accidentally swallowing even the smallest insect and thereby breaching the Jain code of absolute respect for all life, and so I didn't catch all she said. I did gather that the group was on a pilgrimage to Veraval on the coast which would mean two months on the road in the heat of summer and the humidity of the monsoon. That day they planned to reach a village about nine kilometres away. All the nuns carried their meagre possessions wrapped up in a white cloth and something like a floor-mop to sweep away the insects from the ground in front of them. I asked if I could take a photograph and that was politely refused.

I'd always wanted to go to Junagadh because of the fascinating story of the flight of its ruler shortly after India became independent. Under the British, Saurashtra was a patchwork of princely states, they varied from Junagadh with a population of 608,000 and more than three thousand square miles in area to tiny states like Manavadar, whose Khan only ruled over one hundred square miles. Junagadh was the only major Saurashtrian state to be ruled by a Muslim, Nawab Sahib Sir Mahbatkhan Rasulkhanji. He was a ruler who took more interest in his dogs than his subjects, once declaring a public holiday to celebrate the wedding of two of his favourite canine companions. Not being a very decisive ruler, he easily fell under the influence of his *dewan*, or chief minister, Sir Shah Nawaz Bhutto. He, like his son, Zulfikar Ali Bhutto, the executed Prime Minister of Pakistan, had a penchant for plotting. Sir Shah Nawaz's scheme was to get the Nawab to declare that his state would opt to join Muslim Pakistan even though some eighty per cent of his subjects were Hindus. The other major states of Saurashtra had opted the other way which meant he would have been surrounded on all sides either by India or the sea. The Nawab fell for the scheme but lost his nerve and fled when food ran short because neighbouring states refused to trade with him, his subjects became restive, and the Indian army camped on his border. He was in such a hurry that he forgot one of his wives but many of his dogs did manage to board the flight.

The Nawab left behind a city that had been a capital many centuries before his forefathers established their dynasty in the 1730s. The town was built on the plains in the shadow of the hill of Girnar, which had been sacred to Jains for centuries. The hill was studded with temples and the town's long history was marked by many monuments, including Buddhist caves maybe fifteen hundred years old, an ancient fort with a mosque for Friday prayers within its walls, and the mausoleums of the Nawab's own dynasty, each with its own minarets. Most of the monuments remain, but what must have been a colourful small town has been overrun by modern India with its unsightly development so unplanned that the drains in the streets I was driving through couldn't cope with a mere monsoon shower.

I came eventually to a government guest house where, through the good offices of a journalist from Ahmedabad, I was to meet some young party workers from the Bharatiya Janata Party, which was in power in Gujarat and in Delhi. They, I'd been told, had evidence of corruption in the sixty–forty scheme. I found them in the guest house's VVIP bedroom where they were complaining to the local MP, herself from the BJP, that during a recent spot check of nine dams built under the scheme, eight were found to be 'of inferior quality'. The MP was told there was no problem when dams were built by villagers themselves, the problem arose when contractors were brought in.

The workers were surprisingly willing to talk about their own government's corruption to me, although I was a journalist, and deputed Nirbhai Purohit, the young general secretary of the Junagadh BJP, to take me to the site of a dam constructed by a contractor. We drove to the small town of Mendarda where we picked up Mohanbhai, the local secretary of the BJP, a disagreeable looking man, with receding hair brightly coloured by henna. He was reluctant to part with any information beyond the instructions necessary to find our way to the dam. After driving several miles through increasingly desolate countryside, he told the driver to turn off the tarmac road down a bumpy track. There was no sign of civilization or cultivation, not a tree in sight. Suddenly, in the middle of this rock-strewn, barren wilderness, our guide pointed to some figures in the distance, and mumbled, 'That's the dam site.'

Drawing nearer we could see that, as so often happens in India, the hard work was being done by women. Brightly coloured skirts swirling round their ankles, hips swaying, shoulders shifting to balance the metal pans on their heads, they strode confidently across the uneven terrain, miraculously not tripping over their wholly unsuitable sandals. They were a human conveyor belt filling a cement mixer with earth and stone and carrying the resultant unstable compound to the dam site. The dam was almost complete and a young man was busy disguising the true nature of its construction by plastering a thin layer of concrete over the earth and stone embankment. The surly, unshaven supervisor denied all responsibility for the fraud that was being perpetuated. He only did what the contractor told him to do.

'Anyhow,' he asked, 'how do you know this is meant to be a cement dam? The government inspectors came here two days ago and passed it as ninety per cent all right.'

But Mohanbhai knew the contract was for a cement dam.

On the way back Mohanbhai opened up when asked how the scam worked. 'Any eleven people can get together and form a committee to build a dam,' he explained. 'They don't have to be a village panchayat or any recognized body. Officials are too anxious to give the money away.'

'Why?' I asked.

Mohanbhai looked at me as if I was an idiot. 'Because they get a share of it of course. No one checks the dam site, no one checks the estimate, no one checks the dam when it's built. There have been reports of some dams which haven't even been built and yet the contractors get a completion certificate. Money is flowing into the officials' pockets.'

'So how does it work when villagers build dams?'

'That's a different matter. First of all, the committee is not a fraud, then the villagers themselves do the work and watch it to see there is no cheating. After all, they are interested in saving water not making money.'

Before coming to Rajkot I had met the minister for information in Ahmedabad and he'd explained the efforts the government had made to eradicate corruption in the sixty–forty scheme, and other drought relief measures. The drought-stricken areas had been divided into five zones and teams of inspectors had been sent to each one. 'It wasn't just a case of set a thief to catch a thief,' the minister had said. In each team there was a member of the chamber of commerce as well as a senior official, an engineer, and a member of the state assembly.

I asked Mohanbhai whether this was all eyewash.

Before he could answer, the Junagadh BJP secretary butted in, 'No. You heard me tell the MP that the teams had come, but much of the damage had been done by then.'

'So if the teams are so effective why have we just seen an obvious example of corruption still going on?'

'Well, you can't plug every leak of government money, but we have reported this and Mohanbhai will see they don't get a completion certificate.'

'I will most certainly,' said Mohanbhai grimly.

I had to get the official version of the dam scandal, and so I sought an appointment with the civil servant who had been sent to Saurashtra as special relief commissioner. He willingly agreed to see me in his official bungalow opposite what was once Rajkot's racecourse and is now a rather indeterminate open space. I was shown into the sitting room by a servant to wait for the commissioner, but I didn't have to wait long before a small stout man, of an owlish academic appearance, hurried into the room and introduced himself as Pravin Trivedi. He had been posted in Rajkot earlier and everyone described him as 'a clean officer'.

The commissioner blamed misuse of technology in part for the crisis. In the last drought submersible pumps were not available, now the commissioner said they were playing havoc with the water table. They were pumping water from depths of a thousand feet or more, which could only be described as 'water mining'. Ironically Mansukhbhai, the leader of the water-harvesting movement, was able to take leave from the government because of the generosity of his brother who manufactured submersible pumps.

Pravin Trivedi was an enthusiast for the people's movement. Whereas most bureaucrats resent anything that takes power out of their hands, he was all in favour of giving as much freedom as possible to the villagers. 'That's the best part of the scheme,' he said. 'It gives the villagers the responsibility to design and build the dams. It is essential to use the engineering skills of the people. After all, they used to harvest water for centuries without the help of any government.'

'What about the corruption then, what causes that?'

'Corruption? I don't want to magnify it. This is an excellent scheme and it must not be spoilt by unsubstantiated allegations of corruption which you always get with government work.'

'So there is no corruption?'

'No, of course I can't say that. When such a vast movement comes into being there will be irregularities but we must not blame the entire scheme. It really works. The villagers don't just build dams with their labour, they put their souls into them. You must not undermine them by believing exaggerations about corruption.'

'So, why then,' I asked, 'has the scheme been cancelled in Junagadh?'

The commissioner played that back effortlessly, 'It hasn't been actually cancelled in Junagadh or any other district.'

As I was bringing our conversation to an end the commissioner realized that he might have allowed his enthusiasm to run away with him. Remembering that the official line was to rubbish water harvesting in case it detracted from the case for completing the Narmada dam he said anxiously, 'Please don't think that anything I have said can be interpreted as meaning that we don't need the Narmada dam. We must have that water if we are to have an adequate supply because harvesting alone can never fulfil all Saurashtra's needs.'

The Gujarat government had appointed a special minister for the Narmada and he had published a very effective counterblast to his opponents. Reading through it, I had come to realize that there were arguments in favour of the dam, just as there were arguments against it. But the minister had spoilt his argument by falling into the trap of the false alternative, the either-or argument. In stressing the need for Narmada he'd written off water harvesting. In one particular instance he had been manifestly wrong. Unable to ignore the renown of the sarpanch of Rajsamdhiyala which had spread far and wide, he'd stated in his document 'the success of Rajsamdhiyala is due to typical topographical and geological features … the same could not be replicated even in the nearby vicinity due to non-availability of such geological advantage.' But I had seen another success with my own eyes.

On my last day in Saurashtra I took this document to the formidable sarpanch. He was enraged and, ignoring my protests that I didn't understand the satellite maps, insisted on coming back to Rajkot with me to photocopy them so that I could have some scientific evidence with me to refute the minister's claim.

After photocopying the maps Hardevsinh took me to lunch in one of Rajkot's smartest restaurants. During the meal he told me a minister had once attacked him as an enemy of his motherland because he'd criticized Narmada.

'So what do you think about it now?' I asked.

'Well, I'm not sure.'

'That doesn't seem very like you.'

The sarpanch laughed and then fell silent, which was also unusual, before saying, 'I don't see why we shouldn't have both – water harvesting and Narmada. Certainly if we have Narmada that doesn't mean we should waste water.'

That surely is true. The dispute over Narmada will continue long after the court's decision. What can't be disputed here and now is that the way the dam has dominated the water policy of western India is all too typical of India's longstanding policy of seeking large-scale solutions to problems and ignoring the contribution small-scale schemes can also make. Himanshu Thakkar of the South Asian Network on Dams, Rivers and People is an opponent of Narmada, but that doesn't invalidate his description of India's water policy as 'top down, engineer-bureaucrat-politician-contractor driven, dominated by large projects and structures'. But most important of all, according to the NGO leader, is that, 'There is no role for the people.' Hardevsinh and other leaders of the water harvesting movement have forced the government of Gujarat to concede them a role. They have been faithful to the Mahatma who once said, 'I heartily endorse the proposition that any plan which exploits the raw materials of a country and neglects the potentially more powerful manpower is lopsided and can never tend to establish human equality.'

Paradise Lost

In 1968, I think it must have been, I was sitting in Kashmir by the banks of the River Lidder on the lawn of a bungalow built by the British to accommodate anglers. I was drinking beer with Ghulam Mustafa Malik, the director of fisheries and Melville de Mellow, known as the Richard Dimbleby of India for his deep-voiced, picturesque commentaries on national occasions. It had been a good day for Melville and I, but then Malik preserved his trout streams with such efficiency that it was difficult to have a bad day on his rivers. Melville was reflecting on some of the anglers of the Raj he'd known, when from the other side of the high hedge which divided the guests' lawn from the servants' quarters I heard swish and a yelp of pain, swish and a yelp of pain, swish and a yelp of pain, followed by abusive language. I asked Malik what on earth was going on and he explained that one of his river wardens had caught a poacher and was whipping him to teach him a lesson. 'It's better than handing him to the police,' Malik claimed. 'They will whip him too, and then lock him up until his family pay a bribe to get him released.' I have to confess that I did not protest very vigorously against this rough justice. My only excuse could be that I knew that Malik was right in what he said about the police. In those days the Kashmir police were brutal and corrupt, as they are today.

On that visit to Kashmir I was one of thousands of tourists who had fled to the mountains to get out of the summer heat of the Gangetic plain. Kashmir was then one of the most popular destinations for Indian tourists, the early summer was the season for visitors from the west coast, Bombay and Gujarat, they were followed by north Indians who, like me, were seeking refuge from temperatures of over forty degrees centigrade, and then in the autumn Bengalis made the long journey all the way across India to spend their annual puja holidays in Kashmir. There used to be a fair sprinkling of tourists from abroad too, and this number would have been enhanced if the central government had listened to Kashmiris' pleas for an international airport. But when Gilly and I arrived in Kashmir in the summer of 2001 we found we were the only guests staying on Butt's Clermont houseboats. The elderly proprietor received us as though we were royalty, fussing like a motherly hen as his retainers scattered flower petals over our hair and garlanded Gilly. The walls of the wooden hut, which served as an office, were lined with photos of celebrities who had been his guests.

'There's George Harrison,' he pointed out, 'the Beatle, you know. Then Joan Fontaine, so beautiful, and Nelson Rockefeller. I'm told he's one of the richest men in the world. So many came, but now, well, not many because of these troubles.'

Butt's houseboats had always been a favourite resort of Delhi diplomats and I noticed a photograph of the amiable British High Commissioner, Sir Rob Young. But when I asked about his stay, the mournful Mr Butt told me, 'Your high commissioner did want to stay but the security people refused to allow him so he could only pay a brief visit.'

Then Mr Butt led us across his lawn, with its chenar tree whose trunk must have been several yards in circumference and whose age was apparently five to six hundred years, to our houseboat. We were followed on board by a barefooted servant who was introduced to us as 'Ramzan, your valet'. We entered the living room. Its floor was covered with Kashmiri carpets, and a crystal chandelier, on which I was to hit my head from time to time, hung from the low wooden ceiling carved in an intricate pattern, which must have taken heaven knows how many man hours to complete. There were comfortable chairs, a desk, and a dining table too. Mr Butt explained that Srinagar's houseboats originated to beat the Maharaja's ban on Europeans buying land in his kingdom. They chose to live on water instead.

Any tourists who did come to Srinagar in the summer of 2001 hoping to stay on a houseboat and be paddled in a *shikara*, the gondola of Srinagar, across one of the great lakes on which the city is built, or down the waterways that give the city its title, 'the Venice of the East', would take the first aeroplane or bus back home. It was a city under occupation, armed men of the Border Security Force in khaki uniform, with helmets and camouflage flak jackets, were posted every hundred yards on both sides of main roads, they peered through narrow slits in sandbagged bunkers, they manned road blocks, and although few if any of them spoke Kashmiri, they stopped, searched, and interrogated young men. Armoured personnel carriers were parked at some road junctions and we saw the occasional detachment of Indian army soldiers with machine-guns driving through the streets. Khaki washing and underclothes hung from the windows of hotels along the banks of Dal Lake now occupied by the security forces. Officials of the government who didn't want their families to stay with them in Srinagar, were living bachelor lives in the heavily guarded Tourist Reception Centre. The threat from militants fighting to take Kashmir out of the Indian union, had reduced one of the country's finest tourist destinations to a city swamped by jumpy, jittery, security forces.

Much of the blame for the present plight of Kashmir must be laid on what India calls 'the proxy war' it has been fighting for more than ten years against militants who infiltrate from the Pakistani side of the Line of Control and the international border. Although Pakistan denies it has ever trained and equipped the infiltrators or helped them plan their strategy there is strong evidence that it has. Pakistan radio and television, which are of course heard and seen in the valley, back the infiltrators describing them as freedom fighters and calling them martyrs when they are killed. But the mistakes India has made in administering Kashmir have been force multipliers.

Kashmir was always going to be a sensitive issue for India, and Pakistan was always going to play on those sensitivities. At Partition, Pakistan, with some justification, expected to absorb Kashmir. It was, after all, a Muslim majority state bordering Pakistan. But unfortunately for Pakistan it was ruled by a Hindu maharaja, Hari Singh. When the British supervision – the paramountcy – lapsed, a vacuum was created in Kashmir. Hari Singh dithered, unable to convince himself that remaining independent was not an option.

The northern part of his state, and a western enclave, slipped out of his control but it was only when he learnt that Pakistan was sending Pathans from the bellicose tribes of the North-West Frontier into the valley of Kashmir, threatening his capital Srinagar, that the maharaja appealed to India for help and agreed to sign an instrument of accession. Indian troops drove the Pathans out of the valley but the maharajas northern territories and that enclave in the west remained in Pakistan's control. The de facto division of Kashmir which remains to this day was effected within less than three months of Britain resigning its powers over the state.

India had one powerful argument on its side in the shape of Sheikh Mohammed Abdullah, who was the most popular leader in Kashmir and, although a Muslim, favoured joining a secular country rather than Islamic Pakistan. He gave India some grounds for maintaining it had a democratic mandate to incorporate Kashmir at Partition, that its claim to the state didn't just depend on the maharaja's decision. More important than arguments about the accession of Kashmir, was the role Sheikh Abdullah could have played in settling Kashmiris into the union of India, in converting that instrument of accession into the will of the people. But that was not to be. Within six years he was deposed as prime minister of Kashmir, and spent most of the next twenty-two years either under arrest or banned from entering Kashmir. It would be naive to deny that the Lion of Kashmir, as Sheikh Abdullah was known, had proved an easy man to deal with, and he was certainly not prepared to give India all the powers it enjoyed over the other states of the union, but there was no hard evidence to prove the allegations that he had changed his mind about Pakistan or intended to demand total independence. There was evidence, in the form of an agitation against Sheikh Abdullah by a Hindu party, that his land reforms, some of the most effective enacted since independence, had upset middle-class members of that community.

Whatever the rights and wrongs of Sheikh Abdullah's dismissal and arrest, they sowed the seeds of doubt about India's attitude in the minds of many Kashmiri Muslims, and others also connected with the state.

On the lower slopes of the Zabarwan ridge, which towers over Dal Lake, there are three dwellings set in spacious grounds, isolated from the rest of the city, which were once royal residences. The palace was now a hotel, the house the maharaja built for his wife was the residence of the governor, and the house where the maharaja's ADC lived was the residence of the chief secretary, Ashok Jaitly. At one stage it had been converted into an interrogation centre by the Indian security forces. Ashok, well known and popular in Delhi – I had last seen him in the Gymkhana Club – he seemed to be the epitome of the English-educated, secularist elite who had once dominated the Indian Administrative Service, the IAS. But he had sacrificed the prospect of prestigious posts in Delhi, where he was so much at home, because of his loyalty to Kashmir and to Sheikh Abdullah's son Farooq who was currently chief minister of the state. Sitting on the lawn outside his spacious house, its immaculate white walls gleaming in the lights provided to ensure his security, he told us of the frustration he and Farooq Abdullah faced.

'Whatever we want to do we are faced with the fact that Delhi has never trusted Kashmiris. I have always maintained that, and maintained it's because Kashmir is a Muslim state. Farooq misses no opportunity to say in public, "Not all Kashmiris are Pakistanis." And when I ask him why, he says it's because he wants non-Kashmiris to know he knows what they are thinking, what is in their hearts.'

Although members of the IAS owe their loyalty to the central government, not to state governments, the chief secretary was not the only member of that service in Kashmir who believed India had never trusted Kashmiri Muslims.

But successive Indian governments have maintained the opposite. They have claimed Kashmir is proof of their secular credentials. Because it is a Muslim majority state, it disproves the theory that Hindus and Muslims can't live together and are separate nations, the theory on which Jinnah based his claim for Pakistan. Just before we arrived in Srinagar, the Indian foreign minister had gone so far as to claim that Kashmir was 'the core of Indian nationhood'. Yet his Hindu nationalist party, the BJP, creates mistrust of

Muslims, some would argue its ideology is founded on hatred of that community. Meanwhile the secularists, with their paranoia about communalists under the bed, find it difficult to trust anyone who is religious. As for the Congress leadership, with its incessant affirmations of secularism, it has perhaps done more than anyone else to create suspicion in the minds of Kashmiri Muslims.

After more than twenty years of Congress, or Congress-backed governments, Indira Gandhi in 1974 eventually did a deal with Sheikh Abdullah, which was ratified the next year. Sheikh Abdullah got very little more than agreement on retaining the article in the constitution which guaranteed the special status of Kashmir. Most of the special powers which had flowed from that clause were lost, but the Lion of Kashmir did return as chief minister. Because he had been unable to fight the previous election, there were no members of his party in the state assembly, and he had to govern as leader of the Congress, a thoroughly uncomfortable position which strengthened the hands of his opponents who maintained that his deal was a sell-out to India. Indira Gandhi, putting her party's interests ahead of the need to bolster Sheikh Abdullah's position and reassure him of her good intentions, refused to allow an election to the state assembly which would have given the new chief minister his own mandate to rule.

In the end, it wasn't the secular Congress which provided the first wholly free and fair election in Kashmir since Abdullah was first dismissed, but the Janata Party which defeated Indira Gandhi after the Emergency. It's ironic that the Hindu nationalist Jan Sangh, which was later to be reborn as the BJP, was one of the parties that merged to form the short-lived Janata Party. The 1977 election, held under the Janata auspices, gave Sheikh Abdullah's National Conference a majority in the state assembly. It cannot be claimed that he provided good governance but Kashmiris will tell you that when he died one million people turned out to see his funeral procession.

The Lion of Kashmir's son Farooq Abdullah is a doctor who had practised in Britain, he was remarkably open to the press, and often not entirely discreet. He agreed to see us even though he was involved in meetings in Delhi, Jammu, and Srinagar, to discuss tightening security after a series of massacres which had followed a fruitless Indo-Pakistan summit. The day after we arrived in Jammu on the night train from Delhi, twelve people were mowed down at Jammu railway station when militants wearing army uniforms fired into the crowds waiting on one of the platforms.

Inevitably, to get to Farooq Abdullah's office we had to pass through several checks. The only government servant relaxed about security was the sniffer dog, a stout, dusty, golden labrador, asleep behind the desk of a receptionist. The secretariat is one of the few modern buildings in Srinagar. Unlike other Indian hill stations, the capital of Kashmir has not been overrun by developers with their ugly, unplanned, constructions. It is still largely a city of low-rise wood and brick buildings with sloping roofs, not the concrete monstrosities which disfigure Shimla, the capital of the neighbouring state. Property speculators and developers have been deterred by the state's laws against outsiders owning land.

Farooq's office was on the third floor. He charged out of a meeting on security with leaders of the Hindu community which was going on in the next door conference room, sat down, and ignoring my feeble attempt at polite formalities, barked, 'Right, ask me any questions you like.'

The normally jovial, outgoing chief minister seemed to be on an unusually short fuse. He had the height and the handsomeness of his father, but he lacked Sheikh Abdullah's gravitas. In spite of his white hair, which was in short supply, there was still something about Farooq of the impetuous young man who had a reputation for preferring pleasure to politics. In his early days as chief minister he was reported to have ridden round the holiday resort of Gulmarg with a film star on the back of his motorcycle. In her book on Kashmir, the journalist Tavleen Singh confirms the motorbike but says it was her sister who rode pillion.

Put off my stride by Farooq's unusually abrupt manner, I started on a long rambling explanation about our book and its concern with bad governance.

'Bad governance,' he interrupted me, 'bad governance. All of you talk as though Kashmir was particularly badly governed. Delhi is now saying we must provide good governance to win the hearts and minds of Kashmiris. We are fighting a battle, and they talk about maladministration.' He went on scornfully, 'Look at their bloody performance compared with ours. I've had to send people to jail for non-payment of taxes, even some of my friends. I haven't been able to save them. Can they do that in Delhi?' he asked, leaning across his desk and challenging me to answer.

Before I had time to he continued, 'The only answer to this country is decentralization of power to the states. If it becomes a federal structure that will probably save the day. This is a pseudo-federal state. But nobody who comes to power in Delhi wants to give up any powers.'

Farooq had good reason to resent Delhi's hold over the state. Shortly after taking over from his father, he had found himself confronting the imperious Indira Gandhi. Determined to stamp her presence on every corner of India, now that she had taken revenge for her humiliating defeat after the Emergency, she had demanded that Farooq fight the elections in 1983 as her ally but he refused. He had told her, 'This will destroy the very thing we stand for. People will say we have sold their birthright to Delhi.' Any dilution of Farooq's Kashmiri identity was not in India's interest either, because he was the only credible leader from the valley who supported the case for secular India against Islamic Pakistan. But Indira Gandhi didn't bother with any pretensions to secularism. In her anxiety to prevent Farooq's National Conference running away with the election and, destroying her party's base in the state, she took advantage of Kashmir's religious geography. Whilst Muslims are in the majority in the Kashmir valley, in Jammu, the other side of the Pir Panjal range, Dogras and other Hindu communities outnumber Muslims, while remote Ladakh has a sizeable Buddhist population. To compensate for Farooq's following in the valley, she made an all-out bid for the Hindu majority in Jammu region. There she mounted a blatantly communal campaign, encouraging Hindu fears of domination by the Muslims of the valley. One journalist who covered her campaign in jammu has described her as 'outdoing the BJP by miles'. The result was a defeat for the National Conference in Jammu but a sweeping victory in the valley, which gave Farooq a majority in the Assembly. Indira Gandhi and her Congress party, instead of promoting secularism, had polarized politics, creating in the voters' minds a Hindu Jammu and a Muslim valley. What's more, Farooq came back to power.

Worse was to follow. Unreconciled with defeat and angered by Farooq's flirtation with the opposition in other parts of India, Indira Gandhi plotted his downfall by the time-honoured Indian practice of engineering defections from his party. When the governor, her cousin, the wise and experienced civil servant B. K. Nehru, advised against this strategy, he was replaced by Jagmohan, an administrator. He agreed to obey orders and duly dismissed Farooq, barely a year after the election he'd won. It had been a year in which there was evidence of increasing hostility to India in the valley with anti-Indian slogans being shouted during a test match against the West Indies played in Srinagar. The official media reported that spectators also waved Pakistani flags. Some journalists maintained they were flags of a Kashmiri Islamic party. The dismissal of Farooq only heightened that hostility to India. Ved Marwah, a senior police officer, who at one stage served as security adviser to the governor of Kashmir, described the dismissal of Farooq as 'a fatal blow to the pro-Indian forces in the state'. Once again the sentiments of Muslims in Kashmir had been ignored to promote the interests of those in power in Delhi.

Shortly after Farooq's dismissal Indira Gandhi was assassinated. Her son Rajiv, too, could not accept the fact that his party should lose out in Kashmir, or indeed in any other state, so he persuaded Farooq to a deal with the Congress as a condition for his being allowed to return to power. Ved Marwah blamed that deal for 'the rise of the current phase of militancy in the state'. I asked Farooq why he had done a deal with Rajiv when he wouldn't accommodate his mother?

'To repair the damage done by the 1983 election,' he replied as though it was obvious. 'I told Rajiv every election more and more Muslims are voting on a larger scale for my party and Hindus for yours. We should work together so that the state does not get divided on communal lines. But when the election came in 1987, Rajiv and I both recognized our mistake. We should have fought separately. The alliance alienated both our followers and theirs. It was a mistake on both our parts.'

But now Farooq was supporting the coalition government in Delhi, his son was a minister there, and that coalition was dominated by the BJP. Not only was its Hindu nationalism anathema to most Muslims, it had always stood for revoking the article in the constitution which gave Kashmir its special status in the Indian union. Even though the right to fly the red flag of the state, which fluttered above the secretariat, was about the only distinction which remained between Kashmir and other states, the article did provide a basis for Farooq's claim to the right to greater autonomy.

I suggested, 'Surely the alliance with the BJP is far more damaging even than your deal with Rajiv, which you admit was a mistake.'

'People like you can say that. You don't have to run the state,' he shot back. 'If I don't get money from Delhi I won't even be able to pay my staff. I have to really battle with Delhi to run the state. Being in with the government I have one weapon. I can always threaten to pull out and they don't have the majority in parliament to relish losing my MPs.'

Farooq was even more infuriated when I suggested that the alliance with the BJP would undermine his Muslim credentials, and that at a time when he was fighting what amounted to a war against Pakistani-backed Muslim separatists. 'It's not Islam which is in danger here, it's our way of life,' he said with such spleen that I feared he might finally be going over the top. 'Why should I accept their Islam? I am a Muslim, but not a shitty Muslim like them. I don't want their Islam.'

The Abdullah dynasty had never gone unchallenged in the valley. Their traditional rivals were the holders of the ancient office of mirwaiz, a Persian title meaning head preacher. The mirwaiz at the time of the 1987 election, Maulvi Mohammad Farooq, stood for the implementation of the United Nations resolution calling for the status of Kashmir to be decided by a plebiscite, believing the majority would vote for Pakistan. The plebiscite resolution did not allow for independence, the choice was to be between India and Pakistan. The mirwaiz and leaders of other Kashmiri parties opposed to the National Conference who had got together to form the Muslim United Front to fight the 1987 election, claimed that Farooq and Rajiv rigged it. There will always be arguments about the extent of rigging but, as always, it was not what happened, but what people thought had happened which mattered. There can be no doubt that Kashmiris in the valley believed they'd been robbed of a fair election yet again.

The mirwaiz helped create that impression by fulminating against Farooq, Rajiv and the government in Delhi from his pulpit in the largest mosque in Kashmir, Srinagar's Jama Masjid. Built of burnt brick and wood, the roofs of its prayer halls are supported by sixty-foot-high deodar pillars. The courtyard, unusually for India, isn't paved, it's a garden. The customary domes are lacking too; instead the roofs are reminiscent of a pagoda and the dragons jutting out like gargoyles from the roofs are evidence of Buddhist influence. This unusual building symbolizes the particular Kashmiri form of Islam which the mirwaiz preached and practised.

Maulvi Mohammad Farooq was assassinated early in the troubles which erupted after the 1987 election and was succeeded by his son Umar who was only seventeen. By the time we met the young clergyman, he had been preaching from his father's pulpit and leading his party for ten years. The assassinated mirwaiz had been excitable, given to angry outbursts against India for 'treating Kashmir like a colony'. He would speak disparagingly of the Delhi durbar, and of Farooq Abdullah too, describing him as its chamcha, or sycophant. But his son was calm, quietly spoken, and capable of seeing both sides of an argument. Speaking in excellent English, learnt in a Christian school, he didn't accuse India of 'mistreating' Kashmir, but only said it had tried to make the state 'dependent' on it. India, he believed, had thrown the game away in Kashmir.

'At one stage, more or less, people had become reconciled about India and about carrying on their lives within India. But rigged elections, successive governments being thrown out, created the impression that New Delhi has no respect for the political will of the people. It was mostly the wrong doing of the Congress and the Nehru family.'

'What about the 1987 election in particular?'

'That was so obviously rigged that young men who were candidates and agents of the parties belonging to the Muslim United Front took up the gun. They saw there was no hope of a democratic answer to the Kashmir problem.'

The mirwaiz had an orthodox black beard which contrasted with his fair Kashmiri complexion, and his thin, almost pinched features could have been those of a fanatic, but surprisingly he said, 'This is primarily a political struggle, not a Muslim one. A plebiscite with the hope of Pakistan was my father's traditional position but I think things have changed since the movement started. Kashmiris have put so much into it that Kashmiriyat should be accepted.'

Kashmiriyat is the word used to describe the particular culture and religious traditions of Kashmir. Sitting on the small verandah of our houseboat as the rising sun spread a silver light over the jagged shoulders of the mountains which separate the two parts of Kashmir, watching terns beating up and down Dal Lake, a family of dabchicks paddling vigorously between the tall-stemmed pink lotus flowers, and a small kingfisher devouring with some difficulty a not-so-small fish, we heard the rhythmic rise and fall of chanting from a white marble mosque. From a distance it sounded not unlike Hindu bhajans. This, the mirwaiz told us, was part of a tradition established by Mir Syed Ali, the Persian saint who introduced Islam to Kashmir and who is always known as Shah-e-Hamadan, meaning the king, in a spiritual sense, of Hamadan, the town he originally came from. Shah-e-Hamadan found that his Brahmin converts missed their temple worship with its singing and occasional dancing. Silent worship didn't, as the mirwaiz put it, 'give them the feeling that they were near to God'. So Shah-e-Hamadan collected an anthology of verses of the Qur'an and sayings of the Prophet for Kashmiris to chant in their mosques. 'Our preaching is different too,' the mirwaiz explained. 'We don't just talk at the congregation. I will read a verse of the Qur'an and then get the people to repeat it after me. That's why you will find that many illiterate people will know what the Qur'an says, and where it says it, because of this kind of teaching.'

'But surely,' I suggested, 'the Islamic militants fighting here are Wahabites, and they are very strict puritans who would never tolerate your Kashmiri Islam.'

'Yes,' the mirwaiz admitted, 'much of the fighting is being done by fully fledged institutions established in Pakistan and they are Wahabites but they only have a military objective, and the people would not support them if they felt there was any hidden agenda.'

'You would know better,' I said, 'but I wouldn't be so certain, considering that many of these foreign militants are Afghans and you can see the sort of Islam which has been enforced in their country.'

But the mirwaiz would not be moved, 'We will not allow Afghanistan to happen in Kashmir. It's the security forces who are creating an awareness of our Islamic identity because they consider all Muslims as enemies.'

The mirwaiz's contention was borne out by a senior Kashmiri Muslim member of the IAS, who told us how he had been stopped during a cordon and search operation. Although he had shown his identity card and was on his way to an important government meeting, a soldier refused to let him pass saying, 'We have been instructed that all Kashmiris are terrorists.'

But some of the mirwaiz's colleagues in the Hurriyat Conference, an alliance of twenty-five political parties opposed to Farooq and to India, do maintain that this is an Islamic conflict. The chairman of the Conference, Abdul Gani Butt, made no bones about it, telling us, 'We are pro-Pakistan, of course, because we are Muslims.' Sitting in the office of his party, the Muslim Conference, on the first floor of a house tucked away in the back streets of Srinagar, he reverted to his past as a professor of Persian. Treating us as pupils, with much finger wagging and other admonitory gestures, and speaking in language which could only be described as poetic, he told us, 'Justice is like a phoenix in Kashmir, a bird known but seen by no human eyes.' The protests which followed the elections in 1987 were 'India's last chance to hear the beats of our hearts'. Going back to the agreement signed between Indira Gandhi and Sheikh Abdullah, the scrawny, shaven-headed professor scaled new heights of hyperbole. 'When the rat from Kashmir married a snake called Indira Gandhi the people could draw the inference – no child can be born.'

He asked whether we minded his lighting a cigarette and I said we didn't mind but perhaps it wasn't very good for him, which provoked another poetic flourish, 'The life is not worthy of concern that has lost glamour, purpose and dignity. I would prefer death with dignity to life with disgrace.' He warned us against 'denigrating those who lay down their lives for a cause as terrorists', and asked, 'Who kills innocents? Let Amnesty International expose the ugly face of those responsible.' Drawing deeply on his cigarette which was some distance from his mouth, held between two fingers at a right-angle to his clenched fist, he ruled out our theory about good governance. 'Even if angels were brought down from heaven to govern us, the dispute with India would still exist.' As for the role of the Hurriyat Conference, it represented 'the hot red blood of our youth'. But the elderly professor turned politician did admit there were differences within the Conference between the pro-independence and the pro-Pakistan parties.

Successive Indian governments have never seriously considered restoring autonomy to Kashmir. Even when the people of Srinagar came on to the streets at the end of 1989, and there was what can only be described as an uprising, the answer the government came up with was 'crush them'.

The uprising started when the government surrendered to the demands of the Jammu and Kashmir Liberation Front, and released five of the group's leaders in exchange for the kidnapped daughter of the home minister. The capital of Kashmir rose against its rulers. Crowds danced in the streets rejoicing at India's humiliation, shouting slogans against the government and swearing to fight for their independence. Enthused by the defeat of the Soviet army in Afghanistan, the collapse of communism in eastern Europe, and in particular by the fall of Ceauşescu in Romania, the crowds believed their turn had come too.

The Indian government reacted with a crackdown by the security forces, including curfews and shoot-on-sight orders. Police opened fire on a procession marching towards the centre of Srinagar to protest against the brutality of cordon and search operations, and the arbitrary arrests of young men. One hundred people were killed. This massacre brought the foreign press to Srinagar, and I remember the day after it occurred, the sandals of the dead were still littering the bridge where they had been shot. Alarmed by the international coverage of the police brutalities, the government confined journalists to the Broadway Hotel. My resourceful colleague in Srinagar, Yusuf Jameel, had anticipated something like this and had already arranged for me to stay with the family of a fellow journalist opposite his office, and so I was not caught in the press pub. Because of the curfew I couldn't get out and about and wouldn't have been much use to the BBC had it not been for a friendly police officer who, although he knew the authorities were searching for me, dropped by every evening to report on the day's events.

The uprising in Srinagar was in support of the Jammu and Kashmir Liberation Front, which was the most popular and liberal of the Kashmiri secessionist groups, and demanded independence, not accession to Pakistan. The government could well have tried negotiating with them, offering perhaps to restore the autonomy which Kashmiris were given when they acceded, and making the case for staying with India. India did have a case, it did provide access to a large market and an almost limitless source of tourists who needed no passports, no visas, and who had a tradition of holidaying in Kashmir. India had also protected Kashmiriyat and prevented the valley from being overrun by more commercially adventurous communities like Punjabis, Gujaratis, or Marwaris. On the other hand Kashmiris were well aware that Pakistan lost its eastern wing because Bengalis objected to being dominated by Punjabis from the west. Kashmiris also knew that there was still resentment against Punjab's clout in what remained of Pakistan.

Instead of negotiating with the JKLF, the Indian government

demonstrated its respect for Kashmir's autonomy by sending Jagniohan back as governor although it was well known that he would be unacceptable to Farooq. When, as expected, Farooq resigned, Jagmohan was free to carry out the orders of the government of India which were to bring the JKLF to its knees. So the field was left open to the Islamic groups who were guaranteed support and sanctuary from Pakistan just across the Line of Control.

Hindal Tyabji, like Ashok Jaitly an IAS officer who had spent most of his career in Kashmir but was not a Kashmiri himself, believed the new administration was in part to blame for the flight of almost the entire Hindu community known as the Pandits because of their Brahmin caste. Sitting on the roof of his government bungalow, just down the road from the heavily fortified residence of Farooq Abdullah, puffing on an Indian cheroot which he seemed to be having difficulty in keeping alight, Hindal said, 'There should have been no need for the Hindus to leave the valley. After all, we have not had communal riots here like there have been in other parts of India.'

He did admit that the Hindus had reason to be afraid. The uprising had demonstrated the resentment many Muslims felt against Hindus. He also agreed that when Jagmohan 'clamped down' some mosques did broadcast warnings to the Pandits – get out or see what happens to you and your women and children. Some Hindus were indeed killed. They included the judge who had sentenced one of the founders of the JKLF to death. But none of that Hindal felt explained the panic which spread amongst the Pandits and their exodus from the valley. He went on to say, 'Jagmohan has denied that the government deliberately encouraged the Hindus to leave and provided them with transport. What I can say is that the government certainly didn't discourage them. The local police did say things like "The militants will use your houses to hide in, and we don't want you to get hurt." And some of the Hindus did leave in military transport.'

Hindal did not believe the Hindus would come back now, nor did he think the government was serious about persuading them to return. 'It suits the government to have Hindu refugees in Jammu,' he explained. 'They can be shown to foreign visitors as an example of the suffering caused by the militants. At the same time, because their property has not been protected, it has been taken over by locals who have a vested interest – so the problem is a criminal land mafia, not communal.'

Whatever the cause of the exodus, it is difficult to believe that the administration couldn't have done more to give the Pandits a sense of security and persuade them to stay, or indeed to return when the security forces regained the upper hand. Nor can it be denied that Kashmiri Muslims had reason to resent Hindus. Successive governments in Delhi, for all their secular pretension, had made sure that the jobs at their disposal went to Hindus not Muslims. It was widely believed in Kashmir that this was because the government did not trust Muslims. India's cumbersome colonial style of administration was quite incapable of responding sensitively to the feelings of Kashmiri Muslims.

In part, Kashmir can be seen as a tragedy caused by Indian secularists, suspicion of religion and religious people, and the fear, if not outright hatred, of Muslims generated by the Hindu nationalists. A Muslim majority state bordering on Pakistan was always going to need sensitive handling, it could never be just another state of India. But India's failure to come to terms with its own religious identity, meant it was unable to accept that Kashmir should have special treatment.

However, that's not the end of the matter. Pakistan's role cannot be ignored, nor can the impact of a corrupt and inefficient administration, which had never been overhauled since the British left. A senior IAS officer in Srinagar told us that his service was known as the East India Company because Kashmiris felt they were ruled as a colony.

Nowhere is there more evidence of colonialism than in the Indian police forces, who do so much damage to their country's cause in Kashmir. I recently visited the National Police Academy in Hyderabad, where officer cadets in the elite police cadre are trained. In my room I found a copy of the academy's journal. I leafed through it idly, not expecting much more than the usual reports on student activities and glorification of the noble career of policing. To my surprise, I found two articles by senior retired officers bemoaning the continuation of the colonial tradition in the police. One of the former officers maintained that the 1861 act passed by the British Raj 'still governs the organization, structure, philosophy and working of our police forces at the end of the twentieth century, never mind the phenomenal changes in our social, political, scientific, economic, and cultural spheres over the decades'. He pointed out that the pattern adopted by the 1861 act was based on the Irish Constabulary because Ireland was a colony at that time.

The other retired officer, who had commanded the Border Security Force, which is very active in Kashmir, listed the various commissions on police reforms which had been set up from time to time and went on to comment, 'The recommendations received no more than a cosmetic treatment at the hands of the government of India. The political leadership is just not prepared to give functional autonomy to the police because it has found this wing of the administration a convenient tool to further its partisan activities. As for the bureaucracy, control over the police has become an intoxicant they are addicted to and are just not willing to give up. And so the act of 1861 continues to be on the statute book even after nearly one hundred and thirty-nine years – a millstone round the police neck.'

The colonial practice of firing on demonstrators was responsible for Jagmohan's downfall. The occasion was the assassination of the father of the young mirwaiz we met. To this day no one is certain who killed him, but it might well have been one of the Islamic groups who felt he was not sufficiently virulent in his attacks on India and not clear on his stand towards Pakistan. News of the mirwaiz's assassination spread like a forest fire, from mosque to mosque, from tea shop to tea shop, from house to house in the lanes of old Srinagar, carrying with it ugly rumours about the government's role. Thousands of protesters gathered at the hospital. They managed to capture the body from the police and set off to march with it to the mirwaiz's ancestral home. When the Central Reserve Police saw the procession approaching one of their battalion headquarters, they opened fire killing sixty-two people. The government in Delhi had ordered the uprising to be crushed but this was going too far. Without determining the extent of his responsibility, Jagmohan was recalled. In a letter ten senior officers of the Indian Administrative Service belonging to the Kashmir cadre, including Ashok Jaitly and Hindal Tyabji, wrote to his replacement, saying, 'As responsible administrators, we are appalled by the lack of planning, forethought, and consideration for the mourners that led to indiscriminate killing of large numbers of peaceful processionists by nervous and trigger-happy security forces. It is apparent that these security forces did not get the benefit of guidance from their officers and that frantic wireless messages from officers of the state police asking for instructions to be conveyed to the Central Reserve Police to desist from firing were not heeded, which is indicative of a breakdown of the command and control structure of the law and order machinery.'

The new governor, Girish Saxena, was a former head of RAW, the Indian CIA. During his tenure human rights abuses by the security forces continued and on more than one occasion I discussed this with him. A quietly spoken, calm, and very polite man, Saxena always avoided giving a direct answer when I asked why the members of the security forces who committed these abuses were not tried and punished to deter their colleagues and to reassure Kashmiris. Nevertheless I got the impression that the answer was, 'to avoid demoralizing the security forces'. Some members of the security forces were punished but because of another feature of Indian administration, the chronic addiction to secrecy, the public didn't get to hear of those cases. So they were left to believe the worst that they heard about army and police 'excesses'.

Even after the establishment of the Indian Human Rights Commission and a commission in the state too, the authorities continued in their obfuscatory ways. During this visit we were shown a police officer's reply to a complaint to the commission about a man who, according to eye witnesses, had been shot dead by the security forces as he was coming out of the court in Srinagar. The officer dismissed the complaint in standard police jargon as 'baseless, misconceived, and contrary to the facts and records', and gave the standard description of the incident, 'killed in a police encounter'. There was no explanation of the reason for the encounter, nor how it could be that someone coming from the court where he would have been searched for arms could have posed such a danger to the police that they needed to shoot him. A daily paper, the *Greater Kashmir*, reported that there had been thirty-five 'extra-judicial executions' in the twenty days before we arrived. It feared there was no end to what it called 'the most detested and brutal phenomenon'. Relatives of two young men the police claimed they'd shot in an encounter told the paper that the victims had been arrested from their homes and so were in no position to challenge the police. The president of the High Court Bar Association said lawyers had decided not to ask for bail because a détenu in prison was safe but the moment he got bail he was 'killed in a fake encounter'.

Girish Saxena was back in Srinagar for a second term as governor. Sitting on the verandah of the governor's house, looking down on the ink-black Dal Lake and the lights of the city beyond, I reminded him of the conversations we had had during his earlier term. He smiled and said, 'Yes, including the conversation about your friend Yusuf Jameel. That had been embarrassing, I have to admit.' Yusuf had been arrested without a warrant by two army officers, taken to several different locations, interrogated blindfolded and with his arms tied behind his back, and eventually dumped more than fifty kilometres away from Srinagar. During the two days Yusuf was held the government media denied that he had been arrested by any of the security forces, maintaining it was the militants who had kidnapped him.

I told the governor that the high-handedness of the security forces was still alienating the people whose hearts and minds the government claimed it was trying to win. He accepted there was a degree of alienation, saying, 'We have just crossed fifty thousand acts of terrorist violence in the last twelve years. Even if the response to three per cent of these cases have involved excesses by us it means one thousand five hundred cases – a big number. This is the human and political cost we have to pay, people do feel hateful and resentful, it does raise the level of alienation for a time. Hearts are very important.'

'So why is more not done to prevent these excesses?'

'Well, you must accept this is not a beauty pageant, it's a war. The militants emptied three magazines of thirty rounds each in sixty seconds at Jammu station. That's ninety rounds in three minutes. Our security forces are taking casualties too. The ratio between our casualties and theirs is in our favour, but it goes up and down, it's not smooth.'

I had to admit that we journalists often neglect the other side of the story – the 'excesses' of the militants, the plight of the security forces who were their target, and the casualties the Indian army and police suffered.

We seemed very far from the war with the immaculate servants of the governor's residence hovering with their trays of samosas and other snacks, a small bulbul roosting on the top of a rolled blind, and the sound, not of gunfire, but of the call to prayer and of countless click-clacking cicadas. It was hard to believe that the elderly governor, who greeted us as friends, was playing a key role in a war in which brutalities were being committed on both sides. But more than once when I asked him about allegations that the police were arresting young men and then demanding money for their release he admitted, 'We must clean up our act. We should attempt to do security with more imagination and intelligence. There should be gadgets and force multipliers.'

Before we left, Girish Saxena assured us that things were better than when he was last governor. Then fear of the militants' austere Islam had closed all the city's entertainments and driven women to cover themselves from head to toe. He pointed out that cinemas were now open, there were one or two bars, people were picnicking in the Mughal Gardens and, until a recent acid attack on two women whose heads were not covered, the burqa was comparatively rare. 'The fundamentalists are on the retreat,' the governor assured us. 'The old liberal ways are coming back.'

As we drove back we passed several checkposts. I dreaded being stopped because arguing with a trigger-happy paramilitary policeman is not advisable. Fortunately, all the checkposts seemed to be unmanned. Commenting on this, our driver, whose daily encounters with the security forces had left him with a deep hatred of anyone in khaki said, 'This is a cowardly army. They don't dare come on the streets after dark.' But he'd spoken too soon. He failed to get home after dropping us and had to spend the night in Yusuf's office because the security forces wouldn't allow him to pass through the area surrounding the army cantonment.

We too spent a good deal of time in Yusuf's office seeking his guidance on the stories we were hearing, and his help in arranging interviews. It was a small house with a walled garden, or patch might be a better description, bright with English summer annuals, part of a press enclave just five minutes' walk from Lal Chowk, the Piccadilly Circus of Srinagar. The enclave is now named after Mushtaq Ali, a photographer killed when a letter bomb, intended for Yusuf, exploded in his office in 1995. The envelope was delivered by a woman who claimed to be a member of the Dukhtaran-e-Millat, daughters of the Islamic community, an organization which campaigned for women to wear burqas and live strictly orthodox lives. Mushtaq opened the envelope. Yusuf remembers hearing an explosion, seeing a bright yellow flame, realizing that he had been hit in the head, and then reciting verses from the Qur'an because he thought he was dying. Smoke and dust filled the small room. He couldn't see anything, but he heard screams and got to his feet. Stumbling against someone on the floor, he felt his curly hair and realized it was Mushtaq. He staggered outside, still dazed, to get help. Mushtaq was taken to hospital but doctors didn't hold out any hope for him and he died there of a massive wound in his stomach and chest. Yusuf is convinced the woman was not from the Dukhtaran-e-Millat, but was one of the 'renegades' – that is former militants or their supporters who had changed sides and were now working for the government. Shortly before this letter bomb arrived, journalists in the BBC's Delhi bureau and BBC officials in London had warned Yusuf that the Indian authorities were extremely unhappy with his reporting and advised him to be very cautious about his movements. One of the journalists had learned of a conspiracy to implicate him in a recent attempt to assassinate the governor. I knew, from my days in the BBC, how much the government resented Yusuf's courageous and independent reporting from Kashmir, reporting which was widely listened to on both sides of the Line of Control because it was carried by the BBC's Urdu Service.

It was quite possible that the 'renegades', knowing of the authorities' attitudes to Yusuf, had decided to remove him. Uncoordinated, untrained, not subject to the disciplinary code of soldiers or policemen, they had a record of taking the law into their own hands. An elderly civil servant who had risen to the top of the tree in the Kashmir administration had fled from his home after 'renegades' had ransacked it and killed his neighbour. He was now living with his son but still having trouble with the 'renegades'. 'Surrendered militants came to this house too,' he told us. 'They asked us to have hot food ready for them when they came back in the evening and twenty-five thousand rupees in cash. We fled the house and I contacted a major in the local army unit. He apologized and assured us we would not be troubled.'

A young man, who like the retired civil servant didn't want to be identified, admitted that he had joined the militants in the early days of the uprising but he'd left and set himself up in business in Delhi. On a recent visit to his home town in the Budgam district of Kashmir he'd been arrested by the police special task force. He told us what happened then. 'The superintendent of police took me to his room, where there were two sub-inspectors and two constables. He told them to take me away and beat me. After I had been beaten for four days the superintendent of police told me if you get us some money I will let you go. My dad gave an assistant sub-inspector sixty thousand rupees and the next day my dad came to take me away. Now I don't go home if I come to Kashmir, I stay with my uncle in Srinagar.' I asked the young man to tell me about the torture inflicted on him but he refused saying, 'I can't speak about it with a woman in the room.' But he did show us two toes which had been broken when he was beaten on the soles of his feet.

While the security forces continue to alienate Kashmiris, the economic arguments go against India too. Time and again there have been attempts to win the loyalty of Kashmiris by announcing 'financial packages' to accelerate economic development in the state, but it remains without any industry of any significance. The road from the plains into the valley has not been improved since the fifties when a tunnel was bored through the Pir Panjal range to avoid a 9000-feet-high pass that was snowbound in the winter. Indira Gandhi promised the railway would bring trains closer to Srinagar by extending the line from Jammu to Udhampur, but that project has taken more than twenty years and is still to be completed. While international airports are sprouting up all over India, Srinagar's airport is not even controlled by the Civil Aviation Ministry but by the Defence Ministry. There is a chronic shortage of power, and even if tourism had not been ruined by the war with the militants, it would not have come anywhere near realizing its full potential. The director general of tourism in Srinagar, who was manfully trying to breathe some life into the industry, pointed out that China had fifty-six million foreign tourists a year and five million hotel rooms. The whole of India only attracted just under two and a half million tourists and provided just eighty thousand hotel rooms for them. Why was this? I asked. 'Bureaucracy,' he replied, without pausing a moment to think, 'China doesn't have all those licences and clearances we have to obtain in Delhi.' To make matters worse for young Kashmiris who can't get jobs in industry or tourism, they are even penalized by Delhi when they try to go abroad for work. According to the director general, it takes them two years to get a passport.

Pakistan's economy does not suggest that Kashmir would have been flowing with milk and honey if it had been ruled from Islamabad. The size of the local tourist market would have been much smaller, and Islamic injunctions, particularly against alcohol, would not exactly have encouraged foreigners to visit the valley. Pakistan's record on democracy, particularly in the areas of Kashmir it controls, doesn't indicate that it would have allowed free and fair elections in the valley, and corruption is no less a problem in Pakistan than it is in India. But the direct road into the valley from Rawalpindi would have been opened, and the short railway line from Sialkot to Jammu too. Kashmir might also have been allowed to develop the waters of its rivers, the Indus, the Jhelum, and the Chenab. India surrendered the use of their waters to Pakistan in exchange for the waters of the eastern rivers of Punjab. In Pakistan young men are positively encouraged to go to the Middle East so that their remittances help the balance of payments.

Delhi has argued that Kashmir would be prosperous if the financial 'packages' given to the state had not been dissipated by corruption and maladministration. But in Srinagar that argument is not accepted. Hindal Tyabji for instance said, 'For people in Delhi to talk about corruption is laughable. Here it is a small society. Everyone knows if you have made money, there you can do what you like and still have a good reputation. The centre has been playing games with development in Kashmir. We had less money than we deserve.' Ashok Jaitly blamed his fellow members of the IAS in Delhi, saying, 'It's at the bureaucratic level that spokes are put in the wheel. The politicians agree to give us money, then the bureaucrats go to them and say if you give five hundred crores for Kashmir you will have to give it to others and it will become five thousand crores. I sometimes ask them what they do it for. It seems they want us to keep running to them to beg.' The irate chief minister gave us an example of the way the central bureaucracy treated him: 'We have yet another promise of a package,' he spluttered. 'It is lying with them in Delhi right now. Why is it being delayed? Nobody tells me. Even as chief minister I can't find out. My son was until just now minister of state in that ministry but he couldn't find out what had happened to the package. I am continuously being pushed to the bloody wall.'

While we were in Srinagar, parliamentarians in Delhi showed how little they understood the frustration, not just of Farooq but of everyone we met. The heated debate in parliament after the massacre on Jammu railway station followed a set pattern with a leading member of the opposition Congress Party alleging, 'No government in the history of the nation has failed so miserably in maintaining law and order', and the home minister promising even more security forces and extra powers for them too. But the daily *Hindu*, in a biting editorial, castigated the MPs. 'It defies imagination to think we can profitably add to the already overwhelming number of troops deployed in the state of Jammu and Kashmir,' the paper thundered and went on to warn that more security forces would almost certainly mean more human rights violations. Then the *Hindu* made the point the parliamentarians had almost entirely ignored: 'Ensuring security in Jammu and Kashmir is not just about preventing unlawful activities of the militants, it is also about ensuring a climate of economic and social opportunities and not least good governance.' If the *Hindu* is right, India can't put all the blame for the problem of Kashmir on Pakistan.

Conclusion

On 27 February 2002 the Sabarmati Express, getting towards the end of its two-day journey from Varanasi to Ahmedabad, had just pulled out of Godhra Station in north Gujarat when the alarm chain was pulled. As the train came to a halt it was attacked by a mob of Muslims and one of its compartments was set on fire. According to the Gujarat government, fifty-eight people were burnt alive. Many of the passengers on the train were activists belonging to sister organizations of the right-wing Hindu Bharatiya Janata Party, which was in power in Gujarat and dominating the coalition government in Delhi. The activists called themselves *karsevaks*, which literally means volunteers who serve through working. They were returning from Ayodhya where they had hoped to be allowed to start building a temple in honour of the god Rama on the site of the demolished mosque. Some of the karsevaks were among those burnt alive in the Sabarmati Express. Nobody, least of all the government, could provide an accurate report of how a Muslim mob had assembled so suddenly, nor indeed how the fire broke out. There were, however, many reports, including one by the police intelligence, of provocative behaviour by karsevaks who had been coming through Godhra on trains for the previous three weeks. We could well believe those reports having heard the offensive anti-Muslim slogans and seen the provocative behaviour of karsevaks when the mosque was pulled down ten years earlier.

The Vishwa Hindu Parishad, or World Council of Hindus, which is coordinating the Ayodhya campaign, called for a strike throughout Gujarat on the day after Godhra. The government knew this could lead to violence but the BJP still supported the strike. In Ahmedabad, Gujarat's largest city and the state's commercial capital, Hindu mobs of unprecedented size launched brutal attacks on Muslims and their property. There were well-attested cases of rape, many people were burnt alive, mosques and Muslim shrines were destroyed or desecrated. Right in front of the police commissioner's office, the tomb of Wali Gujarati, one of India's most renowned Muslim poets, was razed to the ground and the site then covered with tarmac. The government itself admits that the situation was out of control for three days. The violence spread from Ahmedabad to some other areas of Gujarat and there were a number of retaliatory attacks by Muslims. The government of Gujarat said that seven hundred and nineteen people had been killed. Amnesty International and Human Rights Watch quoted unofficial estimates as nearer two thousand dead.

The National Human Rights Commission, a statutory body which investigated the violence, quoted reports of 'groups of well-organized persons armed with mobile phones and addresses, singling out certain homes and properties for death and destruction – sometimes within view of police stations and personnel'. An independent group of women from different parts of India who visited Gujarat wrote in their report, 'The state – including elected representatives, the political executive, the administration, and the police – abdicated its responsibility to protect *all* its citizens. Far worse, it actually connived in the maiming, raping, and butchering of hundreds of women and children of Gujarat.' Amnesty International suggested that 'the state administration and the police have taken insufficient action to protect the population of the state during the massacres, and in some cases may have even connived with the attackers'. Human Rights Watch said, 'The attacks against Muslims in Gujarat have been actively supported by state government officials and by the police.' The government of Gujarat claimed that, in comparison with four earlier periods of violence in the state when the BJP was not in power, it had called out the army earlier to help restore order, brought the situation under control more quickly, and 'fulfilled its responsibility in a very nice manner'. When we visited Ahmedabad we were told by victims of the violence, by journalists, and by NGOs working in the refugee camps, that the police in most places had done little or nothing to curb the violence in the early days, and that some police personnel and well-known members of the BJP's sister organizations aided and abetted the attacks on Muslims. When I asked a minister who was unwilling to be identified why the government had not at least apologized to the Muslims he said, 'the feeling after the first three days was that Hindus had settled their account for Godhra'.

This is not the first time a government in India has abdicated its responsibility to protect the lives and property of all its citizens. After the assassination of Indira Gandhi, the Congress Party government allowed the attacks on Sikhs in Delhi to continue for several days before taking decisive action. At Ayodhya neither the central nor the state government made any attempt to prevent the destruction of the mosque. In the violence in Mumbai that followed Ayodhya the police were partisan.

The National Human Rights Commission demonstrated one of the strengths of India. It, like some other institutions such as the Supreme Court and the Election Commission, does have the courage to speak out against the failures of governments and to take a stand. The women's group who visited Ahmedabad and produced their courageous report, along with the many NGOs who worked in the refugee camps, speak of the vigour of India's civil society. The press, except for some Gujarati papers, did their job in spite of attacks on journalists, in at least one case by the police, and a sustained campaign against the electronic media by the government of Gujarat. It was once again the politicians and the bureaucrats who failed. It wasn't just the BJP politicians. An elderly journalist who is a follower of Mahatma Gandhi and a prominent member of the Movement for Secular Democracy said to us, 'Congress in Gujarat has not said anything about the riots. It's very heinous. There is a section of the party that is afraid of alienating the Hindu vote.' Politicians played politics while Gujarat burnt.

The civil service and the police went along with the politicians. There were police officers who did their duty in Gujarat and managed to disperse mobs – some of them were transferred. A member of the Indian Administrative Service resigned in protest against what happened in Gujarat. But the police service and the administration as a whole failed. They failed, in part at least, because of the problem of governance that we identified at the beginning of this book, the problem of an unreformed colonial administrative system.

At the end of its report the National Human Rights Commission drew attention 'to the deeper question of police reform, on which recommendations of the National Police Commission and the National Human Rights Commission have been pending despite the repeated efforts to have them acted upon. The commission is of the view that recent events in Gujarat, and indeed in other states of the country, underline the need to proceed without delay to implement the reforms that have already been recommended, in order to protect the integrity of the investigating process and to insulate it from extraneous influences.'

Police reforms have not been implemented because the politicians want to be able to exercise 'extraneous influences', and too many policemen are happy to allow them to do so for a price. R. K. Raghavan, a senior officer of the elite police cadre, recently wrote that 'vestiges of the colonial mentality' survived in the police and identified the basic problem as 'the elected representatives of the people – the MPs and the members of the legislative assemblies – wanting to exercise total control over the civil service at all levels'.

But it's not all the fault of the politicians – the civil service and the police cannot escape their share of the blame. The elite cadres of all branches of the civil service, including the police, have surrendered their autonomy. P. K. Doraiswamy a former head of the bureaucracy in the state of Andhra Pradesh wrote after retirement, 'Honest and outstanding officers are harassed and victimized by the political executive with the shameless assistance of the Judases and the Brutuses in the service who are ready to betray and backstab their colleagues in return for very short-term favours from the powers that be.' The politicians known colloquially as *netas* and the bureaucrats known as *babus* scratch each other backs, and that's why the vacuum the British left has come to be filled by the 'neta-babu raj'.

The civil service and the politicians, instead of keeping an eye on each other, join hands to share the spoils of office and so corruption is an inevitable by-product of this raj. Every Indian complains of corruption, from the poor villager who said to us, 'Whoever I vote for will put my vote in his stomach', to Shashi Tharoor, the UN Secretary General's suave, sophisticated assistant, who has described corruption as 'the biggest enemy to the country's economic progress'. That, of course, is not to say that every politician and every bureaucrat is corrupt. All over India we have found honest and efficient civil servants and police officers, although almost all of them have complained that the system prevented them achieving their potential. We have known many politicians of the utmost probity who have become poorer rather than richer during their careers. But V. P. Singh, the politician whose reputation for honesty was the only reason he became prime minister, admitted to us that he could only be clean because others raised the dirty money which is the currency of Indian politics.

Indira Gandhi once dismissed corruption as a global phenomenon. Was she right, is India any different? We believe it is. Of course money plays a role in politics everywhere, and businessmen openly admit to bribing in many countries. But in India there is almost no aspect of life which has not been corrupted by the neta-babu raj. This is because the government's tentacles spread so widely. The British Raj was known as the Mai Bap Sarkar or Mother Father Government, a government which claimed to do everything for its subjects just as parents do for their children. The government of independent India has been a Mai Bap Sarkar too. In the name of paternalism it has set out to provide everything for its citizens, leaving nothing to their own initiative. In Rajasthan local officials were offended by NGOs helping villagers to harvest water. As officials of the Mai Bap Sarkar they thought water harvesting should be their sole responsibility, and to prove this they ordered a check dam to be destroyed. In the ensuing controversy, which the officials eventually lost, the Rajasthan irrigation minister was quoted as claiming, 'Every drop of water that is received through rains comes under the irrigation department.'

Politicians don't trouble to hide the links between office and money. They talk openly about 'lucrative ministries'. The railways are still a department of the government. As a result, according to M. N. Prasad, a former chairman of the Railway Board, 'Indian Railways has the dubious distinction of being the only major railway system in the world where major decisions on investment policy and organization are taken by politicians according to their whims and fancies'. Time and time again the lure of what the press calls 'the loaves and fishes of office' is blatantly used to 'persuade' legislators in state assemblies to cross the floor. One recent chief minister of Uttar Pradesh found it necessary to reward nearly one hundred legislators with office in order to preserve his majority in the Assembly.

Soviet-style economic planning involves controls and controls spell cash for those implementing them, and so it's not surprising that India did not seriously set about reforming another raj, the licence-permit raj, until it was forced to do so. It was only when India was threatened with bankruptcy in 1991 that it removed controls over investment within the country – controls so absurd that an industrialist could be punished for productivity, for producing more than he was licensed to do – and liberalized the policy on trade and foreign investment. The World Bank and the IMF who prescribed this treatment for India thought that at last the neta-babu raj's grip over the economy would be released. International businessmen and women flocked to Delhi and Mumbai, Bangalore, and Chennai, believing that a liberated economy would provide limitless opportunities to make money out of the middle class, estimated by some optimists at two hundred and fifty million. But I remember saying to an enthusiastic Western diplomat 'this is going to run into the sands', and I have been proved half right, or half wrong, whichever way you look at it.

The economy showed its potential by responding rapidly and strongly to the reforms the 1991 crisis forced on India. But the enthusiasm for reform did not last long and the spurt in industrial growth fizzled away after five years. Ten years after the reforms were launched the editor of the *Business Standard*, T. Ninan, complained, 'attitudes in all too many cases have remained frozen in time, the reformers remain – as they were a decade ago – a hopeless minority'.

Some of that 'hopeless minority' left in disgust. An Indian economist excited by the prospect of reforms returned from America to advise the government, but soon left again disillusioned. The straw which broke his back was a bureaucrat who proudly announced that a procedure had been simplified so that now only five instead of fifteen forms were required, but when the economist asked how many signatures were needed he replied with a self-satisfied, not a sheepish, smile, 'fifteen'.

The complexity of India's bureaucratic procedures, the maze of rules and regulations, the red tape round innumerable procedures, the dreaded discretionary powers which can be used to lock as well as unlock doors, all produce the second by-product of the neta-babu raj – inefficiency. One non-resident Indian industrialist said to me, 'I would prefer to invest in my own country but I go to East Asia instead because there I certainly have to pay but I know I'll get my money's-worth. In India the system is so complicated everything takes so long and you never know whether you'll get what you paid for in the end.' The government's own chief vigilance commissioner has lamented the passing of 'honest corruption', saying 'nowadays you pay a bribe and your work doesn't get done'.

India is now proceeding slowly with what are called the second stage reforms of the economy but even critics of socialist economic management would not say that governments should surrender totally to the market. The conclusion two academics from the London School of Economics, Stuart Corbridge and John Harriss, reached after comparing the economically more successful nations of East Asia with India was that, 'development states have to intervene consistently in "market" relationships and must provide assured financial support for those sectors and institutions (including infrastructure, education, and health-care) which ensure the conditions of existence for long-run economic growth and development'. But government intervention in the market has to be based on sound policies which are efficiently implemented. We recently heard Dr Manmohan Singh, the distinguished economist, who as finance minister introduced the first reforms, argue that India could not have an industrial policy because its standards of governance were so poor. Infrastructure, education, and health are just the sectors where India has so far been least successful.

Corruption and chronic inefficiency are two by-products of the neta-babu raj. Oppression is the third. Because the bureaucracy and the politicians are hand in glove there is no restraint on the government misusing state machinery. Neither the income tax department nor the police raised any questions about the legality of the actions they took against First Global, the Tehelka investors, even though they knew full well that the orders they received and the government's motives were questionable. Aruna Roy's meeting demonstrated the ways that poorer Indians are oppressed when they annoy the government. It would seem absurd to compare freedom and liberty in democratic India with Pakistan, which has been ruled by the army for so many years, but the historian Ayesha Jalal has written, 'Post-colonial India and Pakistan exhibit alternative forms of authoritarianism.' The nurturing of the parliamentary form of government through the meticulous observance of the ritual of elections in India enabled a partnership between the political leadership and the non-elected institutions of state to preside over democratic authoritarianism.'

It is because India's archaic, complicated, inefficient system of government allows money to be diverted, rules to be disobeyed and procedures to be subverted that neither the netas nor the babus have shown interest in reforming it. Perhaps it would be taking this theory too far to suggest that politicians have deliberately opened up other fronts to take Indians' minds off issues of good governance, but it is certainly true to say that caste and communalism, as religion-based politics are known in India, have crowded that issue out. It might have been thought that economic policies, and especially the removal of poverty, would have been the most hotly debated subjects in elections after the reforms started, because there was evidence that economic liberalization was only benefiting the middle and upper classes, but even the three general elections since then have, as usual, been dominated by issues of caste and communalism.

Communalism has been a prominent issue in Indian politics since independence. In the early days, when the constitution was being debated, Nehru said, 'It is a vital problem for us to solve as to whether we are to function fundamentally in regard to our general policy as a composite country or to function as a Hindu country rather ignoring the viewpoints of other groups.' Nehru knew how vital that problem was because he faced strident demands for a Hindu India from within his Congress Party as well as without, and he was surely right to insist on acknowledging that India is a nation of many religions.

Nehru's secularism was in theory wholly laudable. Everyone was to be free to practise his or her own religion, there was to be no state religion, and religion was to be kept out of politics. But in practice Nehru's secularism came to be seen as antipathetic to religion, and the supporters of Hindutva were able to portray it as anti-Hindu. The very word secularism had unfortunate connotations. The *Oxford Dictionary* gives profane as one of its meanings. In India it was often translated as 'dharma nirapekshata' which may, according to L. M. Singhvi, a scholar of constitutional law, mean 'a divorce or hostility between the state and religion'.

Although Nehru hoped that his secularism would keep religion out of politics, it has achieved the opposite. Much of politics is now taken up with a sterile shouting match between secularists and the advocates of the Hinduism which led to the destruction of the mosque in Ayodhya. This is not surprising. Karen Armstrong, in her book on fundamentalism called *The Battle for God*, has written, 'Fundamentalism exists in a symbiotic relationship with an aggressive liberalism or secularism and under attack inevitably becomes more bitter, extreme and excessive.'

Mahatma Gandhi once said, 'It is a delusion to believe that India can ever be served by or can assimilate a message unless it has got a spiritual foundation. It has got to be broad-based upon that foundation if it is to last and permeate the distant villages of India.' India does have a long tradition of religious pluralism, it was a multi-faith society long before the idea was ever conceived in Europe. It was that tradition Gandhi wanted to be the message India assimilated, and writing many years later in the context of the Gujarat violence the British Asian scholar Lord Bikhu Parekh, himself a Gujarati, said, 'We need an overarching notion, not of Hindutva but of Bharatiyata (Indianness), one that affirms and cherishes our rich cultural and religious diversity and embeds it in those public values, sensibilities and institutions that we all do, or should, hold in common. This great historical project requires a historically sensitive imagination, a culturally attuned intelligence, and a shrewd sense of political possibilities. Sadly none of these qualities is much in evidence, either among the fanatical BJP ideologues who are busy destroying the country they claim to love, or among their simple-minded secular opponents whose thinking has advanced little since Nehru's death.'

Caste's prominent role in politics has also distracted the electorate's attention from the issue of governance. In the Indian tradition the community counts for more than the individual, and for most Indians, not just Hindus, but Muslims, Christians, and Sikhs too, caste has been the community which counted. So it's not surprising that Indians have lined up under the banners of their castes rather than their classes to fight their political battles. Nehru, with his Western liberalism, sought to establish a political order with strong rights for the individual, which would encourage Indians to rise above the ties of caste, but his own party could not resist the temptation to practise caste politics.

The elite of India, who are almost entirely upper caste, tend to decry caste politics, although they have brought about a democratic revolution with the lower castes, because of their larger numbers, now dominating the political scene. Power, which for many years was the prerogative of the predominantly upper-caste Congress Party, now has to be shared with parties which represent the lower castes, including the Dalits, formerly known as Untouchables. Unfortunately for the lower castes, the leaders they elect tend to join the club, become netas themselves and take their share of the spoils of the raj. Because it enriches them, they don't want to reform an administration although it oppresses their followers. Nevertheless, there is no doubt that the Dalits and others excluded from the traditional power structures have won considerable benefits from caste politics. The political scientist Ashutosh Varshney has written 'whether or not economic equalities have gone down, social inequalities certainly have, even for the scheduled castes [Dalits]. This is a serious achievement.' But that question mark over the economic gains of the Dalits and other traditionally deprived castes and communities will not be removed until their politicians broaden their agenda. Zoya Hasan, professor of political science at Delhi's Jawaharlal Nehru University was surely right when she wrote, '... north India's recent history and that of Uttar Pradesh in particular indicates that for collective action to become a real force political parties must go beyond caste'.

In spite of the brake the netas and the babus have put on change and progress, India has gone forward since independence and continues to do so. In fact there is evidence that it is at last gathering speed, as we noted in the introduction. This just goes to show the potential of India. If even with the constraints of the neta-babu raj it can achieve one of the highest growth rates, imagine how fast it would grow if those constraints were lifted. If some parts of India can achieve respectable indicators for health and education, imagine what the figures for all India would look like were the backward states not in the grip of particularly virulent forms of the neta-babu raj. But who is going to bell the cat?

So far there is much grumbling among the elite but no sign of a revolt from them or the middle classes. I once heard Aruna Roy argue that they will not revolt because they have the contacts and the cash to bend the present system to their requirements. But that's not always so. Gujaratis are renowned for their business acumen and their state is one of the fastest growing in India; its industrial output doubles every seven years. Those Gujaratis are now counting the damage, worth millions of pounds, that the violence there caused, and regretting the setback to the state's reputation as a good place to invest in. Aruna believes that those who are oppressed by the neta-babu raj will undermine it. The success of her freedom of information campaign buttresses that claim.

Even that public hearing in the village of Janawad led to some change. A committee the state government set up afterwards discovered that only 21 out of 141 public works the village council claimed to have been built had actually been properly completed, and demanded the recovery of 7 million rupees of embezzled funds from local officials. The hearing led to the government ordering that measurement books for local public works were to be written in simple Hindi, which villagers can understand, and therefore question, instead of incomprehensible technical English.

But we believe change is likely to come in a much more Indian way. The neta-babu raj may well gradually wither away. Circumstances will force the politicians and the bureaucrats to relinquish more and more of their powers, and to exercise those they are able to retain in the interests of the public, not of themselves. The economic liberalization of the early 1990s was forced on the government by India's impending bankruptcy, and that liberalization did reduce the government's hold over the economy. Globalization, international competition, the WTO are all forcing the netas and the babus to surrender more of their economic powers. Creeping computerization is making it harder for officials to misuse the powers that remain, to lose files, to hide information, and to deny justice by delay. Politicians are also now all too aware of what has come to be known as the 'anti-incumbency factor'–voters throwing out parties in power because they have failed to deliver. This has at last made politicians realize that caste and creed are no longer enough, that they must perform, and that they can't perform without better governance. Chandrababu Naidu is by no means the only chief minister who has now concentrated on governance, and in particular on devolving power and decentralizing the bureaucracy. The netas and the babus have to be more careful too. The higher courts, particularly the Supreme Court, are keeping a watch on them and even interfering in governance. Delhi, for instance, is less polluted now because the Supreme Court ordered the government to replace diesel with gas as the fuel for running the capital's buses. The free press is another watchdog, and civil society keeps up the pressure too. But wouldn't it be better if the politicians, who are now being told by their voters that they expect better governance, were to remove the brake that is holding India back rather than releasing it gradually and reluctantly? They could make a start by following the advice of the National Human Rights Commission and reform the police. From there they could go to the civil service and the legal system. But that would mean losing the benefits of the present system and neither the netas nor the babus will volunteer to surrender them.

India is often likened to an elephant lumbering along, unstoppable, but never going anywhere fast, and there is a school of thought which says that's no bad thing, that slow and steady does win the race, that India must not endanger its culture by rushing headlong into market capitalism and consumerism. But surely that does not mean that the elephant has to be shackled to the neta-babu raj? The rundown institutions of a colonial past only discredit India's culture, they can't protect it. As for the argument that India's slow progress is the price it pays for democracy, the political scientist Sailendra Sharma has pointed out that democracy shouldn't mean status quo. He has said, 'For India and a host of new and transitional democracies the message is clear: building and reinvigorating the state's administrative and institutional capacities is fundamental to resolving the economic challenges.' For Indians that means dismantling the neta-babu raj so that their country will realize her enormous potential.